Students' Book

Upper Intermediate

Matters

JAN BELL
ROGER GOWER

LONGMAN

Acknowledgements

We are grateful to the following for permission to reproduce copyright material:
H Bauer Publishing Ltd, on behalf of the Editors, for adapted extracts from the articles 'Do you want to live forever?' by Alison Gordon from *Bella* magazine 20.4.91 & 'Exercise Addicts' by Sue Pettit from *Bella* magazine 23.3.91 & an extract from the article 'My man turned into a raging bull' from *Take a Break* magazine 2.3.91; British Broadcasting Corporation for an extract from the news broadcast 'From Our Own Correspondent' with Mark Brayne, Radio 4, 26.3.86; British Broadcasting Corporation & Clare Short MP for an extract from the broadcast 'The Moral Maze', Radio 4, 9.8.91; Channel Four Television Company Ltd for an adapted extract from the article 'The Living Dead' by Adelene Alani from a magazine accompanying the television series *Equinox*; the author's agent for an extract from the poem 'The Oompa-Loompas' Song from *Charlie and the Chocolate Factory* by Roald Dahl (Unwin Hyman Ltd/Penguin Books Ltd); EMAP Metro Ltd for adapted extracts from the article 'How to have the perfect interview . . .' compiled by Gillian Carter from *More!* magazine, Issue 26, 22nd March – 4th April 1989; Faber and Faber Ltd for an extract from *Tell Freedom* by Peter Abrahams (1982); Guardian News Service Ltd for an adapted extract from the article 'Tying the knot: portraits of a modern marriage' by Joanna Moorhead from *The Guardian* newspaper 22.5.91; Hamish Hamilton Ltd & Alfred A Knopf, Inc for a slightly adapted extract from *A Year in Provence* by Peter Mayle, copyright © 1990 by Peter Mayle; Harper Collins Publishers Ltd for the poem 'Happiness' from *In a Marine Light* by Raymond Carver (Collins Harvill, 1988) Hodder & Stoughton Ltd for an adapted extract from *Just Talk* by Hilary Caminer & Deborah Catesby (1987); the author's agent for the story 'A Family Supper' by Kazuo Ishiguro from *Firebird 2*; the author's agent for an extract from *Unreliable Memoirs* by Clive James (Jonathan Cape Ltd, 1980/Pan Books Ltd, 1981); Longman Group UK Ltd for extracts from *Longman Dictionary of Contemporary English* (2nd Edition, 1987) & *Longman Lexicon of Contemporary English* (1981); Marshall Cavendish Partworks Ltd for adapted extracts from the article 'Mars Man's Next Base' from *Quest*, © Marshall Cavendish 1989; The National Magazine Company Ltd for adapted extracts from the article 'When the travel bug bites' by Corinne Sweet from *Company* magazine, September 1989; Newspaper Publishing plc for an extract from the article 'Wedded to the East' by Mihir Bose from *The Independent* magazine 23.9.89, an extract from the article 'Finish to the Fight' by Angela Lambert from *The Independent* newspaper 27.5.89, an adapted extract from the article 'The Mayor has nine wives' by John Lichfield from *The Independent on Sunday* newspaper 21.4.91, the abridged article 'A national lack of tenderness' by Guiliana Mercorio from *The Independent* newspaper 24.12.88, an extract from the article 'A positive channel for natural violence!' by Adrian Whiteson from *The Independent* newspaper 27.5.89 & an adapted extract from the article 'Debutantes say farewell to their well-spent youth' from *The Independent* newspaper 10.4.91; the author's agent for an adapted extract from the story 'The Genius' from *Domestic Relations* by Frank O'Connor (Penguin Books Ltd, 1970); The Observer Ltd for the adapted article 'Journey into the interior' by Rodney Tyler from *The Observer* magazine 29.3.87 & an adapted extract from the article 'Madness on the Motorway', Observer EFL Service; Octopus Publishing, part of Reed International Books Ltd, for adapted extracts from *The World's Greatest Crimes* by Nigel Blundell & Roger Boar (1984); PolyGram Music Publishing Ltd for the lyrics of the song 'I will survive' by Dino Ferakis & Freddie Perren; the author, Amanda Shakespeare for an extract from her article 'Heat and danger in the Peruvian jungle' from *Marie-Claire* magazine, June 1988; Sidgwick & Jackson Ltd for adapted extracts from *Is That It?* by Bob Geldof (1986); Solo Syndication & Literary Agency Ltd for the article 'Killer Son goes Free' by Keith Colling from *Evening Standard* newspaper (date unknown), the abridged article 'Mr Mustard' is jailed' by Jacki Davis from *Daily Mail* newspaper 15.7.87, the adapted article 'The Perils of Pauline' by Liz Gill from *Woman* magazine 16.7.88, adapted extracts from the article 'Nobbled on the final furlong' by Paul Harris from *Daily Mail* newspaper 1.11.89, adapted extracts from the article 'Space Hero "Human Wreck"' by Paul House from *Evening Standard* newspaper 26.1.88 & an adapted extract from the article 'Me and my job' from *Woman* magazine 27.9.89; Sport Newspapers Ltd for an adapted extract from the article 'Little Green Men Beamed Me Up' by Ruki Sayid from *The Sunday Sport* newspaper 10.7.88; Times Newspapers Ltd for an extract & an adapted extract from the article 'Relative Values: Against all odds' by Linda Newman from *Sunday Times* magazine 3.7.88, © Times Newspapers Ltd 1988; Yorkshire Post Newspapers Ltd for adapted extracts from the article 'Giant among the strong men' by Reginald Brace from *Yorkshire Post* newspaper 16.1.90.
We have been unable to trace the copyright holders in the following & would appreciate any information that would enable us to do so:
The article 'Up the Orinoco' by Mary Kemp from *Titbits* magazine, April 1989; the article 'How to you recognise an alien? Twelve feet but only one tiny head' by David Lawson from *Today* newspaper 10.10.89; the article 'Jobs for the boys!' by Mark Weston from *Chat* magazine 14.7.90; the article 'The Big Question Is . . . Is Marriage Old-Fashioned?' from *Catch* magazine 20.5.91; the article 'Could your child be a fruit machine addict?' from *Living* magazine, August 1988.

We are grateful to the following for permission to reproduce photographs:
Ace Photo Agency, pages 4 centre (Benelux Press), 13 below (Bob Taylor), 49 centre (Vibert-Stokes), 49 below left (Paul Steel), 51 (1&2) (Mauritius Bildagentur), 62 above (Mauritius Bildagentur), 81 above right (Phil O'Connor), 109 (Nawrocki Stock Photo); Bryan & Cherry Alexander, page 62 below; Allsport, pages 52 (P. Blondel/ Agence Vandystadt), 114 above left (Simon Bruty), 114 above right (Ben Radford), 114 above centre right (Tony Duffy), 117 (Jon Nicholson); Alpha Photographic Press Agency, page 82 below (R. Pelham); Animal Photography, page 130 above centre; Associated Press, page 76 centre; BBC Books, pages 65 above (J. Charrington), 65 left (Basil Pao), 65 right (Ann Holland); BBC News & Current Affairs, page 76 below; BBC Television, page 22 above right; Barnabys Picture Library, page 25 centre right & far centre right; Barts Medical Picture Library, page 32 above right; John Birdsall Photography, pages 25 above, 94, 96, 105; Ron Boardman, page 81 above right (inset); Gareth Boden, pages 51(4), 140 above, 140 below; Kenneth Bright, page 112; Bubbles, pages 4 above centre right (Loisjoy Thursto); Camera Press, pages 30 centre (Erma), 30 below (Sean Smith), 32 below left (Gianni Marzella), 51(3) (Clive Arrowsmith/SHE); Cephas Picture Library, pages 4 above right (Nigel Blythe), 13 below centre (Mick Rock), 49 below right (Nigel Blythe); Bruce Coleman, page 69; Colorific, pages 4 below (John Moss), 49 above centre right (P. Robert Garvey); Lupa Cunha, page 13 above centre; E.T Archive, page 125 below right; Eye Ubiquitous, page 51(a) (Geoff Redmayne); Ronald Grant Archive, pages 22 below, 23, 86; Sally & Richard Greenhill, page 102 below; Robert Harding Picture Library, pages 4 above left, 25 far centre left, 25 below (Duncan Maxwell), 49 below centre right (Ian Griffiths), 51(5), 51(b), 128(a) (Rainbird), 128(b) (Earl Young), 134 above left & above right; Andrew Hasson, page 120 right; Hutchison Library, pages 10 (Brian Moser), 128(e) (Nancy Durrell McKenna), 130 below right (Carlos Freire), 132 (Sarah Errington), 134 above centre (Jeremy A. Horner), 134 below; The Image Bank, pages 25 centre left (Alberto Rossi), 81 below (Werner Bokelberg), 130 above right (Steve Niedorf); Mike Key, page 51(d); Life File, pages 13 above (Mike Evans), 81 above left (Emma Lee), 81 above left (inset); London Features International, page 5; Simon Marsden/The Marsden Archive, page 30 above; Metropolitan Police, page 125 below left; NASA, page 54; Network, pages 19 (Abrahams), 44 left (Justin Leighton), 76 above (Wendy Wallace); Desmond O'Sullivan, page 91; Picturepoint, pages 102 above right, 130 above left; Pictures Colour Library, page 128(c); Pinsharp, pages 28, 35, 98, 102 above left; Quadrant Picture Library, pages 32 above centre, 49 centre left (Marion Canning), 51(e); Redferns, page 145 (David Redfern); Rex Features, pages 22 above left, 44 right, 49 above right, 82 above (Nils Jorgensen), 114 below centre left (Paul Brown); Bill Robinson, page 120 left; Rolls-Royce Motor Cars Ltd, page 51(c); Peter Sanders, page 128(d); Scope Features, pages 143 (Brian Moody), 144 (Brian Moody); Amanda Shakespeare, page 61; Solo Syndication, page 112 (inset); Frank Spooner Pictures, page 11 (Gamma/John Chiasson); Tony Stone Worldwide, pages 114 above centre left (Bob Torrez), 114 below centre right (Peter Correz), 114 below left (Tim Brown), 125 above (Peter Correz); Telegraph Colour Library, pages 4 above centre left (L. Lawry), 49 above left (Bavaria Bildagentur), 114 below right (Bob Knight); Thames Television, page 22 above centre; Titbits, April 1989, page 124; Malvin Van Gelderen, page 32 below right; John Walmsley, page 32 above left; Zefa Picture Library, page 130 below left.

The photographs on pages 81 below (inset), 115 & 140 centre were taken by Longman Photographic Unit.

Illustrated by
Tim Archbold, Kathy Baxendale, Derek Brazell, Lynn Chadwick, Paul Davies, Pat Fogarty, Pauline Hazelwood, Ian Kellas, Sally Kindberg, Maggie Ling, Gilly Marklew, Bethan Matthews, Harry North, Sharon Pallent, Axel Scheffler, Terry Thomas, Graham Thompson, Gareth Williams, Norman Young.

Contents

Contents chart

Pronunciation	**Writing**
Review of sentence stress Using intonation	Autobiography
Word stress with suffixes Sound: /ə/ Pronunciation chart Intonation of surprise/interest	Personal letter Revising and correcting written work
Weak forms and contractions	Adverbs of degree Strong adjectives Describing a film, play, book, etc.
Sounds: /v/, /w/, silent /w/ Sounds: /p/, /b/	Linking words and expressions: time, addition, contrast, reason, result Narrative
Questions: weak forms and intonation	Sentence patterns Word order Advertisement (job)
Sounds: /æ/ and /ʌ/ Sounds: /ʊ/ and /uː/	Formal/informal language Letter of application (job)
Word linking (consonant-to-vowel; disappearing sounds)	Comparatives and superlatives Advertisement (forms of transport)
Stress in compounds	Complex sentences (linkers and participle constructions) Report, diary or letter to a newspaper
Word linking (vowel-to-vowel, words ending in '*r*')	Indefinite article Personal letter Travel experiences
Sounds: /ʃ/, /tʃ/, /dʒ/	Grammatical and lexical linking words Letter of opinion
Shifting word stress Contractions/stress in conditional sentences	Summary writing Comparing factual and emotional language
Sounds: /ɒ/, /ɔː/ /əʊ/	Description from notes
Corrective (contrastive) stress	Tourist brochure
Intonation of lists Sound: /l/ (*file*/*light*)	Attitude words Dialogue
Homophones	Formal letter of complaint
Word stress in adjectives Pronunciation of the letter *a*	'For and against' essay: organising and linking ideas
Intonation of relative clauses Word stress: words ending in *-ion*	Description of a scene
Weak forms and contractions	Newspaper article

Learning strategies (Unit 1)

Evaluation of speaking abilities, and discussion of activities
Correction of grammar
Discussion of strategies for learning vocabulary

Memories

SPEAKING

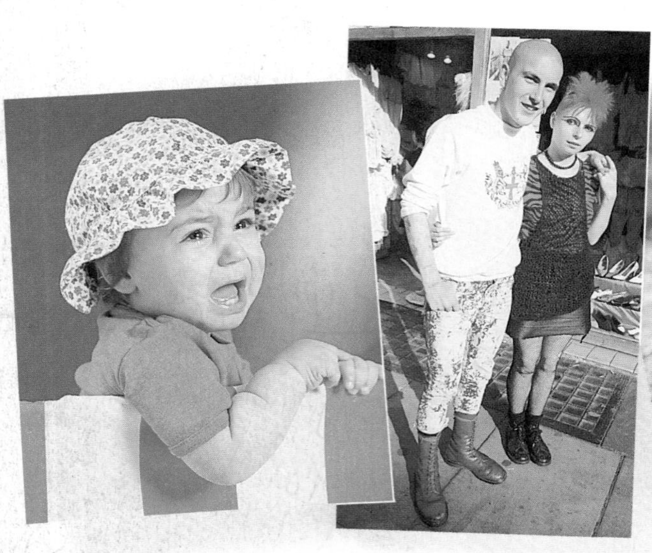

1 Work in groups.

discovery innocence rebellion disappointment love fear freedom insecurity happiness excitement fun cruelty creativity learning selfishness

a) Which of the words in the box do you associate with each stage of childhood? Give your reasons.

b) Talk about your own experiences. For example, an occasion from your childhood when you remember being very happy or frightened.

2 Think about your own childhood. Think of:

- something you used to love (doing).
- a memory of school.
- a person who was important to you.
- an important achievement.
- a place you remember going to or living in.
- a present or possession that you treasured or still treasure.
- a funny or serious event which happened to you.

a) Write notes about four or five of the topics on different slips of paper, as in the examples.

b) In groups, take turns to choose a slip of paper from someone else. Then ask and answer questions about the topics written on it. Example:

A: *Why did you go to Cairo?*
B: *My father worked there for a while.*

Cairo

my charm bracelet

I fell out of a treehouse and broke my arm

SPEAKING REVIEW

1 Think about your strengths and weaknesses when you speak English.

a) Give yourself a mark of 1 to 5 (5 is very good), depending on how good you think you are at each of the following:
- accurate grammar.
- pronunciation.
- use of vocabulary.
- speaking confidently without too many pauses.

b) Discuss your notes with someone else and see if they agree with your assessment.

2 In groups, talk about the kind of speaking activities you: a) enjoy doing b) find useful. Share your views with the rest of the class. Example activities:
- speaking in pairs.
- speaking in groups.
- practising pronunciation in the language laboratory.
- listening and responding to 'real' English (e.g. people, cassettes, video).
- class discussions.

LISTENING

Before listening

You are going to listen to a radio interview with Gloria Estefan. In groups, share any information you know about her.

Listening

1 [1.1] The interview with Gloria Estefan is divided into three extracts. Listen to all three extracts, and say in which extract(s) she talks about:

a) her work.
b) her family.
c) her personality.
d) her childhood.

2 Listen to Extract 1 again. Which of the following adjectives does she use to describe herself?

a) lazy b) determined
c) positive d) pessimistic

3 Listen to Extract 2 again and answer the following questions.

a) What kind of person is Gloria's father?
b) Why did it take her mother a long time to become a teacher?
c) When did her grandmother learn to drive? Why?
d) What quality does Gloria feel she has inherited from her relations?
e) What did her grandmother want to be when she was nine?
f) Why didn't she do it?
g) In what way does she feel her grandmother has influenced her?
h) How has Gloria's husband, Emilio, helped her?
i) Gloria describes herself as a 'couch potato'. What do you think it is, and do you believe her? Give reasons.

4 Listen to Extract 3 again and complete the following sentences.

a) In order to write songs Gloria needs ________.
b) Music has always been ________ to her.
c) She started singing when she was ________.
d) As a child she started singing because she was ________ and ________.
e) She sometimes finds it easier to write when ________.

5 In groups, tell each other anything interesting about members of your family (e.g. their personality and achievements). To what extent do you think you have inherited their qualities?

GRAMMAR REVIEW

1 Look at the sentences below. Match each of the verbs in *italics* to the name of the verb form in the box. Example:
a) Present Perfect Continuous

Present Continuous	Past Perfect	
Present Perfect (Continuous)	*will* + base form	
Past Simple	Past Continuous	Present Simple

a) He*'s been living* there for six years.
b) When he *phones* I promise I*'ll tell* you.
c) What time *does* the train *leave*?
d) Sara*'s* just *left*, I'm afraid.
e) They*'re flying* to India next month.
f) Julia *was crossing* the road at the time of the accident.
g) If I *had* some change I'd give it to you.
h) Brian*'s* still *working* with the same company, as far as I know.
i) I*'ll* usually *leave* the house around eight in the morning.
j) We*'d* already *eaten* by the time Tom *arrived.*

2 Decide whether the verb forms in the sentences in Exercise 1 refer to present, past or future time, or a combination. Example:
a) Present and past time

Check your answers with the table on page 9.

3 Read the text below and find an example of:

a) indirect speech
b) an infinitive
c) a passive form
d) a definite article
e) a participle
f) a conditional
g) a modal verb
h) an auxiliary verb
i) a preposition

I remember believing in Father Christmas – we used to leave our stockings out for him on Christmas Eve and they would always be filled the next day. If we were lucky, our parents would take us to see him in one of the big stores at Christmas time so that we could give him a long list of the presents that we hoped to get. One day, however, when I was about five, my brother told me that he had seen Father Christmas coming into his bedroom at night and it was our father!

4 Complete the following sentences about your own life.

a) I have never . . .
b) I believe very strongly in . . .
c) Next year I . . .
d) If I could buy anything I wanted . . .
e) I used to . . . but now I don't.
f) I can't stand people who . . .
g) The most important thing in life . . .
h) I . . . English for . . . years.
i) I wish . . .
j) At the weekend I . . .

PRONUNCIATION REVIEW

Sentence stress

[1.2] Listen to the following dialogue and underline the words which are most stressed.

A: I'm just going to phone Mum.
B: Can you ask her if she's coming for a meal on Sunday?
A: What time shall we say to come?
B: Oh, around one, I should think. Tell her to bring the car – I've got some plants for her.

Stress and intonation

[1.3] Listen to the following sentences. Underline the correct interpretation in brackets. The first one has been done for you.

a) You're Sandra, aren't you? (*not sure* / *sure*)
b) It's cold there in March, isn't it? (*not sure* / *sure*)
c) I'll have a beer, please. (*polite* / *abrupt*)
d) A gin and tonic, with ice. (*polite* / *abrupt*)
e) You've forgotten your keys. (*statement* / *asking for confirmation*)
f) You've lost your keys. (*statement* / *asking for confirmation*)
g) She's a lovely person. (*fact* / *contradiction*)
h) It's a beautiful garden. (*fact* / *contradiction*)

What helped you to decide? (e.g. Did the voice go up or down at the end? Was the pitch of the voice high or low?)

READING

1 Read the texts as quickly as you can.

a) Which memory is:
- the saddest?
- the happiest?
- the funniest?

b) Which extract:
- do you like the best?
- reminds you of anything in your own childhood?

2 Read the texts again and decide whether the following statements are *True* or *False*, according to the texts.

a) Frank's parents wouldn't explain how babies were born. (Text 1)
b) Frank didn't believe his father's explanation. (Text 1)
c) Peter Abrahams' parents had a happy marriage. (Text 2)
d) Peter was an only child. (Text 2)
e) Phil Collins used to embarrass his brother by what he said. (Text 3)
f) The dog seriously attacked Clive James. (Text 4)
g) The 'dog' was a puppy. (Text 4)
h) Clive still likes dogs. (Text 4)

3 In pairs, discuss the following points.

a) In what way was Frank O'Connor's father joking? When and how are children usually told 'the facts of life'?
b) What do you think made Peter Abrahams' childhood particularly happy?
c) Can you think of an occasion where someone has been embarrassed by the behaviour of a member of your family?
d) Did you ever have any bad experiences with animals when you were a child?

Text 1

Now one of the things I wanted badly to know was where babies came from, but this was something that no one seemed to be able to explain to me. When I asked Mother she got upset and talked about birds and flowers, and I decided that if she had ever known she must have forgotten it. I appealed to my father and he told me that babies were dropped out of aeroplanes and if you caught one you could keep it. 'By parachute?' I asked, but he only looked pained and said, 'Oh no, you don't want to start by spoiling them.' Afterwards, Mother took me aside again and explained that he was only joking. I went quite dotty with rage ...

(from *The Genius* by Frank O'Connor)

Text 2

I remember the family picnics on Sundays. My mother and father would lie on the grass talking. We children would play about in the grass. The grass always seemed very green, the sky was always far away. My mother always had a basket filled with things to eat. And the sun always shone on our picnic Sundays. I remember the cool sweetness of an orange after I had run myself silly.

I remember my father and mother merging into each other in my mind. Together they were my symbol of peace and laughter and security.

37

(from *Tell Freedom* by Peter Abrahams)

Text 3

by CLIVE COLLINS

AT HOME, Phil was *always* playing the drums. He had a set from the time he was three or four and Mum used to pay £3 an hour for him to have lessons. He'd come back and tell his mates what he'd learnt and as soon as he started practising, their parents would call the police to complain about the noise.

I remember one time we went out to a pub in Esher. It was a period when he used to wear his hair in a bow and I felt terribly embarrassed – there I was taking my brother out for a drink and he was wearing a pigtail, and I thought, 'Can I cope with this?'

He doesn't seem to care what other

(Clive Collins talking about his brother, Phil: from *The Sunday Times* colour supplement)

Text 4

UNRELIABLE MEMOIRS

Barking from the stomach, he (the dog) opened a mouth like a great, wet tropical flower. When he snapped it shut, my right foot was inside it. If Bluey hadn't been as old as the hills, my foot would have come right off. Luckily his teeth were in ruins. At the time I was traumatised. I loathed dogs from that day forward.

(from *Unreliable Memoirs* by Clive James)

VOCABULARY REVIEW

Deducing words in context

Look at this sentence from Text 4 on page 7.
When he **snapped** *it shut my right foot was inside it.*

a) What do you think *snapped* means?
b) What helped you to make the guess?

Using a monolingual dictionary

twisting: *a snaky road.*
snap¹ /snæp/ *v* **–pp– 1** (usually of something thin and stiff) to (cause to) break suddenly and sharply off or in two parts: *The branch snapped under the weight of the snow.* **2** to move so as to cause a sharp sound like something suddenly breaking: *The lid snapped shut.* **3** to speak or say quickly, usu. in an annoyed way: *He tends to snap at people when he's got a headache.* **4** to close the jaws quickly: *The dog was snapping at my ankles* (= trying to bite them). **5** *infml* to photograph **6 snap one's fingers** to attract attention by making a noise by moving the second finger quickly along the thumb.
snap² *n* **1** [C] an act or sound of snapping: *The branch broke*

1 Which definition of *snap* is correct in the context? How do you know?

2 How do you pronounce *snapped*? Where in this book can you get help in understanding the phonemic symbols? (Check the *Contents* list.)

3 The words in the box all come from the texts in the previous section. First mark where you think the stress is in each word. Then put the words in columns according to the number of syllables they have. Finally, check your answers in the dictionary. The first one has been done for you.

dotty tropical traumatise ruins bark
rage parachute upset pigtail

ONE SYLLABLE	TWO SYLLABLES	THREE SYLLABLES
	'dotty	

Learning vocabulary

In groups, discuss:
- the strategies you find useful for recording vocabulary (e.g. a special notebook).
- how you memorise new words.
- the advantages and disadvantages of bilingual and monolingual dictionaries.

WRITING

Autobiography

1 Make notes on things such as:
- when you were born and where you grew up (e.g. the country, town, house).
- your family, relatives and friends.
- your schools.
- your early memories.

Date/Place of birth:
16 October 1975; a small farmhouse near Anet
Grew up:
moved to Paris age 8; lived in modern flat
Family:
mother, father, Sophie & Claude
Relatives:
grandmother lived with us
Friends:
Nicole, best friend until I was 12 (cousin)
Schools:

2 Plan how many paragraphs you will have and what you will include in each. Then decide on the order of the paragraphs.

3 Write your first draft and check your work for:
- correct grammar.
- choice of vocabulary.
- spelling and punctuation.

Cut out what is not important. Then revise it and write the final version.

Verb forms as related to time

Verb forms are not always limited to one time frame (e.g. *will* is frequently considered to be a future form but it is sometimes used in the present). The table lists most common uses of each verb form.

Present time

VERB FORMS	USE(S)	EXAMPLES
1 Present Simple	a) Habits	*He **drives** to work most mornings.*
	b) General truths/facts	*Water **freezes** at 0°C.*
	c) States (e.g. feelings/opinions)	*I **like** coffee.*
2 Present Continuous	a) Temporary events happening in the present	*I'**m living** in Madrid at the moment.*
	b) Characteristic behaviour (often irritating)	*She'**s always leaving** the door open.*
3 Past Simple/Continuous	Unreal states/actions	*If I **had** a video I'd record it for you.* *It's time we **were going.***
4 *Will* + base form	Habits (sometimes irritating)	*He'**ll** sometimes **work** until midnight.*

Past time, as seen from the present

VERB FORMS	USE(S)	EXAMPLES
1 Present Perfect Simple	a) Past experiences/actions with present importance	***Have** you **read** that book?*
	b) Unfinished states/habits	*I'**ve lived** in Edinburgh for ages.*
2 Present Perfect Continuous	a) Unfinished temporary actions/situations – focus on the action/situation	*Tom'**s been working** there since 1972.*
	b) Focus on actions in progress leading to present result	*He'**s been cooking** all day. That's why he's exhausted.*

Past time

VERB FORMS	USE(S)	EXAMPLES
1 Past Simple	Completed states/actions/habits (thinking of a specific time)	*I **was** happy when I was young.*
2 *Used to* + base form	Habits and states that no longer exist	*Sue **used to like** living here.*
3 *Would* + base form	Habits that no longer exist	*We'**d** often **argue** when we were married.*
4 Past Continuous	Temporary actions/states/habits in progress	*I **was talking** to her while the TV was on.*
5 *Was going to* + base form	Future in the past (unfulfilled intention)	*They **were going to phone** (but they forgot).*
6 Past Perfect	a) Past states/actions happening before a specific time in the past	*They'**d already gone** to bed when he phoned.*
	b) Unreal states/actions	*If I'**d seen** him I would have told you.*
7 Past Perfect Continuous	Temporary actions/situations before a specific time in the past	*They'**d been listening** to the radio before it stopped working.*

Future time

VERB FORMS	USE(S)	EXAMPLES
1 *Will* + base form	a) Predictions based on personal opinion or conviction	*Lucy **will fail** that exam.*
	b) Spontaneous decisions (offers, promises, etc.)	*Wait. I'**ll help** you.*
2 *Be going to* + base form	a) Predictions based on evidence	*Look at those clouds! It'**s going to rain.***
	b) Plans – decisions already made	*I'**m going to buy** a new car.*
3 Present Continuous	Arrangements already made	*I'**m seeing** the doctor at six o'clock.*
4 Present Simple	a) Fixed events in the future, especially timetables	*The train **leaves** at eight thirty.*
	b) After time expressions	***When** I **see** him I'll tell him what you said.*
5 Future Continuous	a) Temporary events in progress	*Next week we'**ll be sitting** on the beach.*
	b) Inevitable events	*I'**ll be seeing** you next lesson.*
6 Future Perfect	Actions completed by specific time (the past in the future)	*Jo **will have gone** by the time you arrive.*

Cruel to be kind?

SPEAKING 1

1 Look at the photograph and the text. Do you agree with this way of bringing up children? How does it compare to the way they are brought up in your society?

2 Write down five characteristics of ideal parents. Think about factors such as age, personality and behaviour. Use the Present Simple and words like *never* and *always*. Example: *They never lose their temper.*

3 In groups, discuss what you wrote and agree on five characteristics.

'We never hit children or even like to scold them. We like to pick them up or ask them what is wrong, because if we punish them they will grow up to be difficult or bad-tempered. So we bring up our children mainly by talking and explaining things to them.'

(Chief of Amazonian Indian tribe)

REVISION AND EXTENSION 1

Habits and criticism

1 [2.1.] The pictures on the right illustrate comments and criticisms by Lucy and Ben of their families' habits.

a) Listen to them speaking and choose the pictures which best illustrate what they say.

b) [2.2] Listen again and complete the extracts.

EXTRACT 1 (Lucy)

1 My mum's _______ with the windows right down, and it's really embarrassing.

2 My father _______ but sausages and spaghetti, which gets a bit boring.

EXTRACT 2 (Ben)

1 Thomas is the worst, I reckon. He _______ and _______ his own way when he's watching the television.

2 Thomas _______ and taking things or borrowing things.

c) Which verb pattern above implies criticism? Check with Section 1 in the *Language reference*.

2 The adverbs in the box are all adverbs of frequency. Draw a line and position the adverbs along the line in order of frequency starting with *always* (see the example below). If you think they are the same, put one above the other.

always	sometimes	rarely
occasionally	hardly ever	
never	usually	often

always *never*

3 Work in groups of three: A, B and C.

a) Write down on different slips of paper five sentences about yourself using adverbs of frequency. Some sentences should be true and some false. Example:
I never drink coffee.

b) A reads out a sentence and B decides whether it is *True* or *False*. If B's guess is correct he/she takes the sentence. If not, A keeps it. The game continues with B reading out a sentence and C guessing.

c) The person with the most sentences decides if they are written in correct English. If not, he/she should correct the sentences and read them out again. The other two people can challenge these decisions and 'win' a sentence if they are right. The person with the most sentences is the winner.

4 Make a list of irritating habits which your partners, parents or friends have, and put them in order, with the most irritating at the top. Use language such as *He/She keeps + -ing* and *He/She's always + -ing*. Examples:
*'My father's **always leaving** newspapers all over the floor.'*
*'My wife **keeps forgetting** to put the top back on the toothpaste.'*
Find out what other people in the class have written in their lists.

Habit in the past

'I used to loathe the priests and my father and their systems of authority. I would refuse to cooperate in any way. He (my father) was not, in retrospect, a heartless man. He merely carried with him the values of his age. But they were not values that I shared.'

(from *Is That It?* by Bob Geldof)

1 Bob Geldof is a famous pop singer and media personality. Read the short extract from his autobiography.

a) What are the 'systems of authority' that Bob Geldof mentions?
b) What do you think his father's 'values' were?

2 Underline the different ways of talking about habit in the past. Check the pronunciation of these forms. Then check with Section 2 in the *Language reference* to see when *would* cannot be used.

3 In pairs, use *used to*, *would* and the Past Simple to talk about things your parents did, said and believed when you were a child. Did you accept their values or not? Example:
'They didn't use to let me watch television. I thought this was stupid, because . . .'

READING

1 You are going to read a newspaper article which consists of six paragraphs. First read the opening of each paragraph.

a) Guess how the paragraphs will continue.
b) What do you think the article is about?

(1) Perhaps memories of my own childhood have been coloured by time. I grew up during the war and without a father.

(2) I know of no other country where so many crimes are committed against children;

(3) The British tradition of boarding school will always remain a mystery for us poor foreigners.

(4) In public, at least, the British appear cold,

(5) Women friends who travel to Italy with their children come back glowing with praise for the way their children (and they themselves) are treated.

(6) How can I say that the British do not make good parents, when I happen to be married to an Englishman who is a wonderful father and husband, and have many English friends whom I consider to be excellent parents?

2 Read the whole article below quickly.

a) Match the openings in Exercise 1 to the paragraphs (a–f). Example: *a) = 6*
b) What would be the best title for this article?
- The British and boarding schools
- A national lack of tenderness
- Parents' contribution to football violence
- Children in Britain and Italy

3 Complete the following sentences.

a) The writer comes from ________.
b) The British 'national characteristic' is ________.
c) The 'English disease' is ________.
d) The writer had a very ________ childhood.
e) She thinks that being a bad parent can lead to ________.

4 Answer the following questions.

a) According to the writer, what is the British attitude to children in restaurants?
b) What is her opinion of parents who send their children to boarding schools?
c) What does she think about the way her friends bring their children up?

__(a)__ And yet every day the evidence before me in the streets and in the newspapers suggest that they are unusual. Where is the warmth and tenderness between adults and children which is so prevalent in my native Italy, among all classes and types of people? Is this the famous British 'reserve'?

__(b)__ and their children certainly *look* as if they bear the brunt of this national characteristic. In my experience, children thrive on tenderness. I have looked, but there certainly does not seem to be a lot of it among the British. Perhaps in private they are warm and affectionate parents, but in public they seem to go to extraordinary lengths to hide it.

__(c)__ it could almost be called the English disease. It seems almost impossible to turn on the television without some new crime being reported. Of course, there are similar horror stories in other countries, including Italy, but one does not hear about them with such appalling regularity. To what extent, I wonder, is football hooliganism the result of bad parenting?

__(d)__ Not only are they not shunned, but seats are proffered, doors smilingly held open for pram-pushing mothers and tables miraculously appear in crowded restaurants. Why is it that children are so unwelcome – and so rarely seen – in restaurants here?

__(e)__ In the course of our travels, my husband and I have often met British diplomats and foreign correspondents who, between gulps of pink gin at one party or another, would bewail the departure of their eight-year-old child, usually a son. Why were these distressed parents sending their children away? 'It's a beastly family tradition ... a high standard of education ... blah blah blah.' And if they *have* to go, why on earth when they are only eight? Of course some children like it. But what happens when children hate it? From countless melancholic memoirs, biographies and novels it seems that when it comes to tradition children have to do what they are told.

__(f)__ What kept us going was the love and support of family and friends. There was always that feeling of tenderness which I so often find lacking over here.

(from *The Independent*)

5 This is the reaction of some British people to the newspaper article. In groups, discuss your responses.

At least our children have some discipline and good manners and don't demand attention all the time. Francesca's kids think the world revolves around them.

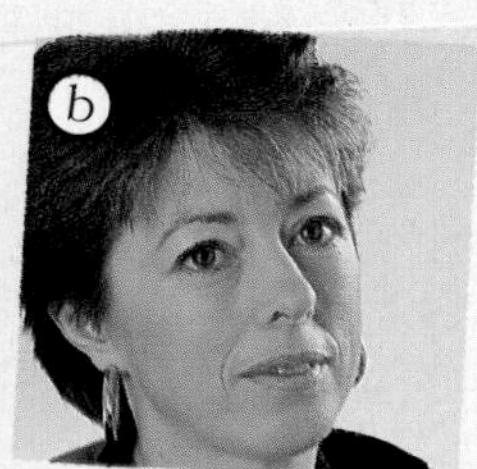

I think we are prepared to spend more time and money on our children's education and extra curricular activities than many foreign parents are.

Well at least we spend our summer holidays together and have our kids' friends back to the house a lot, which is more than can be said for a lot of families abroad.

British children grow up more independent and self-reliant because they're not over-babied and over-protected. Lots of foreign parents are much too possessive.

VOCABULARY

Word building

Guessing the meaning from prefixes

1 Write down as many words as you can which start with the prefixes in the box.

im-	de-	re-	over-	in-	bi-	under-	un-

2 Match the prefixes in the box above to the words in the box below in order to complete the the following sentences. The first one has been done for you.

perfect	paid	sensitive	sleep	frost	print
lingual	dress				

a) When the alarm clock doesn't go off we sometimes *oversleep*.
b) If a book sells out the publisher has to ______ it.
c) Somebody who doesn't consider people's feelings could be described as ______.
d) When you take something out of the freezer you sometimes have to ______ it before cooking it.
e) Before getting into bed we normally ______ and clean our teeth.
f) Someone who speaks two languages perfectly is ______.
g) Workers who think they are ______ often go on strike.
h) If something is faulty it is ______.

Using suffixes

1 Use a dictionary to complete the chart below and mark the stressed syllable in each word of more than one syllable.

ADJECTIVES	NOUNS	VERB
a'ttractive	*a'ttraction*	a'ttract
______	______	en'joy
______	'beauty	'beautify
wide	______	______
'patient	______	–
sweet	______	______
'terrified	______	______
______	dust	dust
'generous	______	–
______	speci'ality	______

2 The following words come from the text in the *Reading* section.

warm*th* tender*ness* fam*ous* nation*al* experi*ence*
horr*or* regular*ity* crowd*ed* educat*ion*

a) On the basis of the chart above, which part of speech is each word?

b) Make other words from those listed. Examples: *tender*, *educate*

Suffixes, word stress and the /ə/ sound

1 Look at the dictionary entries for the words *famous* and *education*.

> **famous** /ˈfeɪməs/ *adj* 1 very well known.
> USAGE compare **famous, well-known, distinguished, emi-**
>
> and therefore likely to be right.
> **education** /edjəˈkeɪʃən/ *n* the process by which a person's mind and character are developed through teaching.

Read the phonemic transcriptions (using the *Pronunciation chart* on page 149 to help you). Notice where the stress is in each word.

2 Work in pairs. What are the words transcribed below? Use the *Pronunciation chart* to help you or check in your dictionary.

a) /ˈtendənəs/ c) /ˈhɒrə/ e) /ɪnˈdʒɔɪəbəl/
b) /ˈnæʃənəl/ d) /ɪkˈspɪriəns/

3 Practise saying the words in Exercise 2, then underline the correct version of these sentences.

a) Suffixes *are / are not* stressed.
b) The /ə/ sound is always *stressed/unstressed*.

REVISION AND EXTENSION 2

Be / get used to (doing)

1 Read the following extract.

> I got used to the climate very quickly, although Jill found it difficult to cope with the humidity at first. We are still not used to starting work at seven in the morning but I'm sure we'll adjust. I'm sure I will never get used to driving on the right. Jill has to keep reminding me...

a) What does *used to* mean in this context?
b) How does *to be used to* differ in form and meaning from *used to* + base form? Check with Sections 2 and 3 in the *Language reference*.
c) What do you think the difference in meaning is between ***I got used to the climate*** and ***We are used to the climate . . .?***

2 In pairs, talk about all the things you have to get used to when:

a) you get your first job after leaving college.
b) you suddenly become famous.
c) you share a flat with someone.
d) you go on a diet.

Be or *get*?

Use one of the expressions in the box and complete the sentences below. Use *be* or *get*, depending on whether you are describing a state or a change in state.

angry	dressed	divorced	lost	ready
engaged	used			

a) I've had my bath and I'm just going to ________.
b) He always ________ at meetings.
c) Our dog doesn't bark in thunderstorms now because she ________ to the noise.
d) They've decided to ________ next year on St Valentine's Day.
e) She used to be married to my boss, but I think she ________ now.
f) I can't read a map so whenever I drive a long way I always ________.
g) OK, I ________. Let's go!

SPEAKING 2

Agreeing and disagreeing with people

1 [2.3] Listen to three short conversations and note what each conversation is about.

2 Listen again to the conversations.

a) Make notes of expressions used to agree and disagree. Example:
I agree absolutely.

b) Put the expressions of agreement and disagreement in order of strength from very strong agreement to very strong disagreement. Check with Section 5 in the *Language reference*.

c) Practise saying the expressions with the appropriate intonation.

Intonation: interest or surprise

[2.4] Listen to this extract from the first conversation and notice the way B's voice goes up when he is showing interest or surprise.

A: Well personally, I'm strongly against mixed education.
B: Are you? Why?

Think of similar 'echo questions' (and add words such as *When*, *Why*, *Where*, etc. if you like) to show interest or surprise in the following statements.

a) I strongly object to compulsory military service.
b) I used to go to boarding school.
c) I've just read an article about capital punishment.
d) They don't agree with sending people to prison.
e) Many old people in this country can't afford to look after themselves.

Having a discussion

1 In groups, give your opinions about the issues talked about in *Speaking 2* Exercise 1.

2 Do you agree or disagree with the following statements? Discuss and give your reasons.

a) Single people do not make good parents.
b) Children of working mothers are disadvantaged.
c) Fathers and mothers should have equal responsibility for looking after their children.
d) Younger people make better parents.

REVISION AND EXTENSION 3

The definite article (*the*)

1 When to use and not to use the definite article causes many students great problems, particularly in writing. Look at these extracts from a student's homework and, in pairs, try to decide when *the* should be used and when it should be left out.

I live in the Brazil where weather is very hot and people are very nice...

I love the music and last year I began learning to play guitar...

Next year I hope to go and study in United States.

2 Check your answers to Exercise 1 with Section 4 in the *Language reference*. Then look at the sentences below and underline the most likely alternative.

a) I enjoy reading *books / the books.*
b) He is reading *books / the books* he got for his birthday.
c) *Poverty / The poverty* seems to be getting worse.
d) Where can you buy *stamps / the stamps*? I haven't got any left.
e) It is a period of great problems for *Europe / the Europe.*
f) We went skiing in *Alps / the Alps* last year.
g) Where's Meg? She's feeding *baby / the baby.* She won't be long.
h) Can you play *violin / the violin*?
i) Is Julie still at *school / the school*? It's after four!
j) What did you have for *breakfast / the breakfast*?
k) Where are you meeting him? At *hospital / the hospital.*
l) He comes from *China / the China*, I think.
m) I can't find *money / the money* I left out for you.
n) *Money / The money* is my biggest worry in life.
o) Sam is really good at *rugby / the rugby.*
p) What did you think of *President's / the President's* speech?
q) *Elderly / The elderly* should be given certain privileges.

WRITING

Personal letter

1 Read the first paragraph of this letter written by a student.

14th may, o/p
30 Linnaen Street,
Cambridge
Boston

Dear Claude,

How are you? It was very kind of you taking me vf
gr/p to airport by your car and Im very greatful. In the sp
end the plane was late by two hours but I had
vf met one of my friends so we enjoyed very much wo
ww talking together. Actually I'm studying English
again – in America!
When I arrived at Rio last month all the family
was there to take me, including dog. We have
talked for hours. But I'm missing you and the
other students at the school in england and I
want coming back there. If Laura has come back
this term say her that I want that she writes to
me. Give my best wishes to our teacher too.
Can you ask him to correct this letter for me?
Please write to me at my adress above.

Yours with affection,

Pedro

P.S. Why dont you come to Boston to see me?
I'm going to stay until 2nd July here and
then return to brazil.

a) What is the purpose of the letter?

b) Symbols identify mistakes in the following areas:
- punctuation
- spelling
- grammar
- word order
- verb forms
- vocabulary
- organisation
- word missing

In pairs, match the symbols with the mistakes. Then correct the mistakes.

2 Look at the rest of the letter.

a) Identify the mistakes which are underlined, and write the symbol in the margin (e.g. if it is a punctuation error write *p*).

b) Correct the mistakes.

3 What are the areas you need to improve most in your own writing? (Use the list in Exercise 1 b) to help you.)

4 Imagine you are Claude.

a) Write a letter to Pedro thanking him for his invitation and giving him news of what has been happening at school.

b) Look back over your letter carefully. Check:
- grammar, including verb forms and word order. (Check that you have used the definite article correctly.)
- punctuation.
- spelling.
- appropriate vocabulary.
- layout and organisation.

Concentrate on your own particular weaknesses.

Language reference

1 Habit in the present

A common way of talking about habit in the present is to use the Present Simple, with an adverb of frequency. The adverb usually comes before the main verb but after the verb *be*:

*He **always goes** to work by bus.*
*She **is usually** late.*

Will is also used to talk about predictable or characteristic behaviour in the present:

He ***won't usually speak*** *to us at breakfast time but he'**ll play** games with us in the evenings.*

The Present Continuous with *always* is often used to criticise annoying habits:

*She'**s always cleaning** the house even when it's not necessary.*

However, the structure is not always negative:

*I like Ali. He'**s always smiling**.*

The verb *keeps* + *-ing* also often implies criticism:

*He **keeps talking** when I'm trying to listen to my music.*

2 Habit in the past

A common way of talking about habit in the past is to use the Past Simple:

*Every morning I **got up, worked** for a few hours and then **went off** to meet Jenny.*

Habits which are no longer true and which are contrasted with present habits can also be described by using *used to* + base form of the verb and *would* + base form of the verb:

*When I was living abroad I **used to swim** for a while before breakfast.*
*My father **would always read** the sports page first.*
***Did** you **use to go out** with Jim?*

Used to (but not *would*) can also be used to talk about discontinued states:

*He **used to live** in Paris.* (NOT ~~*He would live in Paris*~~*.*)

Used to + base form is often confused with *be / get* + *used to* + *-ing* (see below).

3 *Be / Get* + *used to* (+ *-ing*)

In *be used to* (+ noun or *-ing* form of verb), *used* is an adjective, meaning *accustomed* and *to* is a preposition. It implies that something is a habitual state:

*She'**s used to** his strange ways.*
*I **am used to getting up** early.*

Get used to suggests a change in state, when you *become* used to something:

*I have **got used to driving** on the left.* (But I wasn't used to it before.)

Get can also be used with other adjectives and verbs to show a change in state:

*She's going to **get dressed** in a minute.*
*They **got to like** their teacher.*

4 The definite article (*the*)

The definite article is used:

a) Before singular and plural nouns when talking about things that both speakers know about:
*Come and sit by **the** fire.* (It is clear which fire – there is only one.)
*These are **the** books I bought yesterday.* (You have just told me which books you are talking about.)

b) When referring to some public places (especially when talking about them in general, or as buildings rather than institutions):
*I'm meeting him at **the** hospital / **the** cinema / **the** bank.*

c) With some geographical locations:
– collections of states and islands:
***the** United States, **the** Bahamas*
– seas, rivers, mountain ranges:
***the** Atlantic, **the** Thames, **the** Alps* (but *Mount Fuji*)

d) Sometimes, to talk about nationalities, groups of people, animals, musical instruments, etc. in general:
***the** Germans, **the** Italians*
*We're having a raffle to help **the** poor.*
***The** tiger is threatened with extinction.*

e) To talk about unique things (i.e. there is only one):
***the** New York Times, **the** French Revolution, **the** army*

The definite article is NOT used:

a) Before plural and uncountable nouns when talking about people and things in general, and abstract ideas:
Do ***women*** *drive more carefully than* ***men****?*
Poverty *is becoming worse.*

b) For prepositional phrases of place – usually when we are talking about public places as institutions rather than buildings:
*Is Julia still **at school**?*
*My husband is **in hospital**.*

c) When talking about some geographical locations:
– countries (*China, Britain*)
– continents (*Asia, Africa*)
– towns, cities, counties (*London, Essex*)

d) When referring to parts of the body, transport, meals, games, some expressions of time, seasons, months, etc.:
*Mandy's got **big ears**. / I'm going **by car**.*
*Have you had **breakfast**? / The park closes **at night**.*

5 Agreeing and disagreeing

The following expressions of agreement and disagreement are listed in order, beginning with strong agreement and ending with strong disagreement:

I couldn't agree more.
(I agree) absolutely.
Exactly.
So do I. / Neither do I.
Do you think so?
Well, actually, I'm not sure I agree with that.
I disagree entirely.
Rubbish.
You must be joking!

Unit 3

TV or not TV?

LISTENING AND SPEAKING

The most important thing we've learned,
So far as children are concerned,
Is never, NEVER, **NEVER** let
Them near your television set –
5 Or better still, just don't install
The idiotic thing at all.
In almost every house we've been,
We've watched them gaping at the screen.
They loll and slop and lounge about,
10 And stare until their eyes pop out.
(Last week in someone's place we saw
A dozen eyeballs on the floor.)
They sit and stare and stare and sit
Until they're hypnotized by it,
15 Until they're absolutely drunk
With all that shocking ghastly junk.
Oh yes, we know it keeps them still,
They don't climb out the window sill,
They never fight or kick or punch,
20 They leave you free to cook the lunch
And wash the dishes in the sink –
But did you ever stop to think,
To wonder just exactly what
This does to your beloved tot?

(from *The Oompa-Loompas' Song* by Roald Dahl)

1 [3.1] Listen to the recording and read the extract from the poem at the same time. Then answer the following questions.

a) What does the writer recommend doing?
b) What is *the idiotic thing?* (line 6)
c) Find two verbs meaning *watch.*
d) Which verbs describe how children sit while watching TV?
e) What does the writer think of the programmes on TV?
f) What reasons does he give for letting children watch TV?

2 [3.2] Listen to an argument between Gillie and Mark about television. Tick the points Gillie puts forward in the following list.

a) It's a passive activity.
b) It stops kids doing their homework.
c) It's addictive.
d) It causes behaviour problems.
e) It ruins the eyes.
f) It stops people doing other things.
g) The programmes are rubbish.
h) Families never see each other.
i) Children are affected by the violence on TV.

3 Listen again and make a list of Mark's arguments.

4 In groups, discuss which of the arguments you agree with.

Connected speech

1 [3.3] Listen to this extract from the discussion.

And instead of reading, instead of playing musical instruments, what are they doing? They're sitting in front of this television . . .

a) Underline two more weak forms with the /ə/ sound, such as /ənd/, and one contracted form.

b) Put a box (□) above the stressed words.

2 In pairs, practise reading the sentences, trying to focus on the stressed words.

3 Which of the following parts of speech are not normally stressed?

– nouns	– pronouns
– verbs	– articles
– prepositions	– adjectives
– auxiliary and modal verbs	– adverbs

Check with Section 2 in the *Language reference.*

4 Work in pairs, and read the following dialogue.

A: Do you agree that television can become addictive if you're not careful?

B: Yes, I do. Some people are able to be selective and only watch the things that they really want to, but I'd say that the average person just switches it on out of habit and is glued to it all night – just switching from channel to channel until they find something they like.

a) Underline the words which carry most stress.

b) Practise reading the dialogue aloud.

c) [3.4] Listen and compare your version with the recording.

REVISION

Events up to now: Present Perfect

1 Read the article from a TV magazine.

Nureyev:

the man and the legend

Our documentary at 9 p.m. on BBC1 on Sunday looks at the life and career of perhaps the most famous male dancer ever.

Rudolf Nureyev has been dancing since he began taking folk-dancing lessons at the age of seven in his native Russia. After two years with the Kirov School, he graduated at the age of nineteen and soon became one of the stars of the Kirov company. However, he was only with them for three years before making his famous 'leap for freedom' during a tour of Paris in 1961. He has been in the West ever since.

Nureyev has only been back to the Soviet Union twice since his defection – the first time to visit his ill mother and the second time when he went back to dance with the Kirov company in 1989.

For seventeen years his partnership with Margot Fonteyn was the most famous in the world. In more recent years his career has diversified into acting, and he has appeared in several films, such as *Valentino*. He also starred in the stage production of *The King and I* in New York.

He was also director of the Paris Opera Ballet for six years – there is talk that his volatile temperament and the rows that ensued were responsible for his departure. In this documentary you will see ...

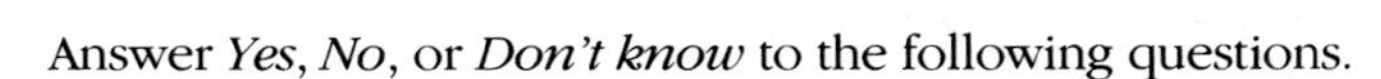

Answer *Yes*, *No*, or *Don't know* to the following questions.

a) Does Nureyev still dance?
b) When did he first return to Russia?
c) Is he still the director of the Paris Opera Ballet?
d) When did he appear in *Valentino*?

2 Look at each pair of sentences and answer the question about them. Check uses of the Present Perfect in the *Language reference*.

a) In which sentence is the past and the present connected?
  i) Nureyev was director of the Paris Opera for six years.
  ii) He has been in the West for thirty years.

b) Which of the following sentences is preferable, and why?
  i) Nureyev has been dancing since he was seven.
  ii) Nureyev has danced since he was seven.

c) Which of these sentences is not correct, and why?
  i) He's had a home in Italy for many years.
  ii) He's been having a home in Italy for many years.

3 These answers relate to the text. Give the questions.

a) Since he was seven.
b) For three years.
c) Since 1961.
d) Twice.
e) For seventeen years.

PRACTICE

1 Look at the list below and find a student who has done one of the things.

a) had dancing lessons
b) played a musical instrument
c) had a Turkish bath
d) walked out of a film because it was awful
e) collected anything as a hobby
f) danced/acted/sung on stage
g) done something embarrassing in public
h) written a poem or a story
i) broken the law
j) gone out with somebody really special

a) Ask for more information, using expressions like *How long, Why, Where.* Example:
A: *Have you ever had dancing lessons?*
B: *Yes, I have.*
A: *Do you still have them?*
How long have you been having them?
How long did you have them?
What level did you get up to? etc.

b) Make notes under headings like those below and collect similar information about five more people.

NAME	WHAT HE/SHE'S DONE	MORE INFORMATION
Marina	*Played musical instrument*	*Used to play the recorder when she was at school. Has been learning the clarinet for 8 years and has passed 3 exams.*

c) Look at the example below. Write similar sentences on different slips of paper, giving the information you found out, without mentioning the names of the people you are writing about.

She has learned how to play two different musical instruments. She played the recorder until she left school and she's been learning the clarinet for 8 years. She's passed 3 exams.

d) Exchange your papers with someone else. Guess the people being described.

e) Finally, look carefully at the sentences and correct them if necessary.

2 The notes below are from a newspaper reporter's notebook.

a) Write a newspaper story based on these notes. Remember they are only notes, so you will have to include extra words such as prepositions, articles, etc. as necessary. Example:
Police have not yet found the 19-year-old university student who vanished while she was on her way to a lecture last week.

Police not yet found 19-year-old university student; vanish on way to lecture last week.
Police all over country look for her 3 days; not have any information yet which help inquiries. They already interview boyfriend and flatmate.
Anyone have information please phone 081 223765.

b) [3.5] Listen to the recording to check your story.

3 In pairs, write similar stories based on the following note.

Film star Jane Carman, romantic wedding south of France yesterday. So far this sixth marriage!
Apparently she divorce last husband - pop star Tim Sullivan - because not show enough affection to her cat.
Carman recently make new film in Hollywood with first husband. Now decide to give up acting.

EXTENSION

Present result: Present Perfect Simple and Continuous

1 Read the caption of the cartoon. Which verb form is used to focus on:

a) the present result of a past activity?
b) a completed activity?
c) the activity itself?

Check with Section 1 in the *Language reference*.

'His eyes have gone square because he's been watching TV all day. So far he's watched three murders, two fights and an armed robbery.'

2 Underline the most likely form below and give reasons for your choice. Check your reasons with Section 1 in the *Language reference*.

a) I've *been deciding / decided* to go out.
b) She's *been writing / written* all morning.
c) She's *been writing / written* four letters.
d) He's *been borrowing / borrowed* money off him three times.
e) Have you *been hearing / heard* the news today?
f) Have you *been watching / watched* that series on BBC1? It's the last episode tonight.
g) Oh no. I've *been tearing / torn* my jumper again.
h) I've *been studying / studied* some Spanish. I think I'll do a course in French next.
i) I've *been learning / learned* loads of vocabulary in class today.

PRACTICE

1 Match the questions in column A with the most likely answers in column B. In pairs, use the cues in column B to make your response. Use either the Present Perfect Simple or the Present Perfect Continuous. Example:
'Why aren't you hungry?' 'I've been eating sweets all morning.'

A	B
a) 'Why aren't you hungry?'	1 talk all day
b) 'Why are you so late?'	2 be on a diet
c) 'Why is Melanie depressed?'	3 break it
d) 'Why is your hair soaking?'	4 eat sweets all morning
e) 'Why are you wearing a tracksuit?'	5 run
f) 'Why is she so brown?'	6 have a drink with the boss
g) 'Why has he lost his voice?'	7 fail her driving test again
h) 'Why is your arm in plaster?'	8 rain
i) 'Why do you look so thin?'	9 come back from holiday

2 Put the time expressions in the box into the appropriate place in the sentences below. Some of them relate to completed actions and some to actions in progress.

recently	yet	just	nearly	so far	already	all day

a) Have you really read that book? That was quick!
b) I've been eating very little.
c) They've finished most of it but they haven't painted the hall.
d) She's been in her room studying.
e) Yes, he's arrived. I can hear his car.
f) They've finished their homework. They'll be ready in ten minutes.
g) He's only interviewed five of them but he's going to see the others tomorrow.

VOCABULARY

Television

Look at the words in the box which describe different kinds of television programmes.

children's programmes	documentaries	drama series	
quiz shows	soap operas	wildlife programmes	news
sports programmes	chat shows	films	current affairs

a) Match the photographs above to the programmes.
b) Which four types of TV programmes do you like and dislike watching most? Add any others you can think of.
c) Compare with the other people in the class. Which types of programmes are most popular? Which are most unpopular?

SPEAKING

Planning a TV schedule

1 As a pre-interview task for a job with Channel 5 TV, the company Controller has asked all applicants to plan and present a typical weekday evening's TV viewing between 4 p.m. and 10 p.m. Applicants will have to talk about the criteria they used for selecting and rejecting programmes.

In groups, plan the kind of programmes to include. The maximum length of a programme should be two hours and the average number of programmes will be eight. Think about the following questions.

a) What range of programmes would appeal to a wide audience?
b) What kind of programmes are suitable for different times of day?
c) Should TV be educational as well as entertaining? Do TV planners have a moral obligation to educate?
d) Should sex and violence be censored, or at least restricted to certain times?

2 One person from each group should present their schedule to the rest of the class, explaining their choice of programmes.

3 Vote on the best schedule. (Do not vote for your own.)

WRITING

Describing something you've seen or read

1 Read the film review.

a) Say in which paragraph the writer talks about: the plot, the performances, whether they recommend the film or not, the background to the film, the film in general.
b) What tense is the review written in? Why?
c) Make a note of the adjectives used to talk about: Laura, the husband, the film in general, the plot, the town Laura moved to.

2 In pairs, choose a film you both know (or a book, TV programme, play, etc.).

a) Decide on adjectives to describe the characters and the story. Examples: *exciting, unconvincing*
b) Use some of the adverbs of degree in the box below to make the adjectives you use stronger or weaker. Example:
*The film was **really exciting** but the actor who played the main part was **rather unconvincing**.*

extremely	rather	incredibly	quite	really	a bit
fairly					

c) Remember to use adverbs to 'colour' verbs and other adverbs as well as adjectives. Examples:
*... which **successfully** disguises ...*
*He was **frighteningly** convincing.*
d) Look at the examples of 'strong' adjectives in the box below and replace them with a normal adjective and *very* or *really*. Write a sentence using them. Example:
(stunning) *The actress was **really attractive**.*

stunning	riveting	hilarious	terrifying	packed
thrilled	brilliant	dreadful	astonishing	

e) Practise saying the adjectives in the box with the intensifying adverb *absolutely* and then choose some of them to describe the film you are discussing. Example:
*The acting was **absolutely dreadful**.*

3 Write a review describing a film, play, TV programme, etc. that you've seen recently, or a book that you've read (it could be the one you discussed earlier).

a) Organise your review something like this:
  i) Introduction (include factual information: title, writer, director, actors)
  ii) The plot, setting, characters
  iii) Your feelings and thoughts (e.g. about the acting, story)
  iv) Conclusion (recommendation)
b) Check what you have written to make sure that you have included a range of adjectives and adverbs.

1 Directed by Joseph Ruben and starring the stunning Julia Roberts as Laura and Patrick Bergin as her obsessive husband, *Sleeping with the Enemy* is this year's spooky thriller and can now be seen at the Odeon in Leicester Square.

2 We first meet Laura at her sea-front home where she is unhappily married to a rich handsome man who dominates and abuses her. She fakes death to escape her nightmarish marriage and adopts a new life in a small delightful mid-west town but inevitably her husband discovers the truth and starts to track her down.

3 Julia Roberts has the difficult task of being a passive victim but manages to come across as innocent and vulnerable. Her reawakening after years of torment is captured extremely sensitively. Patrick Bergin is frighteningly convincing as the psychopathic husband, appearing and disappearing with great economy of movement and sinister menace.

4 The story is, in fact, too similar to *Fatal Attraction* to claim any originality, but the characters are well observed and there are imaginative moments. Although Rubin is a little too free with the fraudulent moments of suspense, the film jangles the nerves effectively with a series of shocks, which successfully disguises a rather feeble plot.

5 I would recommend this as an entertaining film for those who like to be kept on the edge of their seats.

Language reference

1 Present Perfect Simple and Continuous

The Present Perfect connects the present to the past. There are three main related uses:

a) The Present Perfect Simple (*have* + past participle) can be used to talk about a past experience which is important at the time of speaking.
It could be:
– a (very) recent one:
A lorry ***has crashed*** *on the M1.*
*I'****ve*** *just* ***finished*** *my book.*
– one that has happened at some indefinite time in the past:
*I'****ve read*** *that book.*
When thinking of an indefinite time in the past, we use the Present Perfect with adverbials such as *so far, up to now, ever, yet, recently, already* . When we think of something completed at a specific time in the past we use the Past Simple and definite time adverbials such as *last week, two minutes ago*, etc.

b) The Present Perfect Continuous (*has / have + been + -ing* form) and Present Perfect Simple are both used to express actions and activities which began in the past and have continued up to the present. Time expressions such as *for* and *since* are used to express duration, and answer the question *How long . . . ?* (*For* describes the length of a period of time, and *since* refers to the beginning of a period of time.) The continuous form focuses on the activity in progress and the fact that it is often temporary.
Compare:
*I'm English, but I'****ve been living*** *in Lisbon for the last ten years.* (I still live in Lisbon, but it's probably temporary.)

have been living *will probably go home*
PAST *born* ten years ago NOW FUTURE

*I'****ve lived*** *here since I was born.* (I still live here, and I've no intention of moving.)

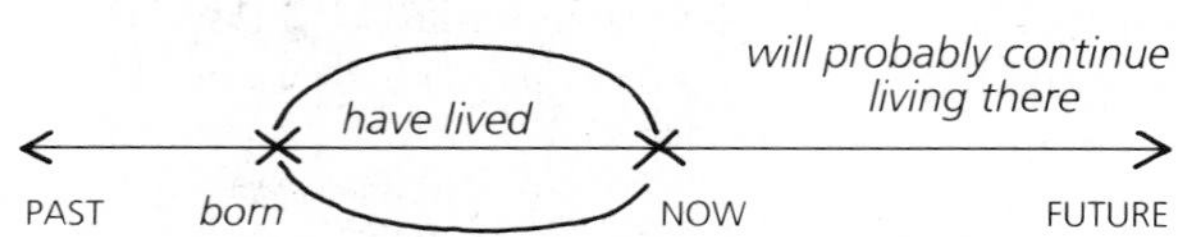

Note that some verbs (sometimes known as 'state' verbs) are not usually used in the continuous form because they do not usually describe activities or processes:
I've known *him for six years.* (NOT ~~*I've been knowing*~~ . . .)

c) Both the Present Perfect Simple and Continuous can be used to talk about present results of past activities.
The Present Perfect Simple emphasises the completed activity:
I'm very pleased with myself. ***I've finished*** *the report and* ***written*** *the letters.* (It doesn't matter when.)
The Present Perfect Continuous focuses on the (usually recent) activity or situation itself which produced the result. The activity itself may or may not be finished:
'Your hair's soaking.' 'Yes, ***I've been swimming****.'*
(The swimming is finished.)
'Your eyes are red.' 'Yes, ***I've been reading*** *all day.'*
(We don't know if she's finished reading.)

2 Weak forms and contractions

In a typical English sentence, content words (nouns, verbs, adjectives and adverbs) tend to be stressed, and grammatical words (pronouns, prepositions, modal and auxiliary verbs, conjunctions and articles) are weak. Words which are weak have reduced vowels – the vowels are usually pronounced with the /ə/ sound:
can /kən/; *the* /ðə/; *for* /fə/
When the grammatical words are at the end of a sentence, emphasised or contrasted, they become strong:
Yes, they ***are***. (/ɑː/)
No, you're wrong. Mary ***can*** *come.* (/kæn/)
Simon can't swim but Paul ***can***. (/kæn/)
Auxiliary verbs are usually contracted in normal connected speech. *He has* for example, becomes *He's*; *They are* becomes *They're*.

Unit 4

But I can't do without it!

READING

'The first time I gambled, I just stayed for an hour. I didn't get addicted until the next day. I can honestly say, from that day on, I was in the casino at two o'clock every afternoon, seven days a week, for the next five years, except when I was penniless. It was a complete obsession.'

(from *Male & Femail*)

1 The man in the picture lost his money gambling in a casino.

a) What other forms of gambling are there? (The pictures below will help you.)

b) Why do you think people start gambling?
c) What kind of people do you think gamblers are (e.g. age, sex, background)?
d) What kind of help or advice would you give them if they wanted to stop gambling?

2 The text you are going to read is about a teenager who became addicted to gambling. Write any questions that you would like to ask him.

Reading

1 Read 'Julian's story' below, and see if your questions were answered.

1 A quarter of all the people who seek the help of *Gamblers Anonymous* are children addicted to fruit machines.

2 Julian started playing fruit machines five years ago when he was 13. Since then he has spent more than £20,000 – money he has earned, borrowed or stolen – on what quickly grew into a frightening addiction.

3 'I was in a bowling alley with friends one day. One of them was playing the electric fruit machines and he kept pestering me to have a go. First I thought it was a waste of money, but somehow I couldn't keep away. At the beginning I used to spend all my paper-round money on the machines, but then I started selling everything I owned – even my records and tapes. I took money from my parents and sold their things, too. I always told myself it wasn't really stealing, that I was just borrowing and would pay them back.

4 'By the time I was 15 I was already spending more than £30 a week on machines. They were my whole life. I used to skive off school every day and play the machine in the local café. I was in a world of my own where nothing else mattered.

5 'Winning wasn't even important; I always knew I was going to lose. There was just something about the machines. They became my friends; friends I didn't owe anything to and who never got annoyed with me. Whatever mood I was in it made no difference to them, we got on fine. I'd go into the arcade feeling tense and excited, but as soon as I started playing I became totally relaxed.

6 'Sometimes I'd spend £20 on a taxi to get to one of my favourite machines. – the bigger and more complicated the better – and I would spend a solid eight or nine hours playing. When I ran out of money I felt completely shattered and was desperate to get more to carry on.

7 'The crunch came the Christmas before I left school when I was 16. I was so frantic to get some money I stole my parents' antiques and sold them. When they found out, they made me show them each shop where I had sold the antiques and they bought them all back. I left home after that, rented a room and found a job in an insurance company. After I'd paid for food and rent I spent every penny I earned on machines – at first it was £350 a month, then it went up to £700 a month.'

8 Julian is one of the lucky ones. He hasn't played for five months now and is determined to keep it that way. 'I had just split up with my girlfriend and was feeling very upset. Quite suddenly I realised how much pain I'd put other people through – it made me feel so bad I wanted to die. It was incredibly difficult, but I stopped playing completely. I didn't get any help – I did it on my own. Now I'll have to live with all the damage I've caused and try to rebuild things. I'm tempted all the time but I know if I go back it'll destroy me.

9 'If you haven't been through it you can't understand what it's like. It starts off as a bit of fun, but it's like a silent drug that eats you up from inside.'

(from *Living Magazine*)

2 Read the text again and find out:

a) how old he was when he started gambling.
b) why he began gambling.
c) what he gambled his money on.
d) where he got the money from.
e) why he liked it.
f) why he gave up.
g) how he stopped.
h) if he misses it.

3 What is the significance of these numbers in the story? Give as much information as you can.

a) 13
b) £20,000
c) 5 years
d) £30
e) £20
f) 16
g) £700
h) 5 months

4 Read the text again. Guess the meaning in context of the words and expressions in *italics*.

a) *pestering me to have a go* (paragraph 3)
b) *a waste of money* (paragraph 3)
c) *paper-round* (paragraph 3)
d) *skive off* school (paragraph 4)
e) a *solid* eight or nine hours (paragraph 6)
f) the *crunch* (paragraph 7)
g) so *frantic* to get some money (paragraph 7)
h) *split up with* (paragraph 8)
i) *put* other people *through* (paragraph 8)

5 Interview each other.

a) Work in groups.

GROUP (S) A
You are a television interviewer. Think of questions to ask Julian, using the cues below. Think of other questions to ask him about his family life.

1 When / start / play / fruit machines?
2 How much / spend?
3 How / get money?
4 How long ago / stop / play?
5 How / feel / while / play?
6 Why / leave home?
7 Why / give up?
8 How long ago / give up?

GROUP (S) B
You are Julian. Read the text again carefully so that you will be able to answer details about your life. Discuss what kind of family life you had (use your imagination!) and be prepared to answer questions about it.

b) Work in pairs to conduct the interview. There should be one member of Group A and one of Group B in each pair.

VOCABULARY

Verbs and nouns (collocation)

'Gambling wrecks lives, smashes marriages, breaks hearts.'

1 *Smash*, *break* and *wreck* have a similar meaning (*destroy*), but they are usually used with different nouns. Complete the following:

a) You ________ a promise, a habit, a rule, the law.
b) You ________ a ship, a career, your chances, a plane.
c) You ________ a car, a window.

2 Link the nouns with the verbs you think are normally used together. The first one has been done for you.

a)

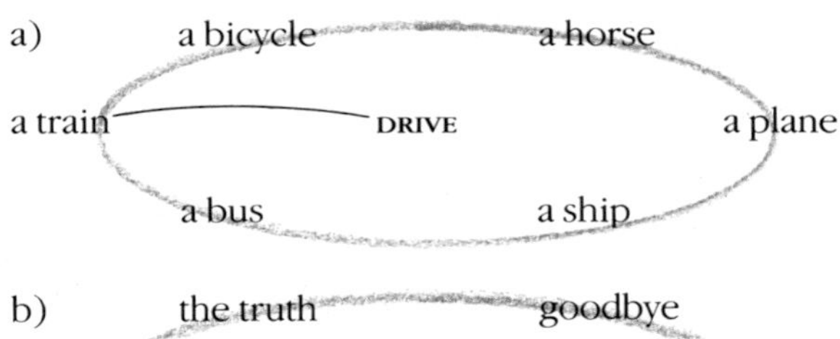

b)

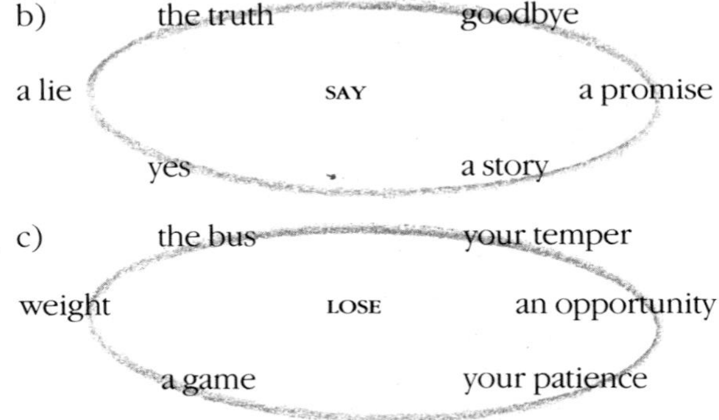

c)

d)

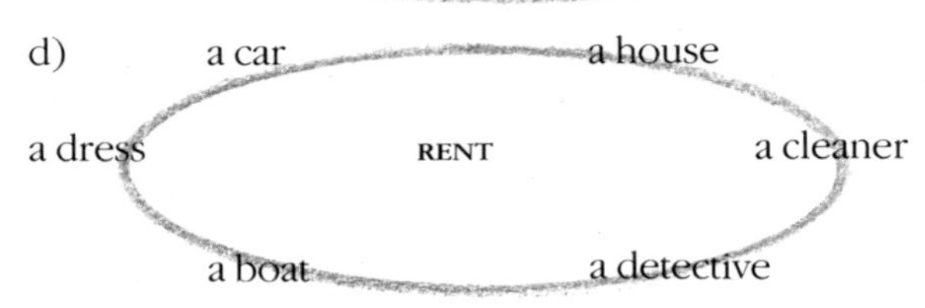

3 Compare your answers.

4 Think of at least three things that you can:

a) miss
b) waste
c) do
d) have
e) keep
f) make

Adjectives and prepositions

1 Which preposition do you need to complete the following sentences?

a) I am addicted ________ chocolate.
b) They are obsessed ________ money.
c) He is dependent ________ alcohol.

2 Complete these sentences using a preposition.

a) I am afraid ________ heights.
b) He's very good ________ sport.
c) I am keen ________ music.
d) I get worried ________ my exams.
e) I am very bad ________ maths.
f) We are interested ________ photography.
g) She's upset ________ the news.
h) He is always very late ________ work.

Sounds: /v/, /w/

1 Practise saying the sentence below. Notice the position of your teeth when you say /v/ and /w/.
He's always very late for work.

2 [4.1] Listen to the sentences below and then practise saying them in pairs.

a) It's the twentieth anniversary of the war, I believe.
b) Would Vera like a glass of white wine while she's waiting?
c) He's very vain but wonderfully witty!
d) We're waiting for William to drive to work.
e) Why don't you and Vicky go for a walk in the woods?
f) The view from the van window is marvellous.

3 Look at the words in the box.

wreck	weather	who	where	white
whole	whisper	wrist	what	

a) In which words is the *w* not pronounced? Check in your dictionary.
b) What is the pronunciation of words beginning with *wr*?
c) What is the pronunciation of words beginning with *wh*?

Check your answers with Section 5 in the *Language reference*.

SPEAKING

1 Look at the photographs. In groups, talk about the following points. Which addictions and obsessions do you think are:

a) commonly associated with a particular age or type of person?
b) a problem in your country?
c) very serious?

2 What do you think causes addictions such as the ones in the photographs. What can help people stop?

REVISION

Past Simple, Past Continuous or Past Perfect?

1 Look at the following sentences.
In 1990, when Julian (1) *was 18 he* (2) *was living on his own in a flat. He* (3) *had already been gambling for five years and his parents* (4) *had thrown him out of their house.*

a) Name the verb forms underlined and numbered 1, 2, 3 and 4.
b) Show on the timeline which of the verb forms (1, 2, 3 and 4) are represented by the marks ●, ✕, ←← and 〰 on the timeline.

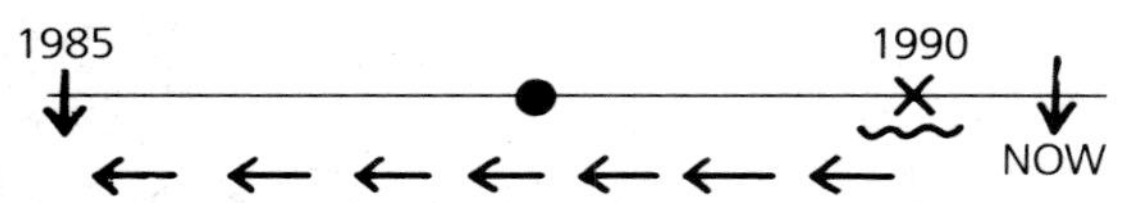

2 Underline the most likely verb forms in these sentences. Discuss reasons for your answers.

a) When he decided to retire Graham Davis *wrote / was writing / had written* twenty novels.
b) The wind *howled / was howling / had howled* outside so I decided to take a jumper with me.
c) I *heard / was hearing / had heard* the phone as I turned the key in the lock.
d) I looked everywhere for my car keys and then I remembered my son *took / was taking / had taken* the car to work.
e) As soon as I heard the news I *phoned / was phoning / had phoned* my mother.
f) 'Why were you outside in the pouring rain?' 'I *brought / was bringing / had brought* in the washing.'

3 Complete the sentences below, changing the cues in brackets to the Past Simple, Past Continuous or Past Perfect. Example:
When she got to her car (*she realise someone break into it*).
When she got to her car she realised someone had broken into it.

a) When I saw Tom last week (*he smoke again*).
b) I had a cup of coffee (*because I run out of tea*).
c) When Penny saw her mother (*she hug her*).
d) (*After I pay for food and rent*) I used to spend every penny I earned on machines.
e) She was very quiet so I asked her what (*she think about*).
f) (*As soon as I see him*) I knew something was wrong.
g) By the time I was fifteen (*I spend more than £30 a week on machines*).

EXTENSION

Past Perfect Simple or Continuous?

1 Why is the Past Perfect Simple used in the first sentence and the Past Perfect Continuous in the second sentence?
*I **had stolen** some antiques from my parents and they found out.*
*I **had been stealing** from my parents for ages and when they found out they asked me to leave home.*

Check with Sections 3 and 4 in the *Language reference*.

2 Look at the sentences below and say which ones are not likely, and why.

a) I *had been splitting up* with my girlfriend, and I was feeling very upset.
b) She *had been cleaning* the car all morning and felt exhausted.
c) Sam had cuts on his legs because he *had been falling over* a lot during the football match.
d) I *had read* the report and I wanted to finish it.
e) Our neighbours called the police because someone *had broken* into their house while they were on holiday.
f) She *had been walking* straight in without knocking so they didn't have time to hide.

3 Read this account of an incident on a train and change the verbs in brackets into the appropriate form.

A funny thing (1 *happen*) to me when I (2 *come*) home from work the other day. The train back from London (3 *be*) very crowded as usual, but anyway I eventually (4 *manage*) to find a seat after I (5 *look*) for ages. It was in a non-smoking compartment, unfortunately, but that was too bad. Anyway, next to me was a very smart looking older woman. A scruffy-looking bloke (6 *sit*) opposite her. After a few minutes this bloke (7 *take*) a cigarette out of his pocket and (8 *start*) to light it. The woman politely (9 *ask*) him not to smoke and (10 *point*) at the no-smoking sign. The bloke (11 *carry on*) as if she (12 *not say*) anything and then (13 *lean*) forward and (14 *blow*) smoke in her face. I (15 *feel*) angry myself by this time but the woman was amazing! She (16 *jumped*) up, (17 *take*) the fire extinguisher and (18 *soak*) him in water. He was so surprised that he (19 *drop*) his cigarette, which the water (20 *put*) out anyway. Then she calmly (21 *pick*) his cigarette up, (22 *put*) it in the bin and (23 *go on*) reading. It was brilliant! The whole compartment, who (24 *watch*) the episode with great interest, (25 *applaud*).

Sounds: /p/, /b/

1 Read the sentence below. Which sound is 'voiced', /p/ or /b/?
*The woman **picked** it up and **put** it in the **bin**.*

2 [4.2] Listen to the following sentences. Which words can you hear?

a) Have you got a *bet/pet?*
b) Do you need a *bin/pin?*
c) Can you see that *cab/cap?*
d) I sometimes dream of a *peach/beach.*
e) Is the cat's name *Pen/Ben?*
f) It's a *bill/pill.*

3 Take turns to read the sentences, choosing either the /p/ or the /b/ word. Ask your partner to say which one it is.

WRITING

Linking expressions

Time

Complete the following sentences and then discuss them with a partner. Make them true about your own life where possible.

a) *As soon as* I was old enough . . .
b) *Until* I met . . .
c) *Before* I began . . .
d) *While* I was living . . .
e) *After* I finish . . .
f) *As* I was having . . .
g) *By the time* I . . .
h) *Since* I started learning English . . .

Addition, contrast, reason and result

1 Use each of the words in the box once to link the sentences below. (The number of sentences you have to write is indicated in brackets.) In some cases more than one answer is possible. Change the grammar and punctuation, word and sentence order if necessary.
Example:
I had a cold. I went swimming. (*One sentence*)
Although I had a cold, I went swimming.

since therefore too however so as well as as although

a) I had had no sun for a long time. I was depressed. I went out and booked a holiday. (*One sentence*)
b) There has been no rain for ages. We have to be very careful how much water we use. (*Two sentences*)
c) He was mad about computers. He gambled on fruit machines. (*One sentence*)
d) Next year I'm going to learn Russian. I'm going to have tennis lessons and take up aerobics. (*Two sentences*)
e) I hated my school. I decided to stay on there. (*Two sentences*)
f) I had no money. I went on a shopping spree. (*One sentence*)
g) It was raining. I decided to stay in. (*One sentence*)

2 In pairs, continue the sentence in italics, using the cues below. Use your imagination! The first one has been done for you.

I screamed at my boss and walked out . . .
a) I also *threw something at him.*
b) Nevertheless, . . .
c) As a result . . .
d) That's why . . .
e) because . . .

SPEAKING AND WRITING

1 Look at the pictures below. In pairs, decide on a story which could link the pictures together, and make notes.

2 Use your notes to write the first draft of the story. Include a range of adjectives and adverbs to describe the place, the people and what happens.

3 Read through your story and check for correct narrative verb forms, spelling and punctuation, use of linking expressions, and organisation of paragraphs.

Language reference

1 Past Simple

The Past Simple is used to talk about completed actions or situations which in the speaker's mind took place at a specific time in the past. It is used with definite time expressions such as *on Tuesday*, *three months ago*, etc.

(See Section 2 of the *Language reference* in Unit 2 for other ways of expressing past habit.)

2 Past Continuous

The Past Continuous (*was* / *were* + base form + *-ing*) is used:

a) To refer to a particular action or event in progress at a time in the past, which is often not completed at the time we are thinking about:
*At two o'clock yesterday I **was coming** back from Oxford.*
This 'longer' activity is sometimes 'interrupted' by a shorter action:
*I **was coming** back from Oxford when the car **broke down** on the motorway.*

the car broke down

PAST *I was coming back from Oxford* NOW

Two longer actions can be simultaneous:
*I **was marking** their homework while Tom **was speaking** to Alan.*
There is often no indication as to whether the action is finished or not (compare *I **marked** their homework.*).

b) For descriptions:
*He **was carrying** a leather briefcase and **wearing** a green shirt.*

c) For describing characteristic behaviour in the past, often critically (see Unit 2):
*He **was** always **smoking**.*

3 Past Perfect Simple

a) The Past Perfect Simple (*had* + past participle) is used to talk about events which happened before a specific time in the past:
*When I saw him I was surprised to see how much he **had changed**.*

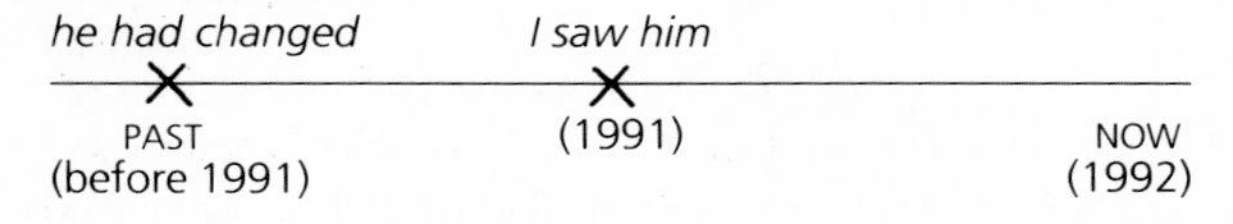

This form is particularly useful when we are writing narrative, so that it is clear when things happened in relation to each other in the past:
He visited his friend in Japan then went to Thailand before he arrived in Hong Kong.
This sentence can become:
*Before he arrived in Hong Kong he**'d visited** his friend in Japan and **been** to Thailand.*

b) The use of the Past Perfect is particularly important when stressing that one event finished before another began:
*I **had finished** the bottle of wine when she arrived.*
(This means that the bottle was finished before she arrived.)
I finished the bottle of wine when she arrived. (This means she arrived and then it was finished.)
Two Past Simple forms are preferred when the second action happens as a result of the first, or when the sequence is obvious. Time conjunctions (e.g. *as soon as*) often make this clear:
*As soon as the thief **saw** the police car he **ran** off.*

4 Past Perfect Continuous

For a longer period of time up to a specific time in the past the Past Perfect Continuous (*had* + *been* + base form + *-ing*) is used:
*Before I came to London **I'd been working** abroad.*

I'd been working abroad *I came to London*

PAST NOW

As with all continuous forms the Past Perfect Continuous focuses on the action in progress rather than on the completed action (NOT ~~*He was depressed because he **had been crashing** his car*~~.). For this reason, 'state' verbs are not usually used in the Continuous form (NOT ~~*I had been seeing him before he arrived*~~.)

5 Pronunciation

a) Voiced consonants
The sounds /v/ and /b/ are examples of voiced consonants in English (other examples are /z/, /ð/, /ʒ/). Voiced consonants are made by vibrating the vocal chords.

b) Pronunciation of *wr* and *wh*
The letters *wr* are pronounced /r/. The letters *wh* are pronounced /h/ if they are followed by *o* (e.g. *who*), but /w/ if followed by *e*, *a* or *i* (e.g. *when*, *what*, *whistle*).

6 Linking expressions

Some linking expressions (conjunctions) connect parts of a sentence together:
***Although** I was tired I got changed and went out.*
Others (adverbs) join ideas across sentences:
*I was tired. **However**, I got changed and went out.*
For details about which linking expressions are conjunctions and which are adverbs, see the table on page 151.

Unit 5

A rare breed

LISTENING

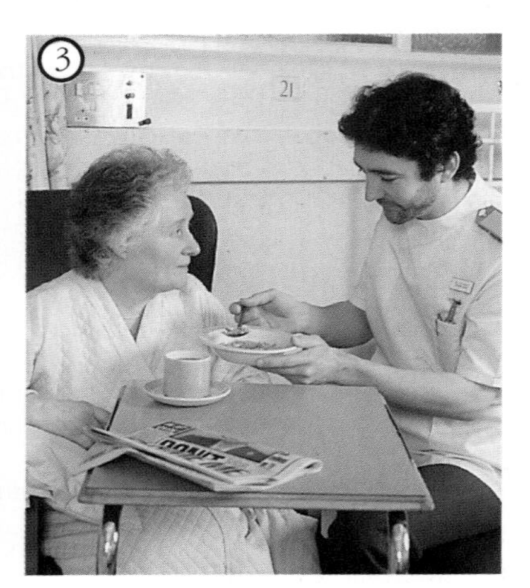

Before listening

1 Which of the jobs in the pictures are normal in your country for both men and women? What is your reaction to these pictures? Give reasons.

2 Read the extract from a magazine article.

a) Guess which picture it refers to.
b) Fill the gaps.

3 Compare your answers and guess:

a) how 'Gwenda's' got its name.
b) how the business started.
c) what women's attitudes to it are, and why.

ME AND MY JOB

You can guarantee the moment you mention you work as a ____(1)____, you become the focus of conversation. People regard you as a bit of a curiosity because ____(2)____ are still such a rare breed.

But the actual job is one I love, especially since I went into business with two other ____(3)____ just over three years ago. We work as a team, there's no boss, so all the decisions are made collectively.

We've called the business 'Gwenda's' and it's based just outside Sheffield city centre in a group of council workshops.

We start work each day at about 9.15 a.m., usually kicking off with paperwork and keeping the books and invoices up to date. We don't have any kind of ____(4)____ help so we share the administrative load, taking it in turns to answer the phone and deal with reps.

After that the customers generally start coming in to drop their ____(5)____ off for the day. We deal with everything from servicing to major ____(6)____. There isn't a job I can't tackle, although you can sometimes get stumped trying to work out what's wrong if you get an unfamilar make.

(from *Woman*)

Listening

1 [5.1] Listen to the recording and check your answers.

2 Are these statements *True* or *False*?

a) The women were unemployed before they opened 'Gwenda's'.
b) They used to keep their own vehicles in good condition.
c) They want their customers to learn some of their skills.
d) Women don't normally get dirty and do heavy lifting.

3 Listen again and answer these questions.

a) What happened last May?
b) Why did they do it?
c) Why do they run classes?
d) What are the advantages of going to 'Gwenda's'?

4 Why does the woman call soap and water an 'amazing sort of invention'? Why does she call heavy lifting 'the usual one'?

Connected speech

1 [5.2] In connected speech, auxiliaries after question words are usually weak. Example: *What do* (/də/) *the **customers** think?* (stress on *customers*)

Practise saying the phrases in the box using the weak form.

Who can you . . . ?
What does she . . . ?
How long have we . . . ?
Why do they . . . ?
How many are there . . . ?
What'll you . . . ?

2 [5.3] Practise saying the following.

a) How does he know what to do?
b) When are we going?
c) Who was that at the door?
d) Where had you been before?

SPEAKING

Intonation

1 [5.4] Listen to two questions that were asked in a different part of the interview in the *Listening* section.

a) Which question is asking for information? (*Question 1* or *2*?) Which one is asking somebody to do something?
b) In which question does the speaker sound more polite? What makes it sound polite? (e.g. Does the voice start high or low?)

2 Work in pairs. Take turns to be Student A and Student B; Student A should use the cues in brackets and practise asking the following questions either politely or impolitely, and Student B should respond according to A's intonation. Example:

A: *Can you give me a hand with my homework?* (impolitely)
B: *No. Why should I?*

a) Why are you wearing (*those shoes*)?
b) Would you mind (*open window*)?
c) When are you (*get married*)?

3 [5.5] Listen to the following questions. For each question is the speaker almost sure or not sure about the answer?

a) Is that the bank over there?
b) Do you like coffee?
c) I'm not late, am I?
d) They didn't reply, did they?

In pairs, practise saying each question using an 'almost sure' intonation and a 'not sure' intonation.

Questionnaire

Answer the questions in the questionnaire for yourself. Then ask the questions to at least two other students, adding two or three of your own. Ask for reasons for each answer.

JOBS FOR THE BOYS OR JOBS FOR THE GIRLS?

1 There are two taxis, one driven by a man, one driven by a woman. Which do you choose?
2 In most circumstances do you prefer the following to be a man or a woman?
 • a waiter in a restaurant • a chef • a hairdresser • a bank manager • a doctor
3 When people work with the opposite sex do you think they use more or less 'bad language'?
4 Are men or women better at jobs which require the following?
 • intelligence • physical skills • feelings
5 At work, do you think men and women should share the same facilities (e.g. meals, cloakrooms)?
6 Your company has few women employees. Should the company employ women in preference to men when their qualifications are the same?

REVISION 1

Asking questions

1 Put the words in the correct order to make questions and match them with the answers below. Use the correct punctuation. Example:
do how do you → *How do you do?*

a) do do want you what to me
b) isn't an he's he actor
c) meet where you say did should we
d) you name didn't her tell she
e) going what her to you tell are
f) was like the what film
g) likes they her everyone don't

1 Great!
2 No, she didn't.
3 Yes, they do.
4 That her husband's not well.
5 To lift this.
6 No, he isn't.
7 By the post office.

2 [5.6] Listen to the recording of a dialogue at a party. At first you will only hear the answers.

A: ________
B: No, this is my first visit to Scotland.
A: ________
B: Only six hours from London.
A: ________
B: In a hotel near the centre.
A: ________
B: Not far.
A: ________
B: It's quiet, but my room's a little small.
A: ________
B: I got a taxi.
A: ________
B: I don't know. It's not mine. I haven't had anything to drink yet.
A: ________
B: Yes, please. A lemonade.
A: ________
B: With a little ice, please.
A: ________
B: Turkish of course, as well as Arabic and a little English.

a) In pairs, invent possible questions for each answer.
b) [5.7] Listen to the complete dialogue and compare your questions with those you hear.

EXTENSION

Subject questions

1 Subject questions (e.g. ***Who speaks Turkish?***) ask the listener to identify a particular person or thing (*Mehmet does.*).
Notice the word order is the same as in statements (*Who likes / I like*).

*'**Who** likes coffee?' 'I do.' ('I like coffee.')*
*'**What** happened at the garage?' 'Nothing.' ('**Nothing** happened.')*
*'**How many people** knew?' 'Not many.' ('**Not many people** knew.')*

Which of the following are subject questions?
a) 'Who sang *Space Oddity*?'
'David Bowie.'
b) 'Whose father came for lunch yesterday?'
'Mine.'
c) 'What plays have you seen recently?'
'Hardly any.'
d) 'How many accidents happened because of the icy roads?'
'Lots.'
e) 'Which dress suited me best?'
'The red one, I think.'
f) 'Why didn't you tell me?'
'Sorry. I forgot.'

2 Which is the correct alternative?

a) Where *she has gone / has she gone?*
b) Who *does live / lives* in this house?
c) What *made you / did make you* angry?
d) What *did you do / did you* that for?
e) How many students *do understand / understand* this exercise?

3 Divide into teams. Each team should think of ten general knowledge questions using subject questions only (e.g. *Which city stands on the River Arno? Who won the last World Championship in motor racing?*) Ask each other. The team with the highest number of correct answers wins.

REVISION 2

Reported questions

1 Read the extract from a magazine article.

According to twenty-five-year-old Stephen Reed there is no difference between men and women – 'apart from the obvious'.

'We're equal... It's your ability that counts, not your sex. I type letters, curriculum vitae and train people on word processors. Most of my bosses have been women and I have no quibbles at all with them. The reaction from family and friends has been positive. In fact, my parents are overjoyed that I've done something for so long,' explains Stephen, who gave up teaching English in Japan to do his present job.

And, when it comes to sitting on the boss's knee for dictation, Stephen chuckles and says: 'That would never happen ... mainly because I don't do shorthand! I've never had a situation with any boss that I thought could get out of hand.'

(from *Chat*)

Give your views on what Stephen says.

2 Stephen has applied for and got a new job. What other questions could be asked in each picture?

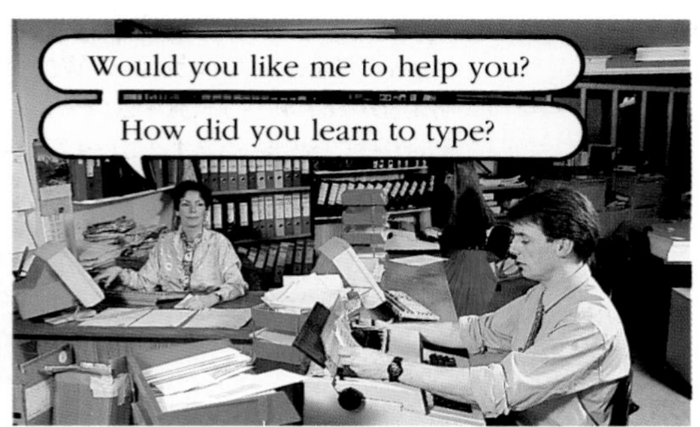

3 [5.8] Stephen's wife, Gillian, is telling a friend about her husband's new job. Listen and note the mistakes she makes. Compare your answers using reported speech.

Less direct questions

Complete the following questions with the names of other students in the class.

a) Is ________ happy?
b) Did ________ get some exercise yesterday?
c) Has ________ ever been to Algeria?
d) What did ________ have for breakfast last Sunday?
e) How long does it take ________ to get dressed in the morning?
f) How much sleep does ________ get every night?
g) What newspaper will ________ buy tomorrow?

a) In pairs, take turns to ask and answer the questions using the expressions in the box to turn the direct questions into less direct questions. (Guess the answers where necessary.)
Example:
A: *Could you tell me if Maria is happy?*
B: *Yes, she is.*

Do you know . . . ? Could you tell me . . . ? Can you remember . . . ? Have you any idea . . . ? I want to know . . . I don't suppose you . . . , . . . you? Do you happen to know . . . ?

b) Check your guesses with the named students.

WRITING 1

Sentence patterns

1 Look at the sentences in the box and complete the statements.

a) Intransitive verbs cannot be followed by ________.
b) A complement is a word or phrase which describes the ________.

> SUBJECT + INTRANSITIVE VERB
> *Her parents argue.*
> *Her parents* (subject) + *argue* (intransitive verb)
>
> SUBJECT + VERB + OBJECT
> *I love you.*
> *I* (subject) + *love* (transitive verb) + *you* (direct object – noun or pronoun)
>
> SUBJECT + VERB + COMPLEMENT
> *My boss is a very clever woman.*
> *My boss* (subject) + *is* (verb) + *a very clever woman* (complement)

2 Put a direct object after the following verbs only where necessary. Use your dictionary to help you. (*Transitive* verbs are usually indicated by [T]; *Intransitive* verbs by [I].) Example:
*Have you cut **the bread**?*

a) Rob laughed . . .
b) You hit . . . !
c) Alex said he enjoyed . . .
d) What time did you arrive . . . ?
e) Children need . . .
f) My back aches . . .

3 Look at the sentences in the box and answer the questions.

a) Some verbs are followed by two objects. Is it the direct object or the indirect object who sometimes 'receives something'?
b) The indirect object normally goes before the direct object. When does the indirect object not go before the direct object?

> SUBJECT + VERB + INDIRECT OBJECT + DIRECT OBJECT
> *Tina gave Andy a new watch.*
> *Andy* (indirect object) + *a new watch* (direct object)
>
> SUBJECT + VERB + DIRECT OBJECT + PREPOSITION + INDIRECT OBJECT
> *I bought a watch for Andy.*
> *watch* (direct object) + *for* (preposition) + *Andy* (indirect object)

4 Using a verb from the box, write at least two sentences for each of the items below, saying what you have done recently. (Invent something if necessary.) Use the patterns in Exercise 3.

> prepare make bring
> give send lend offer
> buy promise sell
> take cook explain
> invite thank describe

a) a birthday, a party or a special occasion.
(Example: *My sister cooked us a lovely meal.*)
b) an occasion when you provided something (e.g. when somebody wanted to borrow something).
c) some correspondence you've had.

Word order

1 Word order is often difficult with adjectives, adverbs and adverbials. For example, it is unusual to put an adverb between the verb and its object. Which of the following are correct?

a) 1 He speaks English very well.
   2 He speaks very well English.
   3 Very well he speaks English.
b) 1 Yesterday I went to the theatre.
   2 I went to the theatre yesterday.
   3 I yesterday went to the theatre.
c) 1 a French tall black woman
   2 a woman tall black French
   3 a tall black French woman
d) 1 Sarah went home after she had finished.
   2 Sarah after she had finished went home.
   3 After she had finished Sarah went home.
e) 1 I went in London to the cinema.
   2 I went to the cinema in London.
f) 1 He put it into his wallet two minutes ago.
   2 He it put into his wallet two minutes ago.
   3 He put it two minutes ago into his wallet.

Check with Sections 8 and 9 in the *Language reference*.

2 Correct these sentences.

a) I have usually my hair cut when I go for an interview.
b) He drives a green small car German.
c) Quietly I've been today sitting in the sun.
d) I when I arrived found the place was full of hooligans horrible.
e) He is a dustman very intelligent who very well dances.
f) English I studied in London in a language school.
g) I can recommend for children a good film.
h) Alison drove off last week quickly.

VOCABULARY

Work

1 Choose one of the following topics: *Finance*, *Building*, *Photography*, *Gardening*. Think of ten words you associate with your topic.

2 Divide the words in the box into the four topic areas above. Use your dictionary to help you.

credit	drill	spade	lawnmower	shares
hammer	darkroom	axe	rake	interest
investment	film	bricks	capital	print
nails	negative	screwdriver	fork	crane

3 Where do the following people usually work? Complete the word puzzle with your answers.

1 stockbroker
2 judge
3 dentist
4 bricklayer
5 secretary
6 machine operator

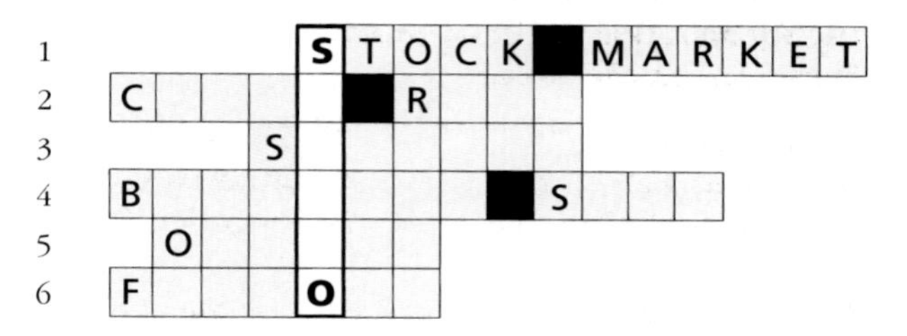

The letters in the box going down spell another word. Who works in that place?

WRITING 2

Advertisement

1 Work in groups. What is the purpose of this advertisement?

2 You want a serious, experienced tennis coach. Rewrite the advertisement to make it completely 'non-sexist'.

3 Compare your advertisements and make improvements.

TENNIS COACH Tall, good-looking man, preferably good physique, required to fill a vacancy for a full-time tennis coach. Hours flexible. Excellent working conditions with lots of opportunity to meet attractive women. Coaching experience not necessary but good tennis skills an advantage. Must dress well and look good on court. If you think you can make the grade, telephone or apply in writing to: The Manager, ACE Tennis Club, Lewisham.
Tel: 081 695-46799 (9 a.m. – 11.a.m.)

Language reference

1 *Yes / No questions*

Questions expecting the answer *Yes / No* are normally formed by inverting an existing auxiliary and the subject (e.g. ***Is he** going?*) or, in the Present Simple and the Past Simple, by adding a form of the verb *do* (e.g. ***Do** you work with other men?*).

To check information we are not sure about we use a rising intonation (e.g. *Is he here?*).

Negative *Yes / No* questions are used to express surprise, to criticise and to persuade:

*'**Haven't you been** to Argentina before?'* ('*No, I haven't.*')

2 Question words and phrases

Questions which begin with questions words are formed:

Question word/phrase (*Where*) + auxiliary (*are*) + subject (*you*) + main verb (*going*)?

When we ask for new information we normally use a falling intonation (e.g. *Where are you going?*)

3 Subject questions

When question words are the subject of the sentence, they ask for the identity of something or someone (e.g. *Who likes coffee?*) and are formed:

Question word (*Who*) + verb (*likes*) + object (*coffee*)?

4 Question tags

Positive statements usually have a negative tag. Negative statements usually have a positive tag:

*It cost a lot of money, **didn't it**?*
*You won't be late, **will you**?*

When we are sure the other person will agree with us, we use a falling intonation (*didn't it?*). When we are not sure we use a rising intonation (*didn't it?*)

To form tags the auxiliary and the subject pronoun in the statement are reversed (e.g. *he has → has he?*). Where there is no auxiliary, a form of the verb *do* is used:

*Kristine lives in Hong Kong, **doesn't she**?*

Note that:

a) We do not use *am not I?* as a tag; we use *aren't I?*:
*I am late, **aren't I**?*
b) Pronouns like *everybody* and *nobody* take plural tags:
*Everybody is happy, **aren't they**?*
c) A positive tag can follow a positive statement when expressing surprise or interest.
*You'**ve been** there before, **have you**?*

5 Reported questions

Reported questions tell someone what was asked. Reported *Yes / No* questions begin with *if* or *whether*. (*'Do you think . . . ?' → She asked him **if he thought** . . .*) Reported questions with a question word begin with the question word. (*'What do you do? → He asked her **what she did**.*)

The word order is question word + subject + verb:

I asked him ***what his name was.*** (NOT ~~*What was his name*~~.)

6 Less direct questions

Less direct questions are questions surrounded by a statement or another question to make them more polite. There is no inversion of subject and verb:

*Do you know **how old she is**?*

7 Sentence patterns

a) subject + intransitive verb: *Her parents argue*.
b) subject + verb + (direct) object: *He parked the car / it*.
c) subject + verb + complement: *She's nice*. (The verb is *appear, become, look, seem, sound, taste, be*, etc.)
d) subject + verb + indirect object + direct object: *She gave Jane the eggs*.

Note that:

a) Indirect objects often name someone who receives something.
b) An indirect object always goes before the direct object (*gave **Jane** the eggs*) unless it is turned into a phrase beginning with a preposition (usually *to, for* or *from*):
*She gave the eggs **to Jane**.*

With some verbs the preposition is never omitted:

*She **explained** the problem **to** me*. (NOT ~~*explained me the problem*~~.)

8 Adverb word order

One position is most common for each type of adverb.

a) Adverbs of indefinite time and frequency normally go in the middle:
*I **often** go to football matches.*
Adverbs of definite time normally go at the end:
*I'll see you **tomorrow**.*
b) Adverbs which say *how well* or *how badly* normally go at the end:
*He drives **very badly**.*
c) When there are two adverbs of position, the larger place goes last:
*I studied **in a language school in England**.*
d) The usual position for adverbial clauses is at the end:
*Sarah went home **after she had finished her work**.*
e) Adverbials usually follow the order: manner, place and time:
*He put it **secretly*** (manner) ***into his wallet*** (place) ***two minutes ago***. (time)

9 Adjective word order

Adjectives normally go before a noun (***rich** man*) or after a verb like *be, look, seem, appear* (e.g. *You look **fantastic**.*). Note the usual order when there is more than one adjective: opinion (*a **beautiful***), size/age (***big**, **old***), colour/pattern (***brown***), nationality/material (***wooden***):

*A **beautiful, big, brown, wooden** cupboard.*

The perfect interview

READING

Before reading

1 Work in pairs. Psychologists say that when you go for a job interview most interviewers have made up their minds whether or not to give you the job within the first four minutes.

a) Look at the people in job interviews. In which pictures are they making a bad impression? Give your reasons.

b) Make a list of the things you *should* do during an interview and the things you *shouldn't* do.
c) Compare your lists.

2 The following sentences come from an article entitled *How to have the perfect interview.*

- **Find out what the company is like before you apply for the job.**
- **Discover as much as you can about the interview.**
- **Think positively and confidently about yourself.**
- **Write an effective CV.**
- **Dress the part.**
- **Be aware of your body language.**
- **Keep a balance of power throughout the interview.**
- **Keep calm before and during the interview.**

a) What reason(s) can you think of for each piece of advice?
b) Which are the most important pieces of advice? Give reasons.
c) What other advice would you give to someone going for a job interview?

Reading

How to have the perfect interview...

1 **Find out what the company is like before you apply for the job.** Are they really the kind of organisation you want to work for?

2 **Write an effective CV.** Keep it brief and simple – a badly written one will lose you the job before you get to the interview stage.

3 **Discover as much as you can about the interview.** This means finding out exactly who will be conducting the interview, what position they hold, and whether it's an informal chat or a formal interview, possibly in front of a whole panel of interviewers.

4 **Dress the part.** Even if the job is in a modern company where the code is casual, you should dress formally for an interview – a suit is always safe. Never keep your overcoat or mac on during the interview – this will make you an outsider from the start. If possible take it off outside the interview room.

5 **Think positively and confidently about yourself.** From the moment you decide to apply for the job think about (and write down) all the qualities you have to offer the company as well as the reasons you would suit the job. Use the interview to discover as much about the job as possible. Even if they offer it to you on the spot ask for some time to consider their offer. Is it right for you AND them?

6 **Be aware of your body language.** Most interviewers don't realise it but they're influenced by your body language the moment you walk into the room. Be assertive, smile, look the interviewer in the eye, and give a firm handshake. Don't lean too far over the desk or slump in the chair with your arms crossed. Practise your 'entrance' at home with a friend so you feel comfortable.

7 **Keep a balance of power throughout the interview.** From a psychologist's point of view this is what interviews are all about! Don't be too timid or allow the interviewer to dominate you because an interview is a two-way process, and you're to decide whether YOU want the job. It's as important for you to ask questions about your potential job as it is for the interviewer to question you. But don't be over-confident or cheeky. No one likes a 'difficult' candidate however good your qualifications are.

8 **Keep calm before and during the interview.** Three-quarters of people feel anxious about job interviews and their nervousness often lets them down. The key is to learn interview skills which are important as job skills, and control your nerves. Remember the interviewer may be nervous as well!

(from *MORE!*)

1 Read the magazine article. Complete the following sentences according to the information in the text.

a) Before you apply for a job you ________.
b) ________ wear a suit.
c) You don't have to ________ long CV.
d) When you go into the interview room you ________.
e) Try not ________.
f) During the interview you mustn't ________.
g) If you are offered the job, ________.
h) You should ________ as well as answer them.
i) Interviewers don't like candidates who ________.

2 Write five *False* sentences about the text. Ask another student to correct them.

3 What do the words in italics mean in context?

a) ... who will be *conducting* the interview ... (paragraph 3)
b) ... what *position* they hold. (paragraph 3)
c) ... give a *firm* handshake ... (paragraph 6)
d) ... or *slump* in the chair ... (paragraph 6)
e) ... and *control your nerves* ... (paragraph 8)

4 Tell each other about any interview situation you have been in and which points in the article you agree or disagree with.

SPEAKING

Job interviews

1 Which of the following suggestions about conducting a job interview do you agree with? Add some of your own.

a) There should be more than one interviewer.
b) The interviewer should sit behind a desk.
c) The interviewer should make notes while the interviewee is speaking.

2 In groups of four, choose one of these advertisements and discuss the points for and against the job.

ADMINISTRATOR

Administrator with experience and word processing skills required to work in our friendly but busy school office. An interest in Shiatsu and Natural Health an advantage.
Please send full CV to:
The British School of Shiatsu,
188 Old Street, London
EC1 9BP.

GOLDEN SKI HOLIDAYS

seeks mature person to run chalet holiday programme in Alps. Outgoing personality and ability to work hard without supervision essential. Good cooking and housekeeping skills an advantage. Modest salary but accommodation and meals provided and abundant skiing time. Apply giving full details to: Golden Ski Holidays Ltd, 2 Ridge Street, Aldershot, Hants.

NURSERY NURSE

Experienced, qualified person required to fill vacancy for full-time nursery nurse. Duties include special responsibility for two-and-a-half to four-year-olds at private nursery. 40 hour working week. Apply in writing to: The Principal, Phoenix Nursery, Pond Lane, Guildford, Surrey GU1 3DD.

Each of you is a candidate for the job your group has chosen. Decide on:
- your qualifications (e.g. university degree, specialised training).
- your experience (e.g. with computers, a similar organisation, children).
- your qualities (e.g. enthusiasm, patience, administrative skill).

3 The interview panel will consist of the three people in the group not being interviewed.

a) Arrange the chairs.
b) Take turns to be interviewed. The candidates should sound interested and enthusiastic. The interviewers should try to find out the candidates' strengths and weaknesses.
c) Vote for who you think should get the job.

VOCABULARY 1

Jobs and duties

1 Work in pairs to complete the following chart. Use your dictionary if necessary.

JOB	DUTIES
traffic warden	_______
_______	repairs electrical apparatus
undertaker	_______
_______	performs medical operations
accountant	_______
_______	flies planes
solicitor	_______
_______	designs machines
plumber	_______
_______	cuts hair
_______	digs for coal

2 Divide the 'duty' verbs in the chart above into those with the final sound /s/ (e.g. *cuts*) and those with the final sound /z/ (e.g. *repairs*).

3 Choose an ending from the box to show what field of work the following people are in. Use your dictionary to help you if necessary.

-ing	-ure	-ancy	-ics	-ry	-ism

a) banker *banking*
b) accountant
c) actor
d) psychiatrist
e) journalist
f) architect
g) economist

4 Work in pairs.

a) Write a brief job description, including working hours, conditions of work and duties. Do not mention the name of the job.
b) Try to guess the jobs of other pairs.

REVISION AND EXTENSION 1

Obligation

1 Look at these sentences and answer the questions below.

I think you ***should*** */* ***ought to*** *wear something smart if you want to impress them.*
*'****Do I have to*** */* ***Have I got to*** *take this horrible medicine?' 'Yes, you have to. The doctor said so.'*
We ***needn't*** */* ***don't need to*** */* ***don't have to*** */* ***haven't got to*** *leave yet; it's only 10 o'clock.*
This cough's getting worse – I ***must*** *give up smoking.*
You ***mustn't*** *tell him I love him – it's a secret.*
You're ***supposed to*** *bring a bottle to this party. Why haven't you?*
We ***weren't allowed to*** *drink in the library (so we didn't).*

a) Which is stronger: *should* or *must*?
b) How do we say something is not necessary?
c) How do we say it's necessary to do something because somebody else says so?
d) How do we say it is necessary not to do something?

Check with the *Language reference.*

2 Work in pairs. You are going to:
a) appear as a guest on a 'chat-show'.
b) train to become a deep-sea diver.
c) be managing director of a big company.

For each situation, talk about:
- the duties (what you have to do, what you are supposed to do).
- the things you don't have to do.
- the things you are not allowed to do.
- the qualities needed (what you need to be able to do).

3 Complete the following sentences.

a) I must go. (present)
We ________ go. (describing the past)
b) You mustn't stay. (present)
We ________ stay. (describing the past)

4 It is April and an open-air concert has been ruined by rain. Complete the dialogue using the past form of the verbs in the following table.

PRESENT	PAST
can't	*couldn't*
don't have to	*didn't have to*
must / have to / have got to	*had to*
mustn't	*wasn't / weren't allowed to*
should(n't)	*should(n't) have*
need	*needed*
needn't / don't need to	*didn't need to / needn't have*

A: You __ (1) __ tried to do something like this now. It would have been much better in July.
B: No, we __ (2) __ have it in April. It was the only time we could get the big stars.
A: Big stars are not so important for this kind of concert. You __ (3) __ worried about that. It's more important that the kids have a good time.
B: No, we __ (4) __ the TV companies to help pay and they said we __ (5) __ have some big names.
A: Why didn't you put up a marquee then?
B: Unfortunately, we __ (6) __. The police thought it would be a fire risk.
A: You're crazy! You __ (7) __ ask the police. This is private property. You __ (8) __ put one up in that field over there.

Sounds: /æ/, /ʌ/, /ʊ/, /u:/

1 How do you pronounce the letter *a* in *have*: *I* ***have*** *to go?*

2 When *must* is weak it is usually pronounced /məs(t)/: *I must go.* How is it pronounced when it comes at the end of a sentence or in the negative? (*Yes, you* ***must***. / *I* ***mustn't*** *smoke.*)

3 [6.1] Listen. Which word do you hear?

a) sang/sung c) swam/swum e) bank/bunk
b) fan/fun d) match/much

4 Compare the short vowel sound in *should* /ʃʊd/ when pronounced strongly (*Yes, they* ***should*** *be.*) with the long vowel sound in *flew* /flu:/. In which of the words in the box is the vowel sound short and pronounced /ʊ/?

book	foot	food	could	shoe	soon
look	moon	would	blue		

5 [6.2] Listen and check your answers.

REVISION AND EXTENSION 2

Asking for and giving advice

1 Look at these examples. Which sentences sound formal?

a) ***Do you think I should** wear a . . . ?*
b) *What kind of . . . **would you advise me to** write?*
c) ***I would appreciate some advice on** the type of . . .*
d) ***Who should I** see when . . . ?*
e) ***It's time you** sent . . .*
f) ***You'd better** not be too . . .*
g) ***I would recommend that you** speak to . . .*
h) ***Try** doing some relaxation techniques before you . . .*
i) ***If I were you, I'd** sit . . .*
j) ***Take my advice and don't** . . .*

2 Work in pairs. Look back at the text *How to have the perfect interview* . . . Take turns asking for and giving advice about a future interview using some of the instructions given in the article (e.g. *Keep calm. Don't lean too far over the desk.*). Make sure your language is appropriate to the situation.

3 Work in groups.

a) Fill in each of the bubbles using expressions from Exercise 1 to give advice.
b) Tell the other groups what the person advised, using expressions such as:
The young man in the restaurant suggested that he should . . .
The woman in the second picture advised her (not) to . . .
c) Which group offered the best advice for each person in the pictures?

1

2

3

4

4 Work in groups of five or six.

a) Each student should choose a different problem from the list below. Consider how you would advise people with problems other than the one you have chosen for yourself.
- It is your first day as a teacher. You have a bad memory for people's names.
- You need a day off work but you haven't got any holiday left.
- You would like to become an actor but you are very shy.
- When you woke up this morning you found you had 500 dollars missing. You had a party last night.
- You are going to be sleeping in a room with three other people. You are worried because you grind your teeth when you sleep.
- You have had an accident in your friends' car which you borrowed. They are coming back in a couple of hours.

b) Ask the other members of the group for advice about your problem. The group should discuss the advice they are going to give.

EXTENSION

Make, *let* and *allow*

1 [6.3] Listen to someone talking about her childhood.

a) What did her parents make her do?
b) What did they let her do?
c) What other things was she allowed to do?

2 Complete the sentences with *make*, *let* or *allow*.

a) Sarah ________ me drive her new Porsche. It was fantastic!
b) We were not ________ to smoke in the restaurant.
c) The soldiers ________ us lie face down. It was terrifying!

3 Work in pairs. Student A is in prison. Student B is in the army. Ask each other questions using *make*, *let* and *allow* to find out who has the best/worst life.

VOCABULARY 2

Using a lexicon

1 Some dictionaries (sometimes called 'lexicons') organise vocabulary according to topic. Look at the (adapted) extracts from the *Longman Lexicon of Contemporary English* and choose the correct alternative in each of the sentences below.

I103 *verbs*: **machines, etc., working**

work 1 (of a machine, moving part, plan, etc.) to be active in the proper way, without failing: *The clock hasn't been working since the electricity was off. Your idea won't work in practice.* **2** to make a machine work: *The machine is worked by hand.*
run told to (cause to) work: *The car engine was running (well/badly).*
operate *often tech* **1** to (cause to) work: *He operates a machine/a factory. The new machine operates day and night.*

I104 *adjectives*: **relating to work**

laborious requiring great effort: *Oh dear! This is very laborious work.*
hard-working working hard: *She is a tremendously hard-working girl.*
industrious *often fml & pomp* hard-working: *What industrious people they are!* **-ly [adv]**
demanding that needs a lot of attention and effort: *A new baby and a new job can both be very demanding.*
strenuous taking great effort; needing a lot of work: *It's been a strenuous day! I don't like this job; it's too strenuous.*
diligent (of people and behaviour) hard-working; showing steady effort: *He's a diligent worker and deserves more pay.*

a) It was a *diligent/strenuous* climb to the top of the mountain.
b) Does this lamp *run/work*?
c) You have to be very *diligent/laborious* to get a good degree.
d) This machine is *worked/operated* by just one man.
e) Learning a new language is very *hard-working/demanding*.
f) Breaking up stones is a very *laborious/industrious* task.
g) It's a very expensive car to *operate/run*.

2 Choose words from the box and put them in the correct form to complete the sentences. There may sometimes be more than one possibility. Use a lexicon or a dictionary to help you.

manage	appoint	recruit	apply	promote	employ

a) I am very pleased that Gloria has been ________ to chairperson.
b) The company received hundreds of ________ for the job.
c) The company's success was due to good ________ year after year.
d) There is high ________ at the moment and many people are looking for work.
e) The new ________ have all been made.
f) We're having a lot of problems ________ well-qualified staff.
g) What are the chances of ________ and a higher salary in this firm?

WRITING

Letter of application

1 Read the letters. Compare their strengths and weaknesses. Comment on:

a) the layout (e.g. Position of address. How the letter should start/finish.)
b) the paragraphing (e.g. How the points should be divided.)
c) the style (e.g. Formal or informal.)
d) the content (e.g. Things you should/should not mention.)

2 These are some of the things you would probably mention in a job application letter.

a) The job and where you heard about it.
b) That you are serious and interested in the place of work.
c) That you are willing to attend an interview.

What would you advise someone *not* to say in a job application?

3 Which of the words and phrases in the box would you *not* expect to find in a job application?

lovely weather here do write!
my references pretty good job
excellent opportunity
suitable vacancy are attached
specialist knowledge
not very happy must stop now
would welcome

4 Match the formal words in column A with the informal words and expressions in column B.

A	B
a) (to) forward	1 the one before
b) prompt	2 letters
c) previous	3 quick
d) assistance	4 send on
e) correspondence	5 help

A

180 Garfield Road,
Levenshulme,
Manchester
M19 3LF

The Principal,
Phoenix Nursery,
Pond Lane,
GUILDFORD
Surrey
GU1 3DD

8th January 1992

Dear Sir/Madam,
I noticed you had this job in the paper for a nursery nurse. Well, I think I could do it and I'd really like to. I'm pretty good with kids.
I'm working in a holiday camp at the moment but I don't much like it and I can't wait to leave. Also, I've always wanted to work in Surrey. They say it's really nice.
I hope you'll drop me a line and ask me for interview. I'm sure I could convince you that I am the person you need.
Yours,

Alison Scott

Alison Scott

B

36 Summerton Road,
GLASGOW G12 8RH
Scotland
9-1-92

Dear Sir,
I would like to apply for the position of full-time nursery nurse, advertised in the 'Surrey Advertiser'. I feel I am well qualified for the position having got four O-levels, four Grade 1 CSEs and having taken an NNEB (National Nursery Examinations Board) course at Nottingham's Basford Hall College. I am an enthusiastic and patient person and I have a genuine affection for young children.
It is sometimes thought unusual for someone my age to apply for such a position but I can assure you I have had considerable experience and very good references from previous employers. A position with the Phoenix Nursery would give me the opportunity to work full-time in the job that I love. A CV giving details of my qualifications and experience is attached. I would be happy to attend an interview at any time convenient to you.

Yours faithfully,

Jean Craig

JEAN CRAIG

5 Rewrite the following sentences to make them more formal.

a) Could you tell me if you have got any jobs going?
b) I'd like to put in for that job you advertised last week.
c) I've put a copy of the ad in the envelope.
d) I'm dropping you a line just to let you know I've moved.
e) Send any letters on from my old address straight away, will you?
f) I need your help. Thanks.

6 Write a letter of application for one of the jobs on page 41.

Language reference

1 Obligation

a) *Should / ought to*

When we recommend or advise somebody to do something we use *should* or *ought to*. (*Ought to* is less commonly used than *should*.):

*I think you **should take / ought to take** a raincoat. It looks like rain.*

We use *shouldn't* when we say it's important not to do something:

*You **shouldn't stay** up so late. You'll be tired tomorrow.* (It's not a good thing in my opinion.)

To express criticism about a past event we use *should(n't) have / ought to have:*

*You **should have told me / ought to have told me** you were coming. Why didn't you?* (NOT ~~must have told~~)

b) *Must / have (got) to*

When we say that something is necessary we use *must / have (got) to:*

*My cough's getting terrible. I **must** give up smoking.* (The speaker thinks it's important.)

*The boss says I **have to / have got to** stay late tonight.* (Someone, not the speaker, says it is necessary.)

Must and *have (got) to* express advice more strongly than *should*:

*I **had to** give up smoking / stay late.* (In the past *had to* is used for both *must* and *have (got) to*.)

When we say it is essential not to do something we use *mustn't:*

*You **mustn't eat** that plant. It's poisonous.*
(*Mustn't* is stronger than *shouldn't*.)

2 Absence of obligation

a) *Needn't / don't have to*, etc.

There are several ways of saying that it isn't necessary to do something: *needn't / don't need to / don't have to* and *haven't got to.*

*She **needn't do / doesn't need to do / doesn't have to do** the washing up. There's a dishwasher.*

*You **haven't got to carry** a driving licence with you in England.* (There is no obligation from anyone else.)

b) *Didn't need to / didn't have to,* etc.

When talking about things it wasn't necessary to do in the past we use *didn't need to* or *didn't have to*:

*I **didn't need to lift / didn't have to lift** any heavy suitcases.* (Perhaps I lifted them but probably I didn't.)

We can use *needn't have* when it is clear the person did something which wasn't necessary:

*You **needn't have lifted** that heavy suitcase. Why did you? It was a waste of time.*

3 Prohibition

When we want to express prohibition in the present we use *can't* and *mustn't*:

*He **can't** go to a night club. He's too young.*
*You **mustn't talk** in the library. Please be quiet!*
(*Mustn't* is usually more like a direct order.)

When we report prohibition we use *not allowed to*:

*My boss **won't allow me to** use the phone.*

To talk about prohibition in the past we use *couldn't* and *wasn't / weren't allowed to*:

*He **couldn't go / wasn't allowed to go** to the night club. He wasn't old enough.*

PRESENT	PAST
can't	*couldn't*
don't have to	*didn't have to*
must / have to / have got to	*had to*
mustn't	*wasn't / weren't allowed to*
should / ought to	*should have / ought to have*
need	*needed*
needn't / don't need to	*didn't need to / needn't have*

4 Duty: *supposed to*

We use *supposed to* to talk about duty:

*Nora **was supposed to water / to have watered** the plants when we were away. What happened?*

5 Compulsion: *make*

Make can have the meaning of 'compulsion':

*Her parents **make** her **wash** the dishes.* (They expect/ compel her to wash the dishes.)

Notice there is no *to* before the second verb except in the passive: *She is **made to wash** the dishes.*

6 Permission: *let* and *allow*

With *let* there is no *to* before the second verb and *let* is not normally used in the passive:

*They **let** her **go** outside.* (She is permitted to go outside.)

Allow is followed by *to* and can be used in the passive instead of *let*:

*She **was allowed to play** in the streets.*

7 Other ways of giving advice

a) Informal

***It's time you** went to class.* (+ past form of the verb)
***You'd better (not)** run.* (+ base form without *to*)
***Try** sending it by fax.* (+ *-ing*, or *to* + base form if it means 'make an effort')
***Take my advice and** give it back to her.*
***If I were you, I'd** get a taxi.*

b) More formal

***I would advise you to** look for a new job.*
***I would recommend that you** change your doctor.*
***I would appreciate some advice on** the car to buy.*

Crawlers, winkers, flashers

LISTENING

Before listening

1 Write down three things that irritate you about other people's driving and talk about them with a partner.

2 Look at the picture and guess what *crawlers*, *winkers* and *flashers* are.

3 Read the following newspaper article and match each paragraph with one of the drivers in the picture above.

1 The crawler is that irritating individual who sticks rigidly to the centre lane of a three-lane motorway, driving consistently at around 50 to 60 miles per hour, and who refuses to move from his comfortable middle road position even when the inside lane is completely clear. He thus effectively blocks two lanes, since British motorway regulations prohibit overtaking on the inside.

2 The winker is protected from reality in his belief that a couple of swift winks on the right-hand indicator will keep him safe when he blasts straight out from a slip-road to join a heavy stream of traffic on the inside lane. The same individual often changes lane in a similarly thoughtless manner.

3 The flasher is that pushy individual who regards the 'fast' lane as his personal property, and insists on staying there, usually with liberal flashing of headlights at those who dare to be in the way at the legal maximum of 70.

(from *The Observer*)

4 According to the article which two things are you not allowed to do on British motorways?

5 Discuss the following.

a) What kind of driver are you / would you like to be?
b) What other types of drivers are there? What is your idea of a good driver? Give reasons.
c) What are you not allowed to do on motorways in your country?

Listening

1 [7.1] Divide into two groups. There has been an accident on the London–Birmingham road.

You are going to listen to the stories which four of the people who were involved gave to the police. One group should listen to speakers A and B, who were travelling to London; the other group should listen to speakers C and D, who were travelling to Birmingham. Each group should:

a) work out what happened (e.g. who hit who).
b) decide what the two characters were doing / trying to do at the time of the accident.
c) make notes on the things the characters agree and disagree about.
d) indicate on the diagram how the accident happened.
e) decide whose fault it was.

2 Each person should join with someone from the other group and compare stories. What differences are there?

a) Agree on what you think happened and who caused the accident.
b) Correct this report of the incident. (Use the word 'probably' if you are not certain.)

Details of incident

At four o'clock, a lorry on its way to Birmingham was slowing down at the bottom of a steep hill. The driver of a BMW was looking to see if she could overtake the lorry before a bend in the road to the right when she crashed head on into a taxi coming in the opposite direction. The taxi had been trying to overtake a Volvo when the crash forced it to spin across the road and end up on the other side of the road in front of the lorry.

Connected speech: word linking

1 [7.2] Listen to four sentences from the interviews and write them down exactly.

2 In the first sentence the speaker says *right on*. In connected speech, words are not spoken separately but linked together. When a word ends in a consonant sound (*right*) and the next word begins with a vowel sound (*on*), or a word beginning with 'h' where the /h/ sound can be omitted, we often move the end consonant to the beginning of the next word: *righ ton*.

a) [7.3] Show the linking in these phrases, then listen to the recording and repeat them. The first one has been done for you.

a) pulls up *pulls‿up*
b) road accident
c) park outside
d) half of
e) he's out of oil
f) get it off
g) Can I have a bit of Angela's ice cream?

b) Mark other consonant-to-vowel linking in the sentences you wrote down in Exercise 1.

3 [7.4] When we speak quickly, /t/ and /d/ sounds at the end of words often disappear when the next word begins with a consonant sound (e.g. *fish and chips* → *fish an chips*). Cross out the letters where the /t/ or /d/ disappears in the following phrases. Then listen to check and practise saying them.

a) Mind the car.
b) And in perfect control.
c) Next time you're here.
d) England lost the match.
e) He must be out of town.

VOCABULARY

Transport

1 Complete the following text with words from the box. Use your dictionary to help you.

windscreen	brake	clutch	overtake	indicate	petrol
traffic jam	slow down	accelerator	licence	gear	
flash	reverse	horn	run over	steering wheel	

Believe me, learning to drive is a terrifying experience. A couple of weeks ago I got my provisional driving ___(1)___ and had my first lesson. The thing I found difficult was that you have to concentrate on everything at once. With one hand you are expected to put the car into ___(2)___ while your left foot is on the ___(3)___. At the same time, the other hand has to hold on to the ___(4)___ and try to keep the car on the road. To get the car to move, whether forwards or in ___(5)___, you have to press the ___(6)___ with the right foot. When you want the car to come to a halt you have to take that foot off and press the ___(7)___ down hard – well not too hard or your instructor disappears through the ___(8)___.

The first day out on the road was a disaster. When I got to the pedestrian crossing I forgot to ___(9)___ and thought I was going to ___(10)___ a little old man who was trying to cross the road. Of course my instructor, who by this time was rather irritated, screamed. Later on there was a van going incredibly slowly so I started to ___(11)___ to let the car behind me know that I was going to___(12)___. Well, you have never seen such a fuss. A car coming the other way started to sound its ___(13)___ and ___(14)___ its lights. How was I to know that up ahead there was a three mile ___(15)___ because some car had run out of ___(16)___ and stopped in the middle of the road?

2 What do you associate with each of the forms of transport on the right (e.g. country, speed, luxury, expense, pleasure)? Give reasons.

3 Link the words in the box with the forms of transport in Exercise 2. Example:
crew: ship, aeroplane, bus

crew	driver	runway
commuter	guard	aisle
filling station	compartment	
dining car	voyage	platform
cabin	windscreen	captain
departure lounge	ticket office	
boarding pass	pilot	

4 Which forms of transport do you use with each of these verbs? Example:
get on: train, boat

get on	get into	land
dock	get out of	get off
park	take off	board

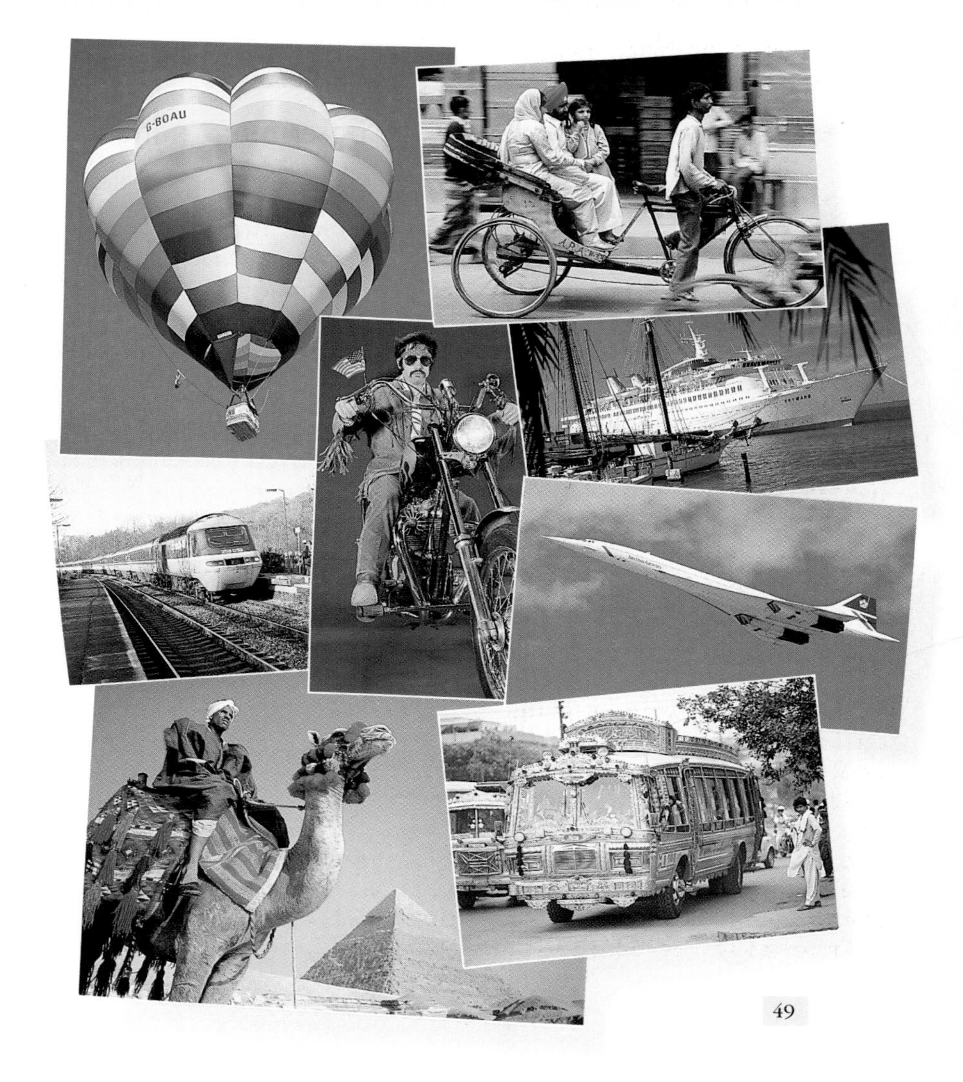

REVISION

The future

1 Look at this example:
I'm sorry I can't come. I'm going to have lunch with my brother tomorrow.

a) Did the person make the decision at the moment of speaking, or before?
b) What difference, if any, would it make to say *I'm having lunch with my brother tomorrow?*

2 Match the following (a–c) with the pictures below and suggest what the people could be saying. Use *going to* + base form, *will*, the Present Simple or the Present Continuous.

a) a sudden decision.
b) a regular fixed event.
c) something started/decided/planned/arranged before now.

PRACTICE

1 What would you say in these situations? Use a future form.

a) Your friend says he has left his money at home. Offer to help.
b) You notice a car coming straight towards you which your driver hasn't seen because he's talking to you. Warn him.
c) Tell Stella you can't meet her tomorrow. Give her a reason.
d) Your mother says you haven't written lately. Promise to do it.
e) Your car is old. You've already decided to get a new one.
f) A new photographic exhibition starts tomorrow. Ask at Tourist Information for the opening and closing times.

2 In pairs, plan a long, luxurious trip around your country.

a) Decide on:
- your method of travel.
- your stopping places and length of stay.
- how long you want to spend away.
- ideas for spending your time.

Plan to do some things individually and some things together.

b) Interview another pair and ask them about their plans.

EXTENSION

Describing changes of plan

1 Look at these sentences and answer the questions below.

*Joanne **was going/hoping/planning to** go to Venice but in the end she decided to go to Bali.*
***Originally, she had/hoped/planned to** stay in a hotel.*
***She was thinking of** getting a dog but she changed her mind.*
***At one time she had thought of** becoming a singer.*

a) Which of these did Joanne do: go to Venice; go to Bali; get a dog; become a singer; stay in a hotel?
b) Correct this sentence: *Kari was hoping of going to the opera and even thinking to go to the ballet.*

2 Work in pairs. On New Year's Day, Leo made some resolutions. Guess from the cues below what the resolutions were and why he broke them. Example:
smoke: He had thought of giving up smoking but someone offered him a cigarette at a party and he accepted.

a) smoke
b) clean the car
c) give to charity
d) buy new clothes
e) watch TV all day
f) bite his nails

3 Work in pairs.

a) You have just heard that the trip you planned in the *Practice* section above can only last two weeks. Also, you have been given a budget of £100 each. What changes will you make?
b) Tell another pair how you changed your plans.

SPEAKING

People and cars

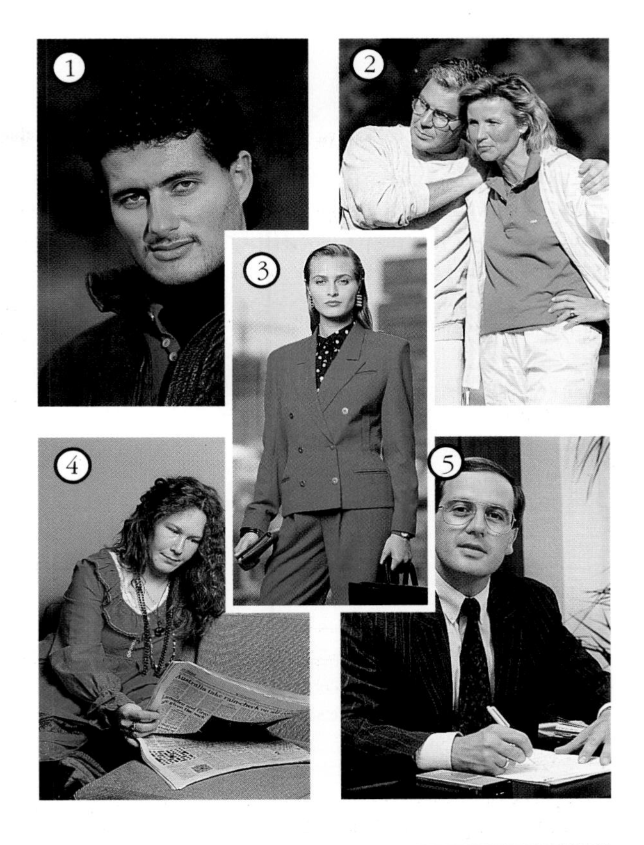

1 Work in groups.

a) Which of these can you imagine being said by the people in the pictures?

A 'I love red cars; they're so sexy.'

B 'Any car I buy has to be big, black and fast. Miles to the litre? No, that's not important.'

C 'The good thing about my car is that you can get the whole family in and it's built like a tank.'

D 'As a director I prefer something large, to make my company look successful and impress the clients.'

E 'My favourite car? One which is economical on petrol – lead-free, of course – doesn't have many gadgets, is easy to park in town and I can use until it collapses.'

b) What does each quote tell us about the person who said it?

c) Which quote do you identify with? (If necessary, write one more for yourselves.)

2 Individually, match the cars on the right with:

a) the people in the pictures in Exercise 1.

b) the people in your group. (Try to guess.)

Then compare your answers with the others in your group.

3 You are going to prepare a television advertisement for one of the cars on the right.

a) Decide which car you will advertise and the features you will draw attention to (e.g. speed, comfort).

b) Decide on the image you will try to convey (e.g. gives a sense of independence, is cosmopolitan, etc.)

c) Decide on the story, the music, the pictures on the screen and *one* caption (e.g. *Takes your breath away.*). You are not allowed to use any other words in the advertisement.

WRITING

Advertisement

1 When we compare two things we use comparatives (*older than*, *more beautiful than*, *more dangerously than*). When we compare three or more things we use superlatives (*the smallest*, *the fastest*, *the most economical*). When we want to say things are equal or not equal we use *as . . . as* (*as cheap as*, *not as shiny as*). Complete the following table.

ADJECTIVE/ADVERB	COMPARATIVE	SUPERLATIVE
______	bigger	______
______	______	the best
comfortable	______	______
______	worse	______
______	______	the easiest
sophisticated	more sophisticated	______
slowly	______	______
______	______	the farthest
few	______	______
______	less	______
______	______	most exciting

2 Compare the following forms of transport, using:
- some of the words in Exercise 1.
- some of the words in the box below.
- some of your own words.

advanced quiet romantic smooth powerful light sexy interesting charming impressive heavy wide old-fashioned prestigious safe

a) motorbike / scooter / moped
b) double-decker bus / coach / tram
c) canoe / speedboat / rowing boat / barge / gondola / yacht
d) spaceship / jet / glider / helicopter

3 Work in groups. You are going to write a magazine advertisement for a form of transport (e.g. to sell a new Harley Davidson motorbike, to advertise a camel ride or a trip on the Orient Express).

a) Choose a form of transport from the pictures on page 49.
b) Discuss the kind of person you are trying to appeal to and make notes on some of the areas covered in the *Speaking* exercise on page 51 (e.g. style, image, special attractions, pictures you will use, etc.) as well as the kind of things you will say.
c) Make a draft of your advertisement, paying attention to your use of adjectives, comparatives and superlatives. Then compare what you have done with another group and suggest improvements.

White water adventure

Bored with your office-bound lifestyle? Join us for an exhilarating raft trip on one of the most spectacular stretches of white water in Austria.

Phone: Action holidays
071 230-6543

Language reference

1 Talking about the future

a) The *going to*-future
When we state an intention based on something we've already decided, we usually use *going to* + base form of the verb:
*I'**m going to buy** a new car.*

b) Present Continuous and *going to*
When we talk about events and arrangements we've already planned for the near future, we often prefer the Present Continuous:
*I'**m taking** my driving test tomorrow.* (A word like *tomorrow* is necessary unless the time is clear from the context.)
We can either use the Present Continuous or the *going to* future to talk about intentions, plans and arrangements which are going to happen soon:
*I'**m going to take** my driving test tomorrow.*

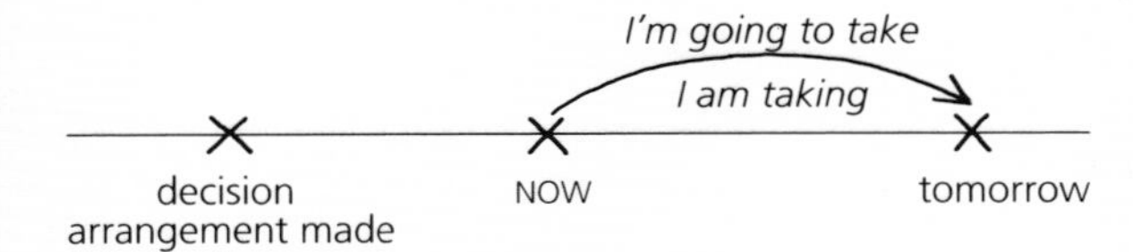

The *going to*-future is used when we predict that something in the present situation will cause something in the future to happen:
*Look at the clouds! It's **going to rain.*** (NOT ~~*It's raining*~~.)
*I feel ill. I think I'**m going to be** sick.* (NOT ~~*I'm being sick*~~.)

c) The *will / shall ('ll)* future
When we make a personal, spontaneous decision (e.g. an offer, a promise) in reaction to a present event we use *'ll* or *shall*:
*That looks heavy. **Shall I help** you? / **I'll help** you.*
We also use the modal *'ll* to express our feeling of personal certainty about a future event:
*I'm sure / I think / I expect **we'll be** there before midnight.*
***He'll be** eighty next week.*

d) The Present Simple
We can use the Present Simple to talk about fixed events in the future, such as timetables and programmes:
*The train **leaves** at nine o'clock tomorrow morning.*
*The course **finishes** next week.*

2 Describing changes of plan

To describe changes of plan we use such expressions as:
We were going / hoping / planning to . . . but . . .
We had hoped / planned to . . . but . . .
She was thinking of doing . . . but . . .
She had thought of doing . . . but . . .

3 Comparatives

When we want to say that things are equal or not equal we can use *(not) as / so . . . as:*
*My car is **(not) as** nice **as** yours.*
When we compare two things and say one is *more* or *less* than the other, we use a comparative construction: *older than, more / less beautiful than, more / less dangerously than.*
*A rickshaw is **cheaper** / **more comfortable than** a bicycle.*
*He drives **more dangerously than** I do.*

a) One-syllable words: add *-er* (*fast* → *fast**er** than*) to the adjective/adverb.
b) Two-syllable words ending in *-y* add *-ier* (*sexy* → *sex**ier** than*).
c) Words with two or more syllables add *more / less* to the adjective/adverb (***more** / **less** elegant than*). (Exceptions: two-syllable words ending in *-y*; also with some two-syllable words you can use either *-er* or *more*: *common – common**er** / **more** common*).

4 Superlatives

When we compare three or more things and say that one thing is more than all the others we use a superlative construction: *the smoothest, the most advanced.*

Add *the* + *-est* to one syllable adjectives or adverbs or two-syllable adverbs ending in *-y*: *wide* → *the wid**est***; *heavy* → *the heav**iest***. If the adjective or adverb has two or more syllables (but not two-syllable adjectives/adverbs ending in *-y*) use ***the most** / **the least** impressive.*
Note that:

a) Some two-syllable words can take either *-est* or *most*:
*the common**est** / **most** common.*
b) Some adjectives and adverbs are irregular in both the comparative and superlative. Examples:
good/well → *better* → *the best*
bad/badly → *worse* → *the worst*

Unit 8

Anyone out there?

SPEAKING

Space quiz

1 Divide into teams and answer the questions in the quiz. The team with the highest number of correct answers wins.

1 When did a man first walk on the moon: 1963, 1969 or 1971?
2 How often does the Earth orbit the sun?
3 Mars is the fourth closest planet to the sun. *True* or *False?*
4 Why was Yuri Gagarin famous in space exploration?
5 How far is the moon from the Earth?
6 What nationality was the first woman in space?
7 Is Mars colder than anywhere on Earth?
8 Which is the largest planet: Saturn, Uranus or Jupiter?
9 What does the atmosphere on Venus consist of?
10 Is the Earth moving through space or is it stationary?

Check your answers on page 149.

2 Discuss the following.

a) If you were given the opportunity to go into space, would you go? Give reasons.
b) What are the most interesting things about space travel? What problems are there?

READING

(1) KILLER ANTS INVADE EARTH

(2) SPACE HERO 'A HUMAN WRECK'

(3) Crippled UFO sends SOS to Earth

(4) Mars: Man's Next Base?

(5) How do you recognise an alien? Twelve feet but only one tiny head

Before reading

1 One of these headlines comes from an encyclopaedia. Which is it? How do you know?

2 Where do the other headlines come from?

Reading

1 There are two types of texts on page 55: one from an encyclopaedia, the other from a 'popular' newspaper. In both, the information and style of writing are different. Ignore the words in *italics* and the numbered gaps at this stage. The texts are mixed together but the paragraphs are in their correct order.

a) Separate the paragraphs into the two texts. Read the texts and select the correct headlines from those above. The first paragraph is given.

TEXT 1 *Headline* ______
1 <u>*para. A*</u> 2 __ 3 __ 4 __ 5 __ 6 __ 7 __ 8 __

TEXT 2 *Headline* ______
1 __ 2 __ 3 __ 4 __

A

Russian cosmonaut Yuri Romanenko, ____(1)____, is mentally unbalanced and has serious physical illnesses after his ordeal, according to a respected Italian newspaper.

B

Apart from the Earth, Mars is the friendliest world we know. *Its* thin carbon dioxide atmosphere is harmless (though not life-supporting), and, with an average surface temperature of minus 23°C, Mars is generally no cooler than the Antarctic in winter.

C

The results of his experiment look likely to put an end to any hopes of sending a man to Mars, ____(2)____, says La Stampa science correspondent.

D

Romanenko returned to Earth on December 29 after a record-breaking stay in space and his condition was said to be 'optimum' by the Russians. But now news is filtering out that all is not well.

E

Even so, the first explorers will need plenty of protection from Martian conditions. Spacesuits will be vital because the atmosphere is so thin that, by Earth standards, *it* is a near vacuum.

F

Although they will not admit it, *his* bones have become seriously decalcified and he has lost a quarter of his blood, down from seven litres to just over five. ____(3)____, have lost weight and function badly on Earth, while he shows signs of mental instability after being subject to cosmic radiation.

G

According to Professor Aristide Scano of a Rome university who lectures in aerospace physiopathology, it is well known that long periods in space lead to a slowing down of the change of calcium in the bones.

H

There is no chance that Mars explorers could survive in *it*. Even if it consisted of pure oxygen, no one could breathe Mars's air. Our bodies require a much greater pressure of gas to breathe. One problem is that, as the atmospheric pressure goes down, so does the boiling point of a liquid. On a high mountain on Earth, water boils at only 70°C. On Mars, blood at body temperature would begin to boil almost immediately. We must be kept safe from these dangers.

I

'After six months in space decalcification reaches up to 10 per cent. After that *we* have no figures. The heart beats slower because the blood weighs almost nothing, so it loses its volume.'

J

One Italian candidate for a future astronaut's place, physicist Cristiano Batalli, says: 'It is clear that Romanenko was used as a guinea pig. We know he was due to stay in space for a year, ____(4)____.'

K

Nevertheless, even in *their* cumbersome spacesuits, the explorers will find that they can move around just as easily as they can on Earth. This is because Mars's surface gravity is much lower. You would weigh only 38 per cent of what you do on Earth.

L

'Gymnastics and radio contact with the Earth are not enough to overcome the physiological and psychological difficulties. Only rockets ten times more powerful than the ones we have today ____(5)____, would make it possible to put a man on Mars. The only solution seems to be a spaceship with artificial gravity.'

carbon dioxide (paragraph B): heavy colourless gas
cosmic radiation (paragraph F): harmful waves of energy found in space
calcium (paragraph G): metallic element, necessary for strong bones and teeth

b) Complete the paragraphs above with the following phrases. (The paragraphs with gaps are all from the same text.)

a) . . . but he had to re-enter because of heart trouble.
b) . . . a voyage taking three years . . .
c) . . . which would reduce the trip to a matter of months . . .
d) . . . who spent 326 days in space . . .
e) His muscles, including his heart . . .

2 Read the texts again and complete the table.

MARS		
	Length	**Problems**
Journey (Text 1)		
Living there (Text 2)	—	

3 On the basis of information from the texts, how do you think life (for human beings) on Mars would compare with life on Earth? Give reasons for your answers.

4 In a text, pronouns can be used to refer to nouns already mentioned or which can be understood from the general context. Match the words and phrases below with the words in *italics* in the text on page 55.

a) the atmosphere on Mars: *it*
b) the first explorers to Mars: ________
c) Yuri Romanenko's: ________
d) the planet Mars's: ________
e) scientists: ________

5 For each of these words from the text mark (') where the stress falls and underline one weak vowel. The first one has been done for you.

'astronaut	explorers
atmospheric	immediately
correspondent	physicist
cosmonaut	require
experiments	temperature

6 The words in the box appear in the texts. Use them to complete the sentences below. (More than one answer may be possible.)

although while even if
nevertheless even so

a) I wouldn't go to Florida ________ I could afford it.
b) I can't go. ________, I appreciate the invitation.
c) ________ I practise a lot, my tennis never seems to get any better.
d) She was reading the paper ________ he was doing the housework.
e) It was raining. ________, I had to go out.

VOCABULARY

Compounds

1 The word *carbon dioxide* consists of two parts (*carbon* + *dioxide*) which have combined to make a compound. In pairs, make as many compounds as you can from the following words.

a) NOUN: ________ *room* (e.g. *bedroom*)
b) ADJECTIVE: ________*-haired* (e.g. *curly-haired*)

2 Look at the examples above. Does the stress fall on the *first* or the *second* part of the compounds in the following?

a) nouns b) adjectives

Check your answers by looking up the example words in the dictionary.

3 Match the words in the list below with the words in the box to make compound nouns, adjectives or verbs. Use your dictionary to help you and to check if the compound is one word, two words with a hyphen or two words without a hyphen.

door room fashioned flow looking paper washer
minded known haired tray walk work

a) sleep*walk*
b) dining ________
c) good ________
d) dish ________
e) house ________
f) old ________
g) well ________
h) long ________
i) over ________
j) wall ________
k) broad ________
l) ash ________
m) front ________

Now put the words you have made into category A or B. (Some might go in either category.)

A: ABOUT THE HOUSE	B: PERSONAL DESCRIPTIONS
	sleepwalk

4 [8.1] Listen to the pronunciation of these compound nouns. Which of them are pronounced differently from the 'rule' in Exercise 2?

a) hitchhiker
b) paper cup
c) front door
d) golf club
e) country house
f) headache
g) lawn tennis
h) science fiction

5 Notice what happens to the word stress when a compound adjective comes before a noun in a sentence. Example:
This bread is homemade. / It's homemade ***bread***.

Practise saying the following:
a) He's first-class. / He's a first-class musician.
b) Jennie's very easy-going. / She's a very easy-going woman.
c) It's old-fashioned. / It's an old-fashioned car.
d) Tom's very hard working. / He's a hard-working student.

REVISION AND EXTENSION

Future Continuous

1 [8.2] Listen to Des talking about what life will be like in fifty years time.

a) What two effects does he think over-population will have?
b) Does he think people will be working in a spirit of cooperation?

2 Look at these sentences.
*'I think we'**ll be eating** very different kinds of food.'*
*'We **might be living** under the sea.'*

Will the 'eating' and 'living' still be in progress in 50 years time or will it be finished?

3 In which of the sentences below does the speaker:
- suggest that the future event has already been fixed or decided?
- make a sudden decision?

a) *I'll write to her tomorrow.*
b) *I'll be writing to her tomorrow.*

Check with Section 1 in the *Language reference* and find out why the Future Continuous can sometimes be used to sound polite.

PRACTICE

1 Put the verb in brackets into the most likely form, choosing either *will* + base form or the Future Continuous. Work in pairs and continue each dialogue in any way you like. Example:
A: ________ (*use, you*) your car tonight?
A: *Will you be using your car tonight?*
B: *No, why?*
A: *I'd like to borrow it if it's OK with you.*

a) A: Tell me. What ________ (*do, you*) at 11.15 tonight?
B: I'll probably be fast asleep. Why?
b) A: Would you like to borrow my camera?
B: Oh, thank you. I ________ (*give*) it back to you tomorrow.
c) A: Would you like me to take Satoshi some chocolates from you?
B: No, don't worry. I ________ (*see*) him tomorrow anyway.
d) A: I've run out of money. ________ (*lend, you*) me £50?
B: As it's Friday I ________ (*go*) to the bank later on. Do you want me to get some money out for you?

2 Work in pairs. Student As should decide what kind of life they lead (e.g. job, home life, leisure activities) and fill in the gaps in their diaries for Sunday to Tuesday next week. Student Bs should do the same. Do not show your partner what you have written.

A

	SUNDAY	MONDAY	TUESDAY
7.00 – 8.30			
8.30 – 9.30		Breakfast	
9.30 – 11.30			Fly to London
11.30 – 12.30			
12.30 – 13.30			

B

	SUNDAY	MONDAY	TUESDAY
7.00 – 8.30			
8.30 – 9.30			Children to school
9.30 – 11.30			
11.30 – 12.30			
12.30 – 13.30			

a) Ask each other questions in order to fill in the gaps in your copy of your partner's diary and to guess what kind of life they lead. Use the Present Continuous (*What are you doing between . . . ?*).
b) Look at the most likely occasions when you can fix up a meeting between you. Only ask questions about what your partner will be doing at exactly quarter to or quarter past the hour in order to use the Future Continuous. Example:
'What'll you be doing at 8.45 a.m. on Tuesday?' – 'I'll be taking the children to school. Sorry.'

EXTENSION 2

Future Perfect

1 In the interview, Des says:
*'I hope that we'**ll have found** a form of transport that won't pollute the environment.'*

a) Does he hope that in fifty years time the 'finding' should still be in progress or that it will be finished?
b) Which of these two diagrams best indicates *will have found*?

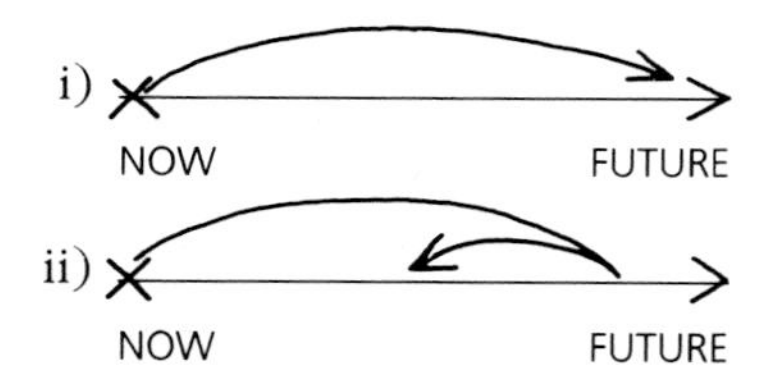

2 Work in pairs.

STUDENT A
You are going to be ruler of the world for the next thirty years.

STUDENT B
You are going to be President / Prime Minister of your country for the same period.

a) Individually, make notes on what you will have achieved:
   - in ten years time (e.g. *You will have made all healthcare free.*).
   - in twenty years time.
   - in thirty years time.
b) Find out each other's achievements (*What will you have done by the year . . . ?*)
c) Decide who will have achieved the most and whether you could work together.
d) Student As should compare their achievements with other As and Student Bs should compare their achievements with other Bs.

WRITING

Complex sentences

1 Look at the following sentences.
***Whenever** it snows in Britain, the railways come to a standstill.*
***In spite of the fact that** there was a slight improvement in sales, the company is still making a loss.*
*Take a coat **in case** it gets cold.*

Join the sentences below using the linking words in the box. Change the order of the sentences and the verb forms if necessary. Example:
Ring first. We might be out.
Ring first in case we're out.

yet	in spite of (the fact that)	in order to	in case
even though	even if	whereas	since

a) Anton has no car. It'll take him a long time to get to his parents' house.
b) Rosa stood on a chair. She wanted to reach the top shelf.
c) Someone passed me at 50. There was a 30 mile an hour speed limit.
d) I enjoyed the disco very much. I had to leave early.
e) Greg drove badly. To my surprise, he passed the test.
f) It wouldn't matter if I had the money. I wouldn't buy you a gold ring.
g) Neil likes hot chocolate. Judith likes coffee.
h) You should insure your jewellery. It might be stolen.

2 Compare the following pairs of sentences.

Since it is Sunday, all the shops are closed.
***Being Sunday**, all the shops are closed.*

Since I've lived here for twenty years, I don't want to move.
***Having lived here for twenty years**, I don't want to move.*

After they got married, they stopped fighting.
***After getting married**, they stopped fighting.*

Although he was not well-qualified, he got the job.
***Although not well-qualified**, he got the job.*

Rewrite the following sentences, using a (present, perfect or past) participle construction. Example:
Before he went to the interview, Deri changed into a suit.
Before going to the interview, Deri changed into a suit.

a) Since I was feeling hot, I took off my overcoat.
b) When we woke up, we saw we had arrived in Moscow.
c) She sat down and went to sleep after she had lit the fire.
d) Now I can see it in close-up, it doesn't look too bad.
e) Since I hadn't eaten oysters before I didn't know what to expect.
f) Although he wasn't very well-educated, he was very well-read.

SPEAKING AND WRITING

1 [8.3] Work in groups and listen to the recordings. Group A should listen to Extract A. Group B should listen to Extract B. Complete as much of the form as you can.

UFO REPORT FORM

1 Name and address:

2 Place: **Date:** **Time:**

3 Other witnesses (names and addresses):

4 Weather conditions:

5 Description of sighting (where seen and for how long):

6 Appearance (indicate size, shape, colour, distinguishing features – draw a sketch):

7 Sound and movement:

8 Description of any aliens (appearance, manner, behaviour, speech, purpose for being here):

9 Conclusions:

2 Interview someone in the other group who saw 'their' spacecraft land. Using the form as a basis, find out the differences between the two incidents.

3 Discuss the following questions.

a) Which of the recorded stories do you believe or not believe? Give reasons.
b) Do you know any UFO stories? (Tell each other.)
c) Why have there been so many sightings of UFOs over the years? Give suggestions.

4 Divide into groups.

GROUP A
You are Whitley Strieber. Write an entry in your diary for the day you saw the aliens. Describe the experience in your own words, talking about your feelings.

GROUP B
You are Mrs Coe. Write a letter to a newspaper talking about your experience. Try to convince the readers it really happened.

Language reference

1 Future Continuous

The Future Continuous is used in the following ways:

a) To describe something you expect will be in progress at a particular moment in the future:
*At 8.15 a.m. on Wednesday I'**ll be taking** the children to school.*

b) To suggest that an event in the future has already been planned. (This is similar to the Present Continuous.):
*I'**ll be writing** to her tomorrow. (I'm writing to her tomorrow.)*
The use of the Future Continuous shows that the event is quite normal and natural and takes away the idea of deliberate intention. (Compare: *I'll write to her tomorrow.* The use of *'ll* indicates sudden decision and a strong intention.)
The Future Continuous can be a polite way of asking about people's plans because it seems to show we are not trying to influence the other person:
*'**Will** you **be using** the car tonight?' 'No. Why?'*

2 Future Perfect

The Future Perfect looks back from a definite time in the future to an action that will have been completed sometime before (we don't know exactly when):
*We **will have finished** before you get back.*
*By the end of next year, we **will have moved** house.*

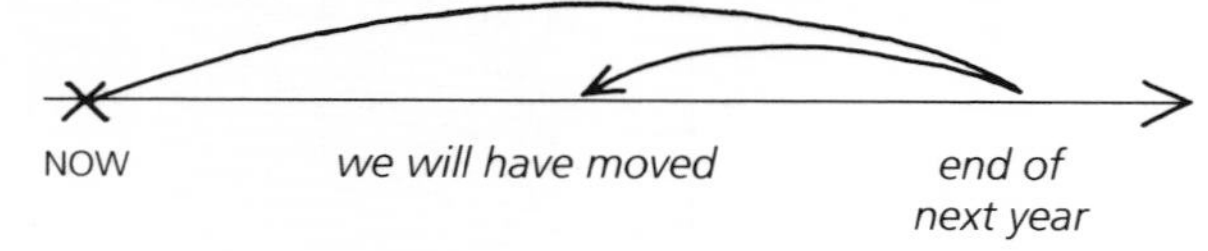

3 Complex sentences

A complex sentence consists of a main clause (*The railways come to a standstill*) and a subordinate clause (*whenever it snows in Britain*).

Adverbial clauses

One type of subordinate clause is an adverbial clause. This kind of clause answers such questions as *Why?*, *When?* and *What for?*

a) Time:
*I'll phone **as soon as I get there**.*
*She was in bed **while he was making breakfast**.*

b) Contrast:
***Although** / **Even though I understand what you say**, I can't agree with you.*
*I wouldn't lend you any money **even if you were broke**.*
*He's a strange person **yet you can't help liking him**.*
*I play baseball **whereas my brother likes tennis**.*
*The company is still making a loss **in spite of the fact that there was a change of management**.*

c) Condition:
*Take a coat **in case it gets cold**.*
*I'd come **even if I were not invited**.*

d) Reason:
***Since you can't answer the question**, let's ask someone else.*

e) Purpose:
*I spent a year in Japan **in order to** / **so that I could learn Japanese**.*

Participle clauses

Subordinate clauses can also be (present, perfect, past) participle clauses:

a) Reason:
***Being Sunday** (Since it is Sunday), all the shops are closed.*

b) Time:
***After getting married** (After they got married), they stopped fighting.*
***Seen on TV** (When it was seen on TV), the film looked old-fashioned.*

c) Contrast:
***Although not well-qualified** (Although he was not well-qualified), he got the job.*

4 Compounds

Words can be combined to make compound words in the following ways:

a) Compound adjectives
Examples: *curly-haired, long-playing*
The stress is usually on the second part (*curly-'**haired***).
When the adjective comes before a noun the stress is moved to the noun (*He's curly-'**haired**. / He's a curly-haired '**boy**.*).

b) Compound nouns
Example: *bedroom*
The stress is usually on the first part (*'**bed**room*). Some have their stress on the second part (*front '**door***).

c) Compound verbs
Example: *undercook*
The stress is usually on the second part (under'***cook***).

Compounds are sometimes written as one word (*bathroom*), two words (*living room*) or hyphenated (*high-class*). In British English, compound adjectives are usually written with a hyphen. However, there are few precise rules about how to form compounds and the same word is often written in different ways. If in doubt, it is best to check in a dictionary.

Around the world

READING AND SPEAKING

1 Look at the introduction to a magazine article. Would you like to go on a journey like this? Give reasons.

HEAT AND DANGER IN THE PERUVIAN JUNGLE

Surrounded by poisonous snakes, marauding jaguars, malarial mosquitoes and huge forest spiders, Amanda Shakespeare began to regret her journey to the jungle.

2 [9.1] Listen to the recording and identify the sounds. What do you think life is like in the jungle? Think of smells, colours, noises, dangers, getting food and drink, the different kinds of towns and houses.

3 Read an extract from the article and find answers to the following questions.

a) What kind of town was Sapito?
b) Why did Amanda's heart miss a beat?
c) What kind of place was Diego's house?

How would you have felt in this situation?

27 June
Although it was dark when I arrived, Sapito smelt the same. I crossed the Plaza de Armas and made for the other side of town. The streets were empty but I didn't feel threatened. I found Diego's house and walked up what I took to be the path, although it was too dark to see. Suddenly something pounced on my shoulders from above. I felt claws dig into my neck and a tail lightly brush my back: my heart missed a beat. But after the initial shock I realised that an overexcited little monkey was squeaking shrilly into my ear. I had great difficulty in disentangling myself from the creature, which insisted on accompanying me to the door. Once inside, I found there was no light and no water, but I knew I was back in the jungle when I heard cockroaches crunch underfoot as I made my way to bed.

(from *Marie-Claire*)

4 Work in groups. Compare life in the jungle to life in the places in the photographs.

5 Discuss the following.

a) Where would you like to go to for an adventure holiday? Give reasons.
b) What preparations would you need to make? (Think about what you want to take, how you would travel, where you would stay.)
c) What would you do when you got there? (Meet local people? Explore caves? Find rare animals to photograph?)
d) Would you prefer to travel alone or in a group? Is this always true? Give reasons.
e) Would you prefer to go as a tourist or as a 'traveller'? Why?

6 Report your conclusions to the other groups.

VOCABULARY 1

Travel

1 Choose the best alternative to complete each sentence. Use your dictionary to help you. Example:
I bought a little doll as a *souvenir* of my visit to India.
(*memory* / *souvenir* / *remembrance*)

a) On the London-Tokyo flight there is sometimes a ______ at Anchorage. (*flying visit* / *stopover* / *stay*)
b) His wife has flown to Singapore on a business ______. (*journey* / *travel* / *excursion* / *trip*)
c) Richard is a very amusing travelling ______. (*companion* / *friend* / *colleague* / *partner*)
d) Have you seen the ancient ______ in the desert? (*remainders* / *remnants* / *ruins* / *wrecks*)
e) Nothing happened at all. It was a very ______ holiday. (*uneventful* / *insignificant* / *incidental*)
f) From the top there was a wonderful ______ of the whole valley. (*spectacle* / *sight* / *view* / *look*)
g) In the 19th century, David Livingstone, the Scottish ______, tried to find the sources of the Nile. (*explorer* / *tourist* / *globetrotter* / *rambler* / *sightseer*)
h) The company arranges daily ______ to the island to see the penguins. (*pilgrimages* / *campaigns* / *itineraries* / *excursions*)
i) St Tropez is one of the most popular tourist ______ in the South of France. (*spas* / *resorts* / *packages* / *charters*)

2 Keep a record of any words you would like to remember under the heading *Travel*. Make sure you write down each word in a phrase, showing which words go with it (e.g. the preposition that can follow *souvenir*: *buy a souvenir of*...).

SPEAKING

Selling a holiday

1 Work in groups. If other students have had a holiday in the same town or country as you, work with them as a group. Students with no holiday places in common should agree where they would be prepared to 'sell'.

2 You are going to try to persuade other students to go on holiday to 'your' location. Decide on the main 'selling points' (e.g. food, climate, culture, things to do, attractive sites).

3 Design a poster to illustrate the attractions of your holiday location and make notes for a talk.

4 Make your presentations, showing the poster and using your notes to help you. Agree on the most attractive place to visit.

REVISION AND EXTENSION

Using phrasal verbs

Phrasal verbs are verbs followed by a particle, e.g. *look up* – *look* (verb) +*up* (particle). The particle can be an adverb and/or a preposition. Examples: *turn into* (verb + preposition); *get ahead* (verb + adverb); *look forward to* (verb + adverb + preposition).

In order to use phrasal verbs correctly you need to know:
- whether the verb takes an object (i.e. is it *transitive* or *intransitive*?) – See Unit 5.
- where the particle is placed in the sentence.
- the position of the object pronoun (e.g. *him, it*) in the sentence.

There are rules you can follow, depending on whether the particle is an adverb or a preposition. The dictionary will also help you.

1 Look at the sentences on the right. (Ignore the underlined words at this stage.) In which sentence(s):
- is the verb intransitive?
- can the particle be separated from the verb?
- are the particle and the verb never separated?
- are the particle and the verb always separated?

a) I am *looking forward to* my holiday.
b) I *looked up* the word in the dictionary.
c) Fortunately the travel business is *looking up*.
d) The children *looked after* their rabbit very well.
e) He *talked* Natalie *out of* going home early.

2 Look at the dictionary definitions and check your answers to Exercise 1.

keeps one's good position.
look up *phr v* [T] (**look** sthg. ↔ **up**) to find (information) in a book: *Look up the word in the dictionary.* | *I'll look up the times of the trains.*
look up to sbdy. *phr v* [T] to respect; admire

The hat looks well on you.
look after sbdy./sthg. *phr v* [T] to take care of; be responsible for: *Who will look after the baby while they're out?* | *I can look after myself.*
look ahead *phr v* [I] to plan for the future.

look to our own work.
look up *phr v* [I] *infml* (of a situation, business, etc.) to get better, esp. after being bad; improve: *Trade should look up later in the year.* | *Things are looking up!*
look sbdy. up [T] to find and visit (someone) when

see also UNLOOKED FOR.
look forward to *phr v* [T] to expect with pleasure: *I'm really looking forward to your party.* [+ v-ing] *I'm looking forward to going to your party.*
look in *phr v* [I (on)] *infml* to make a short visit

until there is no time left for voting.
talk sbdy. **out of** sthg. *phr v* [T] **1** to persuade (someone) not to do (something): *See if you can talk her out of it.* [+ v-ing] *The policeman talked the man out of jumping from the top of the building.*
talk sthg. over *phr v* [T (with)] to speak about thoroughly

a) How does the dictionary indicate the way these phrasal verbs are used grammatically?
b) Which one(s) would not be used in a more formal situation?

3 Replace the nouns which are underlined in Exercise 1 with a pronoun. What changes, if any, have to be made to make the sentence grammatically correct? Check your answers with Section 1 in the *Language reference*.

PRACTICE

1 Work in pairs and take turns to say alternate sentences below:
- substitute the phrasal verb in brackets. (Where possible, separate the particle.)
- substitute a pronoun in place of the noun where it is underlined.

Guess the answers and then check in your dictionary.

a) The fire fighters *extinguished* the blaze. (*put out*)
b) The alarm clock *rang* early. (*go off*)
c) We've got *no more* petrol *left*. (*run out of*)
d) Do you know he *rejected* the job? (*turn down*)
e) Don't *destroy* that letter! (*tear up*)
f) He really *resembles* his mother, doesn't he? (*looks like*)
g) I won't *tolerate* this situation any longer! (*put up with*)
h) The police have promised to *investigate* the burglary. (*look into*)
i) We'll have to *postpone* the meeting until next week. (*put off*)
j) I can *give* Tom *a bed* for the night. (*put up*)

2 Look at the pictures.

a) In groups, choose a verb from the box (e.g. *pick*), add a particle (e.g. *up*), and match the resulting phrasal verb to the pictures (e.g. *pick up* can be used in picture 1). Try to use one of the following particles when making the phrasal verbs: *off, out, up, across, in.* There may be more than one possibility.

make	pick	come	do	fill	turn

b) Make a sentence to accompany each picture. Example:
1 Gary is going to ***pick up*** *the hitchhiker.*

c) Call out one of the phrasal verbs to the class. Someone in another group must give you a sentence which corresponds with one of the pictures. Decide whether they are correct or not.

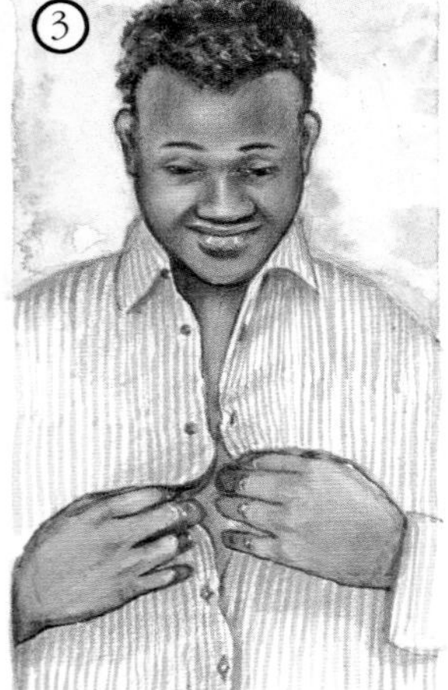

3 Work in pairs. Student A should say a verb (e.g. *get*) and Student B should mime a phrasal verb which can be made from this verb (e.g. *get up*). Decide on a time limit, and refer to your dictionary if necessary.

LISTENING

Before listening

In 1988 the actor Michael Palin set out from London to film a journey round the world in 80 days for the BBC. He was not allowed to use an aircraft. These photographs were taken on the journey.

a) Which of his experiences while travelling do you think photographs 1 and 2 show?
b) Which of the photographs does the certificate in 3 relate to?

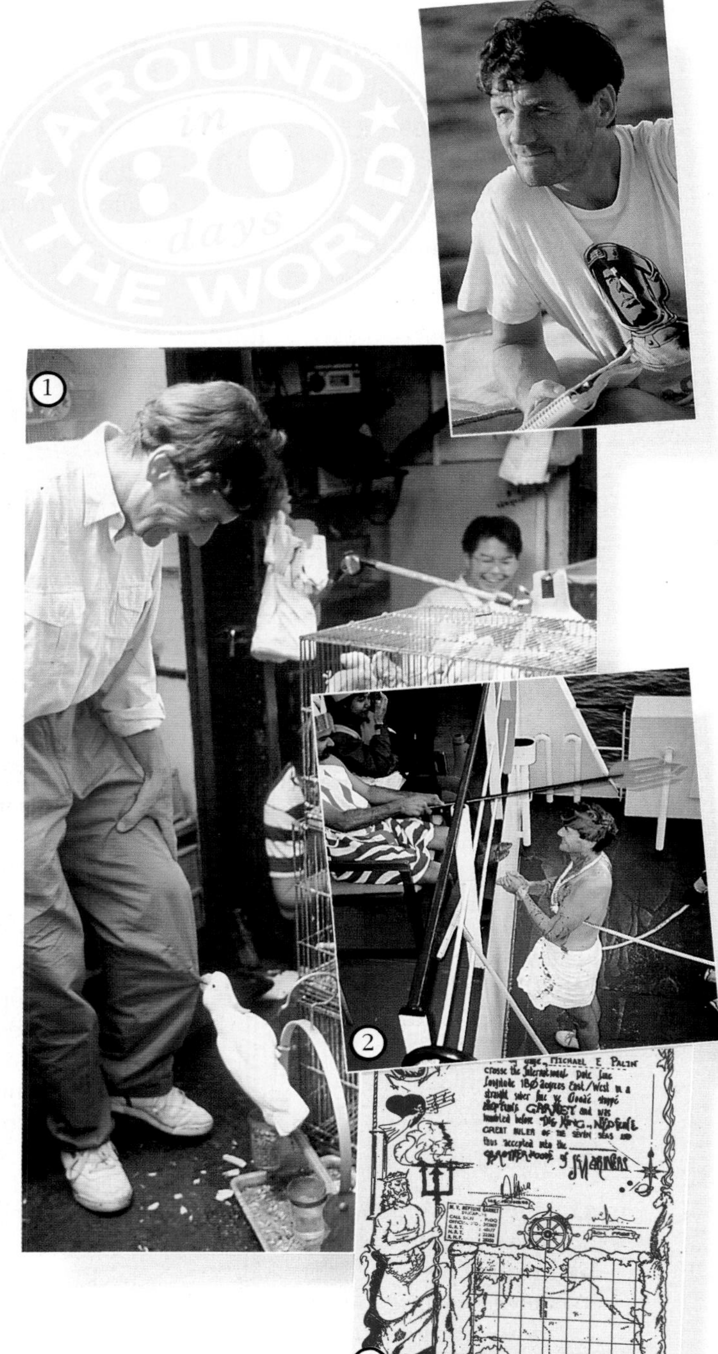

Listening

1 [9.2] Listen to a radio interview with Michael Palin. (Note that he refers to a TV programme he was in called *Monty Python's Flying Circus* with the actor John Cleese in which there was a comic sketch about a parrot.)
Find out exactly what happened in photograph 1.

2 Listen again. Work in pairs.

a) Student A should make a list of the things Michael Palin enjoyed about the journey. Student B should make a list of the things he didn't enjoy so much.
b) Compare your notes. Were there any things Michael both did and didn't enjoy?

3 Complete the following sentences.

a) Michael thought it was important to make friends with the crew of the boat (*dhow*) because . . .
b) When he was ill . . .
c) There's a street in Hong Kong where . . .
d) He made a mistake with the cockatoo. Instead of being . . .
e) The interviewer asked Michael if . . .
f) As smaller hotels are more typical of the country . . .

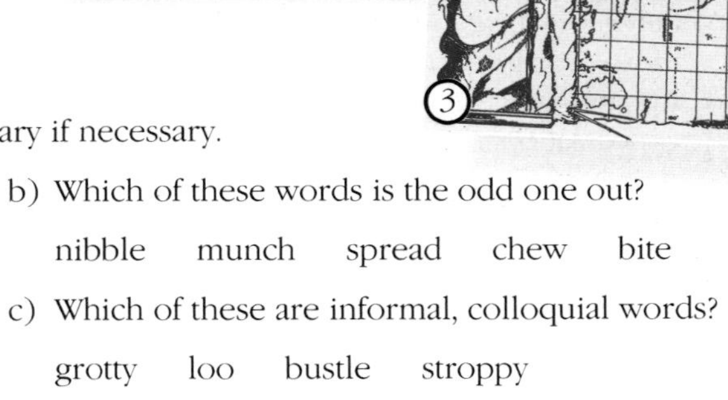

4 Answer these vocabulary questions, using a dictionary if necessary.

a) Make words from the following using one of the suffixes in the box below.

reflect resemble private friendly

-ship -ion -acy -ance

b) Which of these words is the odd one out?

nibble munch spread chew bite

c) Which of these are informal, colloquial words?

grotty loo bustle stroppy

Connected speech

1 [9.3] In the interview Michael Palin says: *very uncomfortable*. Words ending in a vowel sound (*very*) are often linked to words beginning in a vowel sound (*uncomfortable*) with a small /w/ or /j/ sound depending on the first vowel sound.
Listen to the following phrases and write a /w/ or /j/ sound between the words. The first one has been done for you.

a) to (/w/) eat
b) I (/__/) am
c) she (/__/) is
d) you (/__/) ought
e) no (/__/) other
f) very (/__/) unhappy
g) who (/__/) are

2 [9.4] In the interview you will also hear the words *They were on* . . . Notice that words ending in the /r/ sound are linked to words beginning with a vowel. Listen and repeat the following phrases.

a) anywhere else
b) we're out
c) more or less
d) sooner or later
e) beer is

3 [9.5] Dictation.

a) Listen and write Lucy and Mike's conversation.
b) Mark all possible links between words (including those practised in Unit 7).
c) In pairs, practise reading the conversation.

VOCABULARY 2

Looking up idiomatic expressions

Idiomatic expressions are fixed groups of words which have a different meaning to the individual words in the expressions. However, you can sometimes guess the meaning of idiomatic expressions from the context.

1 In pairs, guess what the expressions in *italics* mean.

a) No, he's got it wrong. I think he's *barking up the wrong tree*.
b) I don't think she's going *for good* – just a couple of years.
c) He's been working for ten hours *at a stretch* every day this week, only stopping for a cup of coffee.
d) We agreed that we'd *go halves* on the bill. How much is it?
e) I really *couldn't face* doing the washing up that night so I left it till the morning.
f) That job's just *up your street* – you'll be perfect for it.
g) After the second boring visit I *put my foot down* and refused to go again!

2 Check your guesses for Exercise 1 in the dictionary. In order to check, identify the key word and then look it up. Example: *bark up the wrong tree*.

> **bark** /bɑːk/ ... **3 bark up the wrong tree** *infml* to direct one's efforts or actions at the wrong person or in the wrong direction; have a mistaken idea: *You're barking up the wrong tree if you think she'll be able to help you.*

Bark is the key word, but if you had looked up *tree* you would usually be directed to the right place.

Notice the expression *infml* (meaning *informal*) after this idiomatic expression, which means you should be careful not to use it in formal contexts.

WRITING

The indefinite article

1 A magazine is going to publish different people's travel experiences. Expand the following notes into full sentences using *a/an* where required. (You can check with Section 2 in the *Language reference* to find out when to use the indefinite article.) The first one has been done for you.

a) Helen Baker. English. Works as English teacher in London. Recently had interesting experience in Japan.
Helen Baker is English. She works as an English teacher in London and has recently had an interesting experience in Japan.
b) Jo-Anne Campbell. 24-year-old pianist from rural part of Australia. Recently returned from travelling round Kenya in Land Rover. Met beautiful African singer called Winnie.
c) Jean-Paul Mitterand. French–Canadian engineer with well-known company. Loves unusual adventures. Travels everywhere by motorbike. Last year had two-month ride round Mongolia.
d) Diyangui Nkama. Angolan lawyer with six-year-old child. Had bad back for years. Earlier this year stayed in lodge in wildlife park in remote region of India. Needed medical assistance. Had to visit local doctor. Made sensational recovery.

2 Read the text about Helen Baker's trip to Japan. Fill in the gaps with *a/an* or *the*. Leave a blank if no article is required.

When I finished ____(1)____ university I became ____(2)____ English teacher. My boyfriend Junju wanted me to go back home to ____(3)____ Japan with him and I thought it was ____(4)____ ideal opportunity to travel. We took ____(5)____ cheapest flight possible and went to Nagoya by ____(6)____ bullet train. ____(7)____ journey was fantastic – smooth, fast and punctual. It's only delayed if there's ____(8)____ earthquake. ____(9)____ only problem was later, when I was travelling alone and I couldn't understand ____(10)____ station names.

We stayed with Junju's father in Okazaki, just outside Nagoya, but it was ____(11)____ disaster. He just could not accept my travelling, unmarried, with his son, and felt I should do ____(12)____ housework as is traditional in Japan.

Surviving in Japan made me ____(13)____ lot more confident. I realised I had ____(14)____ strengths I hadn't known I possessed, like ____(15)____ determination and ____(16)____ optimism. ____(17)____ main reason I came home after ____(18)____ year and ____(19)____ half was because I felt ____(20)____ homesick.

(from *Company*)

Personal letter: making arrangements

1 [9.6] When Helen was in Japan she invited her parents to come and stay. Listen to this phone conversation with her mother.

2 You are going to write Helen's letter confirming the arrangements. Listen to the phone conversation again and take notes. You are going to enclose the map below and explain how to get to the house.

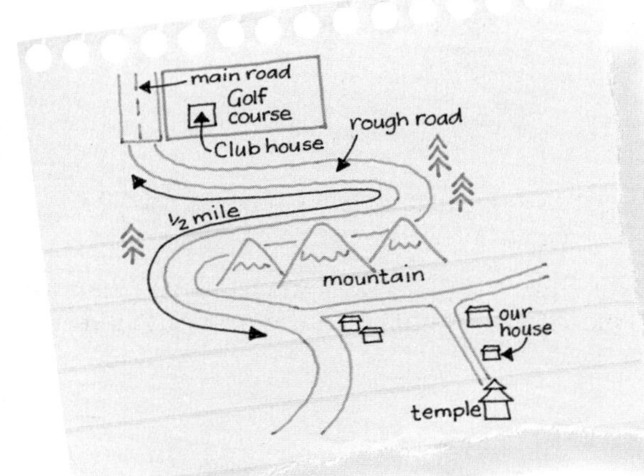

3 Write the letter including some of the details from the phone conversation but try not to use the exact words. Pay particular attention to:
- the layout of the letter.
- the level of formality. (Remember: Helen is writing to her mother.)
- the use of the article.
- the use of imperatives and prepositions when giving directions (*take the . . . to*; *at the . . . go*; *next to . . . there is*; *walk along the . . .*).
- reported speech (if appropriate).

4 Exchange letters with a partner and try to improve each other's letters.

Language reference

1 Phrasal verbs

Some verbs combine with an adverb particle or a preposition to make phrasal verbs (sometimes called 'multi-word verbs'). These combinations are often idiomatic, with more than one meaning. The meanings are often very difficult to deduce from the individual parts.

Type 1: VERB + PREPOSITION

These are transitive and are sometimes called 'prepositional verbs':

*The children **looked after** their rabbit / it.*

Here the direct object (*the rabbit, it*) must come after the preposition (*after*). (NOT ~~*They **looked** the rabbit **after**.*~~)

Type 2: VERB + ADVERB

a) Intransitive:
*Business **is looking up**.*
Here *up* is an adverb (adverbial particle). The phrasal verb is not followed by an object.

b) Transitive:
*I **looked up** the word in the dictionary.*
*I **looked** the word **up** in the dictionary.*
Here the phrasal verb (*looked up*) is followed by an object (*the word*), so the adverb (*up*) can come before or after the object (*look up the word / look the word up*).
However, when the object is a personal pronoun (e.g. *it*) the personal pronoun must come before the adverb (*up*):
*I **looked it up** in the dictionary.* (NOT ~~*I **looked up it**.*~~)

Note that in the sentence *I **looked up** the chimney, up* is a preposition and must come before the direct object.

Type 3: VERB + ADVERB + PREPOSITION

These are transitive and are sometimes called 'phrasal-prepositional verbs':

*I'**m looking forward to** my holiday.*

Here the phrasal verb consists of an adverb (*forward*) followed by a preposition (*to*). The object (*my holiday, it*) must come after the preposition.

2 The indefinite article (*a/an*)

The indefinite article (meaning 'one' or 'one of a kind') is used with singular countable nouns:

a) When something is indefinite:
*Would you like **a** cup of tea?* (It doesn't matter which one).

b) When something is mentioned for the first time:
*He has **a** three-month-old baby. The baby is very fat.* (Use *the* for the second mention.)

c) To say what something is or someone does:
*This is **a** Swiss penknife. Helen works as **an** English teacher.*

d) Before a certain number or quantity expressions (***a** few, **a** great many, **a** half, **a** hundred*) and to contrast with more than one (*two biscuits and **an** ice cream*).

We can also use *a(n)* to talk about 'all examples of a kind' instead of the plural noun:

***An** old house is* (OR *Old houses are*) *more expensive than **a** new house* (OR *new houses*).

Compare with the definite article in Unit 2. Note there is no article (sometimes called the 'zero article') before plural or uncountable nouns when talking about things in general:

Travel books are very interesting. Travel broadens the mind. BUT ***The** travel story I like the best is . . .* (the specific story).

3 Connected speech: word linking

(See Unit 7 for words ending in a consonant sound which are followed by words beginning with a vowel sound.)

Words ending in a vówel sound pronounced with a rounded lip position (e.g. *t**o***) are often linked to words beginning with a vowel sound (e.g. ***ea**t*) with a small /w/ sound (*to* /w/ *eat*).

Words ending in a vowel pronounced with a spread lip position (e.g. *Why . . . ?*) are often linked to words beginning with a vowel sound with a small /j/ sound (e.g. *Why /j/ are they . . .?*).

Unit 10

A Family Supper

READING 1

1 Read the opening paragraphs of this story by Kazuo Ishiguro. Answer the following questions.

a) Why is it dangerous to eat fugu?
b) Why do you think it became popular?
c) What were the circumstances of the writer's mother's death?

A Family Supper

Fugu is a fish caught off the Pacific shores of Japan. The fish has held a special significance for me ever since my mother died through eating one. The poison resides in the sexual glands of the fish, inside two fragile bags. When preparing the fish, these bags must be removed with caution, 5 for any clumsiness will result in the poison leaking into the veins. Regrettably, it is not easy to tell whether or not this operation has been carried out successfully. The proof is, as it were, in the eating.

Fugu poisoning is hideously painful and almost always fatal. If the fish has been eaten during the evening, the victim is usually overtaken by 10 pain during his sleep. He rolls about in agony for a few hours and is dead by morning. The fish became extremely popular in Japan after the war. Until stricter regulations were imposed, it was all the rage to perform the hazardous gutting operation in one's own kitchen, then to invite neighbours and friends round for the feast.

15 At the time of my mother's death I was living in California. My relationship with my parents had become somewhat strained around that period, and consequently I did not learn of the circumstances of her death until I returned to Tokyo two years later. Apparently, my mother had always refused to eat fugu, but on this particular occasion she had 20 made an exception, having been invited by an old schoolfriend whom she was anxious not to offend. It was my father who supplied me with the details as we drove from the airport to his house in the Kamakura district. When we finally arrived, it was nearing the end of a sunny autumn day.

2 In what order did the following events happen to the writer? Number the events 1–6. Example: *1 – c)*

a) He came back to Tokyo.
b) He found out how his mother had died.
c) He went to California.
d) His mother died.
e) His relationship with his parents got worse.
f) He arrived back in his father's house.

3 The title of the story is 'A Family Supper'. What do you think the story is going to be about?

4 Read the next part of the story and find evidence for or against the following statements.

a) The writer's father is a businessman.
b) Watanabe was a relation of the writer's father.
c) Watanabe killed himself because his firm failed.
d) Kikuko is the same age as the writer.
e) The brother and sister did not get on very well.

5 Look at the pictures.

a) Decide which picture is most like the father. Give reasons for your answers.
b) Which of the adjectives in the box do you think could describe the father? Give reasons.

emotional	talkative
serious	affectionate
traditional	proud
relaxed	informal

c) Are there any other adjectives you can think of?

'Did you eat on the plane?' my father asked. We were sitting on the tatami floor of his tea-room.
'They gave me a light snack.'
'You must be hungry. We'll eat as soon as Kikuko arrives.'

My father was a formidable-looking man with a large stony jaw and furious black eyebrows. I think now in retrospect that he much resembled Chou En-lai, although he would not have cherished such a comparison, being particularly proud of the pure samurai blood that ran in the family. His general presence was not one which encouraged relaxed conversation; neither were things helped much by his odd way of stating each remark as if it were the concluding one. In fact, as I sat opposite him that afternoon, a boyhood memory came back to me of the time he had struck me several times around the head for 'chattering like an old woman'. Inevitably, our conversation since my arrival at the airport had been punctuated by long pauses.
'I'm sorry to hear about the firm,' I said when neither of us had spoken for some time. He nodded gravely.
'In fact the story didn't end there,' he said. 'After the firm's collapse, Watanabe killed himself. He didn't wish to live with the disgrace.'
'I see.'
'We were partners for seventeen years. A man of principle and honour. I respected him very much.'
'Will you go into business again?' I asked.
'I am – in retirement. I'm too old to involve myself in new ventures now. Business these days has become so different. Dealing with foreigners. Doing things their way. I don't understand how we've come to this. Neither did Watanabe.' He sighed. 'A fine man. A man of principle.'

The tea-room looked out over the garden. From where I sat I could make out the ancient well which as a child I had believed haunted. It was just visible now through the thick foliage. The sun had sunk low and much of the garden had fallen into shadow.
'I'm glad in any case that you've decided to come back,' my father said. 'More than a short visit, I hope.'
'I'm not sure what my plans will be.'
'I for one am prepared to forget the past. Your mother too was always ready to welcome you back – upset as she was by your behaviour.'
'I appreciate your sympathy. As I say, I am not sure what my plans are.'
'I've come to believe now that there were no evil intentions in your mind,' my father continued. 'You were swayed by certain influences. Like so many others.'
'Perhaps we should forget it, as you suggest.'
'As you will. More tea?'
Just then a girl's voice came echoing through the house.
'At last.' My father rose to his feet. 'Kikuko has arrived.'

Despite our difference in years, my sister and I have always been close. Seeing me again seemed to make her excessively excited and for a while she did nothing but giggle nervously. But she calmed down somewhat when my father started to question her about Osaka and her university. She answered him with short formal replies. She in turn asked me a few questions, but she seemed inhibited by the fear that her questions might lead to awkward topics. After a while, the conversation had become even sparser than prior to Kikuko's arrival. Then my father stood up, saying: 'I must attend to the supper. Please excuse me for being burdened down by such matters. Kikuko will look after you.'

My sister relaxed quite visibly once he had left the room. Within a few minutes, she was chatting freely about her friends in Osaka and about her classes at university. Then quite suddenly she decided we should walk in the garden and went striding out onto the veranda. We put on some straw sandals that had been left along the veranda rail and stepped out into the garden. The daylight had almost gone.

Chou En-lai: Premier and Foreign minister of China in the time of Mao

6 What do you think the following phrases tell us about the events or characters in the story?

a) *Inevitably, our conversation since my arrival at the airport had been punctuated by long pauses.* (line 15)
b) *... upset as she was by your behaviour.* (line 36)
c) *I appreciate your sympathy.* (line 37)
d) *You were swayed by certain influences.* (line 39)
e) *My sister relaxed quite visibly once he had left the room.* (line 55)

7 Discuss the following.

a) How and why does the father think that business is changing?
b) What is the father's attitude to Watanabe's suicide?
c) What do you think the son feels about the suicide?
d) Why do you think Kikuko suggests going into the garden?

LISTENING 1

1 [10.1] Listen to the next part of the story.

a) What part do the pictures and words play in the story?
b) Which topics do Kikuko and her brother *not* talk about?
   - Kikuko's future
   - the father's future
   - the writer's future
   - the mother's death
   - Watanabe's suicide
   - the 'ghost'

2 Listen again and continue these sentences based on the story.

a) Kikuko said she was not sure that she wanted to go to America with her boyfriend for three reasons: ...
b) The mother had tried to convince them that the 'ghost' the writer had seen was ...
c) Kikuko told her brother that their mother had blamed herself and her husband for ...
d) The writer is not sure he'll return to California because ...

3 Answer the following questions.

a) When the writer says *'Yes, Father was just telling me how Watanabe was a man of principle.'* What is his attitude to what Watanabe did?
   i) He agrees with his father.
   ii) He is being ironic (i.e. he means the opposite of what he says).
b) What did the writer say he had seen in the clearing?
c) Why do you think Kikuko takes *unnaturally theatrical puffs on her cigarette*? What is her personality like?

READING 2

Read the next part of the story and answer the following questions.

a) Why do you think the father wanted to show his son the house?
b) What can you deduce from the words *For some moments my sister did not move*? (line 6)
c) How does the father occupy his spare time?
d) What significance, if any, do you think the battleship has to the story?
e) What does the father blame himself for?
f) Why does the father think his wife died? What were her 'disappointments'?
g) What is the son's reaction to why his mother might have died?

We found my father in the kitchen. He gave us a quick glance, then carried on with what he was doing.
'Father's become quite a chef since he's had to manage on his own,' Kikuko said with a laugh. He turned and looked at my sister coldly.
5 'Hardly a skill I'm proud of,' he said. 'Kikuko, come here and help.'
For some moments my sister did not move. Then she stepped forward and took an apron hanging from a drawer.
'Just these vegetables need cooking now,' he said to her. 'The rest just needs watching.' Then he looked up and regarded me strangely for
10 some seconds. 'I expect you want to look round the house,' he said eventually. He put down the chopsticks he had been holding. 'It's a long time since you've seen it.'

As we left the kitchen I glanced back towards Kikuko, but her back was turned.
15 'She's a good girl,' my father said quietly.

I followed my father from room to room. I had forgotten how large the house was. A panel would slide open and another room would appear. But the rooms were all startlingly empty. In one of the rooms the lights did not come on, and we stared at the stark walls and tatami in the
20 pale light that came from the windows.
'This house is much too large for a man to live in alone,' my father said. 'I don't have much use for most of these rooms now.'

But eventually my father opened the door to a room packed full of books and papers. There were flowers in vases and pictures on the walls.
25 Then I noticed something on a low table in a corner of the room. I came nearer and saw it was a plastic model of a battleship, the kind constructed by children. It had been placed on some newspaper; scattered around it were assorted bits of grey plastic.

My father gave a laugh. He came up to the table and picked up the
30 model.
'Since the firm folded,' he said, 'I have a little more time on my hands.' He laughed again, rather strangely. For a moment his face looked almost gentle. 'A little more time.'
'That seems odd,' I said. 'You were always so busy.'
35 'Too busy perhaps.' He looked at me with a small smile. 'Perhaps I should have been a more attentive father.'
I laughed. He went on contemplating his battleship. Then he looked up. 'I hadn't meant to tell you this, but perhaps it's best that I do. It's my belief that your mother's death was no accident. She had many worries.
40 And some disappointments.'
We both gazed at the plastic battleship.
'Surely,' I said eventually, 'my mother didn't expect me to live here for ever.'
'Obviously you don't see. You don't know how it is for some parents. Not
45 only must they lose their children, they must also lose them to things they don't understand.' He spun the battleship in his fingers. 'These little gunboats here could have been better glued, don't you think?'
'Perhaps. I think it looks fine.'
'During the war I spent some time on a ship rather like this. But my
50 ambition was always the air force. I figured it like this. If your ship was struck by the enemy, all you could do was struggle in the water hoping for a lifeline. But in an aeroplane – well – there was always the final weapon.' He put the model back onto the table. 'I don't suppose you believe in war.'
55 'Not particularly.'
He cast an eye around the room. 'Supper should be ready by now,' he said. 'You must be hungry.'

VOCABULARY

Ways of doing things

*He looked up and **regarded** me strangely.* – *regard*, in this case, means to look at thoughtfully.
*Kikuko **giggled**.* – *giggle* means to laugh in a silly or childish way.
*... then **skipped** on ahead of me.* – *skip* means move in a light dancing way.

1 Use your dictionaries to help you sort the words in the box into three categories: *smiling*, *looking* and *walking*.

glance	stagger	limp	
laugh	stroll	grin	watch
creep	march	gaze	peer
glimpse	crawl		

2 Choose a suitable word from the box to complete the sentences below. (You will have to change the verb into the appropriate form.)

a) I'm afraid I didn't see it very well. I just ________ it through the window as I was passing.
b) The baby was asleep so Jo ________ quietly upstairs.
c) The dog had hurt his leg – he was ________.
d) Luke ________ quickly round the room but he couldn't see them.
e) Mark ________ for the camera, showing his beautiful teeth.
f) We ________ into the well, but we couldn't see the ghost.

3 In groups, take turns at miming a type of look or walk. The others should guess what you are miming.

LISTENING 2

Before listening

Look at the picture and the extract from the listening text. Then, in groups, guess what is going to happen next.

He took some fish to his mouth and started to eat. Then I too chose a piece and put it in my mouth. It felt soft, quite fleshy against my tongue.
'Very good,' I said. 'What is it?'
'Just fish.'

Listening

1 [10.2] Listen to the next part of the story and answer the following questions.

a) What is the significance of the photograph?
b) What was in the large pot on the table?
c) Who had cooked it?
d) Who began eating it first?
e) Who ate the last piece?

2 What do you think the fish was?

3 Look at these key extracts from the story. What could each of the speakers be thinking?

a) *'Who is that? In that photograph there?'*
b) *'Your mother. ... Can't you recognize your own mother?'*
c) *'Very good,' I said. 'What is it?'*
d) *'Just fish.'*
e) *'Here,' I said to my father, 'you have this last piece.'*

Connected speech

1 Look at the short extract on the right, which comes from the listening text. You are going to practise reading it aloud for maximum dramatic effect. Think about how you are going to read it by first reading the text silently and making notes.

a) Underline the word(s) which are stressed.
b) Look up the pronunciation and stressed syllable of any words you are not sure of.
c) Think about how the sentences will be said. (Your intonation will depend on whether you think the person speaking is surprised, angry, etc.)

The first sentence has been marked up, as an example.

2 In pairs, practise reading the text dramatically.

3 [10.3] Read the text while listening to the recording and note any major differences.

At first I continued eating, then my hands became still. The others noticed and looked at me. I went on gazing into the darkness past my father's shoulder.
'Who is that? In that photograph there?'
'Which photograph?' My father turned slightly, trying to follow my gaze.
'The lowest one. The old woman in the white kimono.'
My father put down his chopsticks. He looked first at the photograph, then at me.
'Your mother.' His voice had become very hard. 'Can't you recognise your own mother?'

READING 3

Read the last part of the story and discuss the following in groups.

a) When the father says *'There are other things besides work'* what do you think he means?
b) Does the conversation between father and son change your mind about the probable ending to the story? Give reasons.
c) What motive would the father have for an unhappy ending?
d) What do you think the father really wants to say to his son?
e) Do you have any sympathy for the father?

When we had finished the meal, my father stretched out his arms and yawned with an air of satisfaction. 'Kikuko,' he said. 'Prepare a pot of tea, please.'
My sister looked at him, then left the room without comment. My father stood up.
'Let's retire to the other room. It's rather warm in here.'

I got to my feet and followed him into the tea-room. The large sliding windows had been left open, bringing in a breeze from the garden. For a while we sat in silence.
'Father,' I said, finally.
'Yes?'
'Kikuko tells me Watanabe-San took his whole family with him.'
My father lowered his eyes and nodded. For some moments he seemed deep in thought.
'Watanabe was very devoted to his work,' he said at last. 'The collapse of the firm was a great blow to him. I fear it must have weakened his judgement.'
'You think what he did – it was a mistake?'
'Why, of course. Do you see it otherwise?'
'No, no. Of course not.'
'There are other things besides work.'
'Yes.'

We fell silent again. The sound of locusts came in from the garden. I looked out into the darkness. The well was no longer visible.
'What do you think you will do now?' my father asked. 'Will you stay in Japan for a while?'
'To be honest, I hadn't thought that far ahead.'
'If you wish to stay here, I mean in this house, you would be very welcome. That is, If you don't mind living with an old man.'
'Thank you. I'll have to think about it.'
I gazed once more into the darkness.
'But of course,' said my father, 'this house is so dreary now. You'll no doubt return to America before long.'
'Perhaps I don't know yet.'
'No doubt you will.'

For some time my father seemed to be studying the back of his hands. Then he looked up and sighed.
'Kikuko is due to complete her studies next spring,' he said. 'Perhaps she will want to come home then. She's a good girl.'
'Perhaps she will.'
'Things will improve then.'
'Yes, I'm sure they will.'
We fell silent once more, waiting for Kikuko to bring the tea.

SPEAKING AND WRITING

Discussion

1 In groups, give your opinions on the following points.

a) Do you agree that parents often find it difficult to 'let their children go'?
b) Do you think that children should do what they think is best for themselves, regardless of what their parents want for them?
c) To what extent do you think children should be responsible for looking after their parents when they are older or alone?

2 Work in groups. Imagine that Kikuko, instead of speaking to her brother about her possible future plans, decides to write him a letter telling him about her worries and asking for advice.

a) Discuss the things she might write about (including what her father's reaction might be).
b) Write a draft of the letter and compare with the drafts written by other groups.

Planning a film 'trailer'

Work in groups. Imagine that a television film has been made of this story and that you are planning a 'trailer' to advertise it.

a) Decide on the most interesting or exciting moments from the story and work out a two minute 'advert', using these scenes, to persuade TV viewers to watch the film.
b) Decide what you will say in the 'voice-over'. This should give a brief summary of the main issues of the film as the images are being shown.
c) Present your trailer to the rest of the class, explaining the scenes you have chosen and reading the voice-over. Decide which group has the best trailer.

Unit 11

Scoop or snoop?

LISTENING

Before listening

The photograph on the right was taken during a famine in Africa and the one below it during the Vietnam war. They raise the issue of the role of the journalist at such times.

A journalist was asked the questions below. Work in groups and give your opinions. What do you think a journalist would say?

a) Does 'giving the facts' of what is happening mean the journalist should avoid personal 'colouring' in reports?
b) Are photographs necessary if the report is good enough?
c) How does a journalist feel when photographing or reporting on events such as the ones on the right?
d) Do you think journalists should simply report the news or do they have a humanitarian duty to try to change the situation?
e) Do you agree that some journalists seem to exploit human suffering while looking for a story?

Listening

1 [11.1] Listen to the interview with Michael Buerk, which is divided into five extracts. Each extract is his reply to one of the questions discussed in *Before listening*. Match the extracts to the questions.

Michael Buerk is a well-known BBC news presenter, who was responsible for the report on the Ethiopian famine in 1984-85. This report led to unprecedented world aid for the starving. Michael Buerk is also a radio and newspaper journalist.

2 Listen to each extract again and decide which of the following are an accurate summary of what Michael Buerk said. Correct the ones which aren't.

EXTRACT 1
Journalists should only give the facts. It's up to the people listening to decide for themselves what to do about these facts.

EXTRACT 2
In the 1984–85 famine Michael Buerk felt it was his job to avoid any emotional 'colouring'.

EXTRACT 3
While he was in Ethiopia Michael Buerk felt that reporting on the famine was a useful job to do.

EXTRACT 4
There is always a danger of journalists exploiting human suffering in the interests of a good story, although many of the victims do not in fact feel exploited.

EXTRACT 5
A good journalist doesn't necessarily need pictures to make his point.

3 These are some quotes from Michael Buerk's interview. Decide what the words in *italics* might mean and then check in a dictionary to see if you were right.

a) as clear and *unambiguous* a factual account . . . (Extract 1)
b) to *convey* a feeling of what it was like to be there . . . (Extract 2)
c) it's very difficult to be an *impartial* observer . . . (Extract 3)
d) we may feel very sensitive to the *crass* actions of journalists in disasters . . . (Extract 4)
e) relatives of the victims don't have the sort of sensitivity that we *impute* to them . . . (Extract 4)
f) whose interest is merely to focus attention on their particular *plight* so that help may come. (Extract 4)
g) outside observers might think that this misery was merely being exploited for *titillation* purposes. (Extract 4)
h) (pictures are) absolutely *vital*, aren't they? (Extract 5)

4 Work in pairs. Give your opinion on the following questions.

a) How are disasters, accidents and murders reported in your country? Do you think journalists are usually quite sensitive or do they exploit suffering? Give examples where possible.
b) Do you think TV viewers are becoming so used to seeing disasters on TV that it no longer has an effect? Give reasons.
c) Are people who report on and take photos of events such as those you've just discussed in any way 'inhuman' or 'uncaring'? Give reasons.

Sounds: /ʃ/, /tʃ/, /dʒ/

1 Find examples of the sounds /ʃ/, /tʃ/, /dʒ/ in these phrases from the interview.

a) *the actions of journalists* (Extract 4)
b) *in a famine situation* (Extract 2)

2 [11.2] Listen to the following sentences. Which words can you hear?

a) Look at those *chips/ships*.
b) Did you *wash/watch* it?
c) Have a *sherry/cherry*!
d) I think they're *sheep/cheap*.
e) Has he got a big *gin/chin*?
f) He began to *joke/choke*.
g) Don't *cheer/jeer*.

Practise reading the sentences to someone else and see if they can hear which word you are saying.

3 In pairs, practise these dialogues with the sounds /ʃ/, /tʃ/ and /dʒ/.

a) A: Watch Sheila chopping up that large chicken. I'm sure it'll be delicious with chips.
B: Actually, I'll just have a jam sandwich.

b) A: Shall I take a message?
B: Yes. There's a change to our arrangements. The children are at the pictures so we're going to rush to the shops before they shut.

READING AND WRITING

Grammatical and lexical linking words

One of the results of Michael Buerk's report was a big rock concert in aid of Ethiopia, organised by Bob Geldof. Later, Geldof went to Ethiopia to see how the money was being spent.

1 Read this extract from Geldof's autobiography and answer the following questions. (Ignore the words in *italics* for the moment.)

a) What are the photographs that Kenny Lennox wants to take?
b) How does he justify it?
c) Who or what does Bob Geldof think are:
   i) fat and concerned?
   ii) sensational?
   iii) cheap?
d) What does he agree to?

2 Which point of view do you agree with – Geldof's or Lennox's? Give reasons.

3 In pairs, read the text again. Discuss what each of the grammatical and lexical expressions in *italics* refers to.

Before we left I called all the photographers and the TV cameramen together 'You really do have to understand *this*. I do not want any pictures taken of me with starving children. We've seen *them* before, visiting politicians looking fat and concerned as they hold a child in (5) their arms who is near the point of death from malnutrition, who may well die the day after *the Western celebrities* and their photographers have left the camp.'

'Christ, Bob, you know *that's* what we've been sent to get, you with one of the children who Band Aid is trying to help. That IS the (10) picture,' said Kenny Lennox of the 'Daily Star'.

'I know it is. And *it* is the picture I don't want. Can't you see how cheap it is. It's disgustingly sensational. It degrades the people involved. It's exploiting *their* misery to give you a nice shot.'

'But it's not like that. You're not here for publicity, we know that. (15) You're here because you're trying to help. All *we* are doing is recording the horror which is the reality of the situation.'

'That's not how *it* will appear to people at home. It will simply be construed as shameful, distasteful and patronizing. You can take pictures of me in the camp. You can take pictures of *the kids*. But not (20) *the two* together.'

(from *Is That It?* by Bob Geldof)

4 Complete the sentences below with one of the words or phrases in the box. Use each of them once only.

mine	this	these	one	theirs	then	there	it	the ones

a) It's not your book. It's ______ . I bought it yesterday.
b) What are the apples like? ______ over there are good but ______ here are awful.
c) It was 11 p.m. and he still hadn't got home. I knew ______ that something was wrong.
d) He left the windows open. ______ was a mistake, as the house was broken into.
e) Does this car belong to Carol and Ray? No, ______ is the blue ______ over there.
f) I knew I'd be late for the show. When I finally got ______ the door was shut.
g) Did you like the film? Yes, ______ was very nice.

REVISION 1

Conditional sentences

1 Read the following examples.

i) *If you are European, they think you are a doctor.*
ii) *If a 'non-journalist' went to report on a famine, they would find it very difficult to remain impartial.*
iii) *If you take a photo like that, people will feel it is patronising.*

Which of the example sentences express the idea that:
a) something is likely to happen?
b) something is a fact?
c) the situation is unlikely?

2 Which of the example sentences are zero, first or second conditional? How are they formed?

3 Look at the following sentences and say how they are similar to or different from the example sentences.

a) Unless you have a rest, you'll be ill.
b) If you've finished, you can go.
c) If you could do anything you wanted, what would you do?
d) If I were you, I'd buy this one.
e) Tim would be happier if he were living abroad.

If or *when*?

Is it possible to use *if* and *when* interchangeably in any of the following examples?

i) ***When** I am older, I'm going to buy a dog.*
ii) ***If** you drop a glass, it breaks.*
iii) ***If** you live to be 100, you'll get a telegram from the Queen.*

Check your answers with Sections 1-4 in the *Language reference.*

PRACTICE

1 Work in pairs. Take turns at making questions from the cues below and asking your partner. Example:
if/you find some money in the street/you take it to the police?
If you found some money in the street, would you take it to the police?

a) if / you not like / your friend's new dress / tell her?
b) if / your best friend's partner / ask you to go out with them / you go?
c) when / you finish eating / we go?
d) if / you break something valuable / in your parents' house / you blame the dog?
e) if / you rule the world / what you do?
f) if / choose an ideal partner / what they be like?

2 Think of a possible reason for the following situations. In groups, discuss who has the best reason. Decide whether you should use *if* or *when.* Example:
take on a new identity
I might take on a new identity if the police were looking for me.
I might take on a new identity when I am older.

Why might / would / will you:
a) be very happy?
b) improve your English?
c) get married/divorced?
d) get really angry with someone?
e) have a party?
f) receive a large amount of money to spend?
g) become famous?
h) have seven years bad luck?

3 Underline the best alternative in the following sentences.

a) Go to bed before 11, please. And *when/if* you go to bed remember to turn the lights out.
b) *When/if* the meeting starts on time, I'll be home by 8.
c) *When/if* you do that again, I'll scream!
d) *When/if* her son starts school, she is going to look for another job.

4 Complete the following sentences.

a) We'll probably go out for a picnic tomorrow if . . .
b) Remember to turn on the heating if . . .
c) When the programme finishes, . . .
d) Plants die if . . .
e) If you don't give them any water, those plants . . .
f) Water turns to ice when . . .

VOCABULARY

Non-idiomatic phrasal verbs

Phrasal verbs can be divided into two types:
- those where the meaning can be understood from the main verb and the particle (e.g. *She* ***picked up*** *the pen.*)
- those where the meaning is not obvious from the verb or particle because it has an idiomatic meaning (e.g. *She* ***picked up*** *the language very quickly.*)

Match three of the verbs in column A with a different particle from column B, in order to complete the captions for the pictures below. The choice of particle is clear from the context. Be careful with the position of the particle.

	A	B
a)	put	off
b)	turn	away
c)	pull	out
d)	throw	on
e)	go	down
f)	stay	up
g)	take	in

... It's cold outside.

I think they should ... They're dangerous.

Could you ... I can't see.

① ② ③

Idiomatic phrasal verbs

1 [11.3] Listen to the recording and write down the sentences.

2 Work in pairs. Rewrite each sentence using a phrasal verb with idiomatic meaning from the box.

take after	run out of	get over	pick up
break down	bring up	look forward to	

Check in your dictionary to see if you were correct.

REVISION 2

Wanting situations to change

1 Look at the pictures above.

a) Can she swim?
b) Has he got a book to read?
c) Is he at home?
d) Are they happy or depressed? Why?
e) Are they talking about the past, present or future?
f) Is there a difference between *wish* and *if only*?

2 What verb form follows *wish* or *if only* when you are talking about unreal or hypothetical situations in the present? Check with Section 5 in the *Language reference.*

3 Look at the pictures and guess what the people are thinking. Use *if only* or *wish*. Example:
If only I had more time!

4 What do you wish about yourself?

a) Write two sentences on a slip of paper describing what you would like to be different about your behaviour, appearance and life in general. Do not write your name. Examples:
I wish I didn't have a bad memory.
I wish I were taller.

b) Work in two groups. Mix the slips of paper and take turns to choose one. Ask questions to find out whose it is. Then ask him/her to explain their wishes and give reasons. Example:
If I had a good memory, I would find exams easier.

EXTENSION

Wanting things (not) to happen

Wish + would

IT DRIVES ME MAD

‘I WISH PEOPLE would keep their dogs on a lead. Not everyone likes dogs jumping all over them, and it can be dangerous.’

‘I WISH PEOPLE wouldn't eat crisps and rustle paper in the cinema when other people are trying to watch the film. It really irritates me!’

‘THE POPULAR PRESS write about nothing else but the Royal Family. It really gets on my nerves!’

‘CAR PARKING FACILITIES in our towns are terrible. Why can't the government build more car parks?’

‘WHY DO SUPERMARKETS insist on putting sweets and chocolate near the checkouts so that children can see them?’

1 In the newspaper *Letters column* above, look at the two extracts on the left and answer the following questions.
a) Are the writers talking about the present or future?
b) What form of the verb follows *would*? Can you use both ‘state’ and ‘action’ verbs?
c) How do the speakers feel?

2 Look at the last three extracts.
a) How could these feelings be expressed using *wish*, as in the previous examples?
b) Talk about things that annoy you, using *I wish . . . would* or *I wish . . . wouldn't*.

3 Think of as many complaints as you can about someone you know (e.g. your teacher, a relative, a friend). Example:
I wish my teacher would start the lesson on time.
I wish Javier wouldn't talk so much.

SPEAKING AND LISTENING

Discussion

1 [11.4] The MP Clare Short was recently attacked about her personal life. Listen to her defending why she thinks people in the public eye such as herself do not deserve to have their personal life made public by the 'gutter press' (popular newspapers) and answer the following questions.

a) In what situations does she think her life deserves to be exposed? Give examples.
b) What does she object to the popular press doing, and why? Give examples.
c) What would she like to see and what would happen as a result?

2 In groups, discuss the following questions.

a) Do you agree that there should be a privacy law? Think of the arguments for and against.
b) What actions can people in your country take if the newspapers print stories about someone which are untrue and cause that person to suffer?
c) What compensation should people like Clare Short get?
d) What are your opinions on the view that people get the kind of newspapers they deserve?

WRITING

Letter of opinion

Elton John awarded £1 million damages after *Sun* allegations about his private life

READERS' RIGHT TO REPLY

THIS WEEK in the news there has been a lot of publicity about the huge compensation given to a certain pop singer after he proved that a popular newspaper made untrue claims about his personal life. However, are readers aware that:

- There is no legal aid for libel. Only reasonably wealthy people can sue. An 'ordinary' person could not afford the £30,000 needed to take a newspaper to court. Is it fair that famous people can defend their reputations and stand to win a lot of money when ordinary people can't?
- Damages in libel actions are decided by a jury rather than a judge so they are based entirely on their opinion and can result in people being given very large sums of money. However, if you are blinded, or lose an eye or a leg, the judge decides and there are clear calculations made.

Write and give us your opinion on the issues above. Say what you think of the popular press's invasion of privacy. Suggest if and how you think the law should be changed with regard to privacy and compensation.

1 Read the newspaper article and give your opinions.

2 In groups, make notes for a letter in reply to the article. Then write the letter.

3 Exchange your letter with other groups. Decide which letter is the best.

Language reference

1 The zero conditional

Two present forms are used when something happens normally and is a fact:

*If you **are** European, they **think** you are a doctor.*
*If you **don't water** plants, they often **die**.*

2 The first conditional

The first conditional is used when talking about situations which are likely to happen in the future and their probable results:

*If you **take** a photo like that, people **will think** it is patronising.*

If (or *when*, or *unless*) is followed by a present form (simple or continuous) and sometimes the Present Perfect:

*When you **have finished**, we'll go.*

The main clause (which is used to make predictions, promises, etc.) can consist of modals such as *will, may, might, should,* other future forms (such as *going to*) or the imperative form:

*If you're going to the post office, I'**ll come** with you.*
*When you get to the traffic lights, **turn** left.*

3 The second conditional

The second conditional is used to talk about imaginary situations in the present or future and their possible results:

*If a non-journalist **went** to report on a famine, they **would find** it hard to be impartial.*

It is also used for situations which are impossible:

*If I **were**/**was** you, **I wouldn't do** it.*

If is followed by a past form (simple or continuous) and the main clause is followed by a modal such as *would / might / could.* The order of the clauses can be reversed:

I might not see him if I wasn't wearing my glasses.

4 *If* or *when*

If we are sure that something will happen we use *when*:

***When** I leave school, I'm going to join the army.*

If there is an element of doubt in the condition we have to use *if*:

***If** it rains tomorrow, we'll have to put off our trip.*

If the sentence expresses something that is always true (e.g. a scientific fact), *if* and *when* mean the same thing:

***If**/**When** water freezes, it turns to ice.*

5 Wish

a) *Wish* + past forms

Wish + the past (simple or continuous) is used to express dissatisfaction with a state, habit or action in the present, and a wish that it was different.

*I **wish** I **had** dark hair.* (state)
*I **wish** you **didn't drive** so fast.* (habit)
*He **wishes** he **wasn't**/**weren't sitting** in a classroom right now.* (action)

Could is used to talk about ability.

*She **wishes** she **could swim**.*
*I **wish** I **could speak English**.*

If only is often used to express the same feelings and is a little stronger.

***If only** I **had** dark hair.*

b) *Wish* + *would*

Wish and *would* (+ base form) expresses the hope that an action or habit will change in the near future. It is often used for complaints:

*I **wish** you **wouldn't work** so hard.*
*I **wish** you **would go away**.*

6 Pronominal forms

Demonstrative pronouns, (*this / that / these / those*, etc.), personal pronouns (*it / her*, etc.) and possessive pronouns (*mine / theirs*, etc.) and *one / the ones* are often used to avoid repeating a noun:

*Is this your car? No, this is **mine**.*
*Which do you want? **The one** in the window.*

There/then are also often used to avoid repeating the noun:

*I was meeting him at the cinema. When I got **there** he'd gone.*
*It was 11 p.m. I knew **then** that something was wrong.*

Pronouns like *that* and *this* can also replace complete sentences and refer forwards or backwards in the text:

*I decided not to do the exam. **That** was the most stupid decision I ever made.*
*You really have to understand **this**. I do not want any pictures taken of me.*

Crime and passion

READING

Before reading

1 These headlines accompany two newspaper articles which are both about 'crimes of passion'.

a) Make guesses about:
   - why the 'houseproud husband' snapped.
   - what he did when he snapped.
   - why he is called 'Mr Mustard'.

b) In what situations might a son attack his father? Why do you think the boy went free?

c) Make a note of any questions you'd like to ask about either of the stories connected with the headlines.

2 What irritating habits might provoke a partner or relative to violence? Discuss in pairs.

3 Do you think 'crimes of passion' should be punished differently from crimes which are planned? Give reasons to support your opinion.

Reading

1 Work in two groups. One group should read Text A and the other group should read Text B. While reading your text note down the answers to the following questions.

a) How was the victim killed?
b) Why was the victim killed?
c) What was the victim like?
d) What is the accused like?
e) What was the punishment?

KILLER SON GOES FREE

Probation for youth who stabbed father

'Mr Mustard' is jailed

Houseproud husband snapped over supper

Text A

Mild-mannered Thomas Corlett, the houseproud husband who strangled his wife after a row over a tube of mustard, was jailed for three years yesterday after denying murdering his wife.

It took the jury just ten minutes to find the 58-year-old balding civil servant not guilty of murder, but guilty of manslaughter on the grounds of diminished responsibility.

Corlett, described as a man of 'impeccable character', had gradually taken over the household chores during his 26-year marriage, including cooking and cleaning. After his wife became ill with asthma, their relationship had deteriorated.

Medical witnesses at the trial said Corlett was like a houseproud housewife with a craving for perfection. A pent-up rage built up in him over his wife's untidiness. His wife started going on holidays with a friend, never asking if he wanted to join them and never telling him when she would be back. In 1985 she forgot to send him a birthday card for the first time. Five weeks later the trivial row over the mustard led to her death.

The snapping point came when the couple sat down to a supper of sausages, green beans and mashed potatoes at their home in Middlesex on December 12, 1985.

On the spot on the table where he normally put his newspaper was a tube of German mustard. He moved it. His wife, Erika, 63, picked it up and slammed it down in its original place. During the quarrel Erika stood up and started flailing her arms. Corlett grabbed her by the throat and the couple fell to the floor. Corlett called an ambulance when she fell unconscious but minutes later Mrs Corlett was dead.

Defence counsel David Farrington handed over a glowing reference from Corlett's boss. The barrister said that Corlett would be extremely unlikely to offend again, and asked for him to be sent home. Judge Gerald Butler accepted that Corlett acted out of character but said that he could not take the lenient course being urged upon him.

(from the *Daily Mail*)

Text B

Sixteen-year-old Peter Stone went free yesterday after admitting killing his father with a home-made knife.

5 He stepped in as his parents were arguing one night and stabbed him through the heart.

He told the police, 'He hit my Mum in the face. When I 10 was younger he used to hit her and I could do nothing.'

But after his arrest the catering student said of his father, 'He always loved me.'

15 Stafford Crown Court was told that there had been a strong bond between father and son, but this broke down as 49-year-old Leonard Stone 20 tyrannised his wife for four years after losing his job.

Stone, said to be 'quiet, well-spoken and non-violent' by police, is the youngest of 25 six children.

His father became violent towards his 40-year-old wife Sylvia after losing his lorry-driving job because of a drink-30 driving conviction nearly four years ago.

He became depressed and made several half-hearted suicide attempts – but always 35 when someone was close by.

He frequently attacked his wife – although several months could go by without him raising his fists – and he 40 spent periods in a psychiatric hospital.

Yesterday Peter Stone, from Walsall, was put on probation for three years 45 after he pleaded guilty to manslaughter. Mr Justice Kenneth Jones told him, 'You are on the threshold of your life. This is inevitably a burden 50 you will have on your conscience and will have to carry over the years. I do understand the position in which you found yourself.

55 I accept your father was a difficult man. Any father must understand nothing is quite so insupportable in the eyes of a son as violence 60 offered by a father to a mother.'

And the judge referred to his courage in admitting the offence, and said he was taking 'a perhaps exceptional 65 course'.

He said, 'I do it because I have faith in you. I hope you will in the future do everything in your power to 70 justify the faith I am showing in you.'

(from the *Evening Standard*)

2 Ask someone who read the other text to give you answers to the questions in Exercise 1, and make notes. Find out anything else you want to know about the crime, the criminal or the victim.

3 Read the text that you didn't read before and then work out the questions which go with the following answers to both Text A and Text B.

TEXT A

a) Manslaughter.
b) Ten minutes.
c) 26 years.
d) Sausages, beans and potatoes.
e) He called an ambulance.

TEXT B

a) A home-made knife.
b) Quiet, well-spoken and non-violent.
c) Because the father was violent to Peter's mother.
d) Because he was convicted of drinking and driving.
e) Four years ago.

4 Discuss the following questions.

a) Is it fair that the boy went free? Why do you think the court was sympathetic to him?
b) Do you agree with the verdict of manslaughter for 'Mr Mustard'? Why do you think he was not accused of murder?
c) Do you think the law is too 'soft' where domestic violence, such as the 'Mr Mustard' case, is concerned?

5 Look at the phrasal verbs (in *italics*) and express them in another way. Refer to your dictionary if necessary.

a) He had gradually *taken over* the household chores . . . (Text A, line 15)
b) She *slammed* it *down* . . . (Text A, line 43)
c) He *handed over* . . . (Text A, line 52)
d) He *stepped in* . . . and stabbed him through the heart. (Text B, line 5)
e) (the bond) *broke down* as 49-year-old . . . (Text B, line 18)

6 Read the texts again and find an equivalent word or expression for each of the following:

TEXT A

a) household jobs (line 16)
b) strong desire (line 23)
c) anger (line 24)
d) took hold of something quickly (line 46)
e) gentle, not severe (line 59)

TEXT B

a) something that unites people (line 17)
b) not really interested (line 33)
c) a heavy weight (line 49)

VOCABULARY

Law and order

1 Look through the texts again and underline all the words you can find connected with law and order. Compare with a partner.

2 Use the words you found in Exercise 1 to complete the following definitions.

a) If you commit a crime the police ________ you.
b) You have to go to ________ for a trial.
c) You can ________ guilty or not guilty.
d) A person who sees a crime being committed is a ________.
e) For serious crimes the people who decide if the accused are guilty or not are the ________.
f) The man who sentences the accused is called the ________.

3 In pairs, look at the words and expressions in the box below.

a) Which are against the law in your country?
b) Which are the *most* and *least* serious in your opinion? Give reasons.

dropping litter	jaywalking	drug pushing	fraud
spitting in public	suicide	arson	libel	kidnapping
manslaughter	treason		

4 In your country, which crimes in Exercise 3 are punished by:

– a fine?
– jail?
– death?
– some other method?

5 What do the following mean?

a) to be given a suspended sentence
b) to be put on probation
c) to be out on bail

Shifting word stress

1 [12.1] Listen to the following sentences and mark where the stress is in the word *convict*.
The police arrested the ***convict****.*
The police had to ***convict*** *him.*

2 Look at the following sentences and mark the stress in the words in *italics*.

a) The *protest* was fairly peaceful.
b) I want to *protest*.
c) *Imports* are rising sharply.
d) We need to *import* more coal.
e) Have you bought your mother a *present*?
f) They *presented* him with a gold watch.
g) If you don't work you won't make any *progress*.
h) He has *progressed* at an amazing rate.

3 [12.2] Listen to the recording and check if you were correct.

4 Decide whether the following words have the same stress pattern when they are nouns and verbs and then check with your dictionary.

a) arrest
b) produce
c) contrast
d) witness
e) debate
f) attack
g) permit
h) appeal

WRITING

Summary writing

1 Look back at Text A on page 84. The writer of this article is not just describing facts but trying to create a dramatic feeling.

a) In column A make a note of the most important facts in the article and in column B make a note of any facts which you think are not directly relevant to the crime. One has been done for you.

A
Thomas Corlett strangled his wife.

B
He was 'mild-mannered'.

b) In pairs, compare your notes.

2 Use your notes from A to write a short summary of the original article. Decide in which order to put the points and divide them into different paragraphs. If possible join the points together, using your own words and including linking expressions. (See page 150.)

EXTENSION 1

Regrets and criticism

Third conditional and *wish*

1 Read these examples.
If she hadn't moved the mustard, he wouldn't have killed her.
Corlett really wishes he hadn't lost his temper.
Are the following sentences *True* or *False* according to the examples?

a) Corlett killed Erika.
b) Erika didn't move the mustard.
c) Corlett didn't lose his temper.
d) Corlett regrets what he did.

2 Look at the examples above and complete the notes below.

a) When talking about imaginary past events *if* is usually followed by *had (not)* + ________ .
b) The main clause, which talks about imaginary consequences in the past, is usually formed by *would* (or *may/might*, etc.) + ________ + ________ .
c) To talk about wishes and regrets in the past we can use *wish* + ________ + ________ .

Past hypothesis

Look at the following examples.
If this had happened here,
i) *the boy would have gone to prison.*
ii) *the boy may/might have gone to prison.*
iii) *the boy would be in prison now.*

a) Which of these example sentences is the least definite?
b) Why is the second part of the sentence sometimes *would have* + past participle, sometimes *would* + base form and sometimes *may* or *might* instead of *would*?

Check with Section 1 in the *Language reference.*

Connected speech

1 [12.3] Listen to the following sentence and underline any words which are contracted or weak.
If this had happened here, the boy would have gone to prison.

2 Underline the words which are weak or contracted.

a) If it had been working properly, I could have done it.
b) She might have agreed if the job had paid more.
c) If I were you, I wouldn't even think of it.
d) He would have had a shock if he had seen her.
e) I couldn't really go unless the boss agreed to it.

3 [12.4] Listen to the recording and check if you were correct. Then practise reading the sentences in pairs.

PRACTICE

1 Look at the sequence of events and consequences below.

a) Match the two parts of the sentences and practise saying them.

a) John wouldn't have woken up late . . .
b) If he hadn't been driving so fast, . . .
c) If he had calmed down before getting to work, . . .
d) He might still have his job . . .

1 if he hadn't lost the business for his company.
2 if he had remembered to set the alarm.
3 he might not have had the accident.
4 he might not have forgotten his appointment.

b) Imagine you are John. Talk about your regrets, using *wish* or *if only*. Example:
***I wish / If only** I'd remembered to set the alarm.*

2 Look at the newspaper extracts.

a) 21-year-old Sylvie Forrest had a lucky escape yesterday when she arrived at Liverpool Street Station 3 minutes late for her train after being held up in a traffic jam. This same train was later de-railed, severely injuring many passengers.

b) Trainee merchant banker Tom Willis's life changed dramatically while he was on holiday last year in Russia After meeting his future wife, Ludmilla, he threw up his well-paid job and sold his London home. Unfortunately he was unable to find a job in Russia, and Ludmilla has since left him. He has now returned to Britain but has not been able to find a job.

c) 20 years ago the tiger population had dropped dramatically and was in danger of disappearing completely because of the destruction of the tropical forests. Thanks to the intervention of the World Wide Fund for Nature, who have set up reserves to protect them, the population has now doubled.

d) Footballer Steve Perry blames his bad performance in yesterday's match against Arsenal on a fish restaurant he went to the previous night. 'It's my fault we lost the match,' he said later. 'I was feeling terrible all day. I'm sure I had food poisoning.'

a) Use the third conditional to talk about the consequences of the imaginary situations. Example:
If Sylvie hadn't arrived late for her train, she might have been seriously injured.

b) Imagine you are Tom Willis and Steve Perry. Talk about your regrets, using *wish* or *if only*.

3 Write down at least three things you regret about your past. In groups, discuss what you wrote. Use *wish / if only* and the third conditional as in the speech bubble on the right.

I wish I'd stayed on at school. If I had, I could have gone to college and been a vet.

REVISION AND EXTENSION 2

Should / shouldn't (have)

1 Sam has decided to get married. What advice do you think his friend gave? Use *should/shouldn't*. Example:
You should try not to travel abroad so much.

2 [12.5] Sam's marriage didn't last. Listen to the first part of the conversation he had with his friend five years later and write down the following.

a) Two things that Sam regrets doing.
b) What the friend says Sam did wrong.

3 [12.6] Listen again and note how Sam expresses regret and how his friend criticises him.

a) Write down exactly what they say.

b) Practise saying the three expressions, focusing on the appropriate intonation and weak forms, e.g. *should've* /ˈʃʊdəv/.

4 [12.7] Listen and note how Sam continues. Work in pairs to guess what his friend said to him.

5 Louise, a company director, was supposed to go on a business trip to Japan last week but she missed the plane. Look at the pictures below which show what happened on the morning of her trip and say what she should and shouldn't have done.

SPEAKING

Moral issues

Work in groups. Read the five court cases below. Imagine you have to make decisions about some or all of them.

a) Decide what the people concerned should and shouldn't have done.
b) Decide what sentence you would impose, if any (e.g. jail).
c) Present your opinions to the rest of the class.

CASE 1
A teacher is doing project work with a class of ten-year-olds and gives a pair of scissors to each group. Unfortunately, one of the girls is severely injured by a pair of scissors and the girl's parents claim compensation.
Your decision
Should the family get compensation? If so, how much and who should pay? Is the teacher in any way responsible?

CASE 2
Mrs Anderson is driving her car, keeping to the speed limit, when a dog suddenly runs across the road in front of her. She brakes to avoid the dog. A man in a Jaguar behind her, driving quite fast, crashes into her and causes a lot of damage. Both drivers are slightly injured.
Your decision
Who is to blame for the accident? Should Mrs Anderson have braked to avoid the dog? Who should pay for the damage?

CASE 3
Mr and Mrs Davies were married for 18 years and had one daughter. When they got divorced in 1977, Mr Davies re-married and his new wife looked after him through his illness until his death in 1990. In his will he left £100,000 to his daughter, £50,000 to his first wife, £50,000 to a lover in London and £50,000 to his golf club. His second wife demanded that the will be changed.
Your decision
Should the will be changed in any way?

CASE 4
Mrs James is stabbed by Mr Jordan during a row, and starts to lose a lot of blood. She is taken to hospital where it is said that her condition is not critical but she needs a blood transfusion. However, she belongs to a religious sect which does not believe in blood transfusions. She refuses to have one, and dies.
Your decision
Should Mr Jordan be charged for murder or manslaughter? What should his punishment be? Are the hospital at all responsible?

CASE 5
Mrs Williams, aged 85, was terminally ill and in great pain. She was given an overdose of sleeping pills by her daughter, who could not bear to see her mother suffering.
Your decision
Should the daughter be prosecuted?

Language reference

All the grammar points in this unit are concerned with unreal situations in the past in contexts which often involve regret and criticism.

1 The third conditional

The third conditional is used to describe and speculate about an imaginary past situation and its imaginary consequences. It consists of two clauses:

a) the conditional clause:
   i) *if* + Past Perfect (*had (not)* + past participle), or
   ii) *if* + Past Perfect Continuous (*had (not)* + *been* + *- ing*)

b) the main clause:
   i) would *(n't)* + the perfect (*have* + past participle), or
   ii) *would (n't)* + *have been* + base form + *-ing*:
      If she ***hadn't moved*** *the mustard pot, he* ***wouldn't have killed*** *her.*
      I ***wouldn't have been driving*** *if the train* ***had been*** *on time.*

May (not) / *Might (not)* / *could have* are used instead of *would (n't) have* if the result is not so sure:
  The boy ***might have gone*** *to prison in my country if he'd committed this crime.* (*But I'm not sure.*)

However, *would/might/may/could* + base form (or *be* + base form + *-ing*) is used if the situation is still possible now:
  In many countries, if Corlett had murdered his wife he ***would still be (serving*** *his sentence) in prison.*

Have and *would* are usually contracted or made weak:
  If ***I'd*** (/aɪd/) *seen him, I* ***would have*** (/wʊdəv/) / ***I'd have*** (/'aɪdəv/) *stopped.*
  If ***I'd*** *been feeling tired, I* ***wouldn't*** *have continued.*

2 *Wish* + Past Perfect

Wish + Past Perfect (Continuous) is used to express regrets in the present about something which happened or didn't happen in the past:
  I ***wish*** *I* ***had gone*** *to university.* (*But I didn't.*)
  I ***wish*** *you* ***hadn't said*** *that.* (*But you did.*)
  He ***wishes*** *he* ***hadn't been sitting*** *by the window.* (*But he was.*)

If only expresses a stronger regret in the past:
  If only *I* ***hadn't said*** *that!*

3 *Should(n't) have*

Should(n't) have expresses regret or criticism about the past. The expression is used to talk about something that was necessary but didn't happen or when somebody did the wrong thing. It is formed with *should (not)* + *have* + past participle (or *have been* + base form + *-ing*). The auxiliary *have* is pronounced weakly (/əv/):
  You ***shouldn't have*** (/'ʃʊdəntəv/) ***left*** *the door open.* (*But you did.*)
  You ***should have*** (/'ʃʊdəv/) ***been watching*** *the road.* (*But you weren't.*)
  I ***should have stayed*** *on longer at school.* (*But I didn't.*)

Unit 13

Just a piece of paper?

LISTENING

Before listening

Read the headline and caption.

a) Why do you think that some young Asian couples in Britain have two weddings?
b) Why are the young couple only allowed out together for the 'occasional pizza'?
c) Do you think parents should choose marriage partners for their children? Suggest advantages and disadvantages.

Wedded to the East

At a bureau in Southall, Asian parents choose marriage partners for their children. If status and background prove suitable and a deal is agreed, the young couple may be allowed out together for an occasional pizza in the months between their English and Asian weddings.

Listening

1 Satish, a Gujarati Indian brought up in Britain, and his Swedish wife, Barbrő, had two weddings, one in England and the other in Sweden. How do you think the two wedding ceremonies differed?

2 [13.1] Listen to Satish and check your answers. Which wedding was more important for:

a) Satish? b) his parents?

3 [13.2] Listen to Satish as he continues. What does he mean by the following phrases?

a) '. . . it wasn't for me'
b) '. . . your love will develop'
c) '. . . you've been checked out'
d) '. . . it's not necessarily forced'

4 Complete the following sentences according to the interview.

a) Satish ________ in Sweden.
b) During the Hindu wedding Satish ________ by the priest to do things he didn't understand.
c) At the wedding, future marriages ________.
d) When living abroad, marriages in registry offices ________ as a bureaucratic necessity by Asian families.
e) An 'arranged marriage' ________ not necessarily ________.
f) In an 'arranged marriage' family backgrounds ________.

5 Discuss the following questions.

a) Have you changed your views on 'arranged marriages'?
b) How is a Hindu wedding similar to or different from a wedding in your country?

REVISION

The passive

1 In the *Listening* section Satish uses several passive constructions. Example:
*My older brother's marriage **was arranged**.*

a) How is the passive formed?
b) Which words in a passive construction are stressed and which are weak forms?

2 In which contexts would you expect to find the following examples of the passive? Why is the passive used? Example:
Strips of wood are put through a machine.
Description of a process.
Because knowing who does it is not important.

a) Passengers are requested to remain seated.
b) Oh, yes, *Risk*. It was written by Dick Francis.
c) Unfortunately taxes have had to be increased by another two per cent.
d) Famous Politician Arrested.

3 Why is the passive not used in the following sentences?

a) Gascoigne shoots and scores!
b) I've heard of Dick Francis. He wrote *Risk*, didn't he?

Check with Section 1 in the *Language reference*.

4 When a verb has two objects, two different passive constructions can be formed with either the direct or indirect object as the subject. Examples:
i) *Catherine was given a prize.*
ii) *A prize was given to Catherine.*
(In (i) we have probably already been talking about Catherine – *a prize* is new information. In (ii) we have probably been talking about the competition – *Catherine* is new information.)

Rewrite the following sentences with another passive construction.

a) The invigilator was handed the papers. (*The papers* . . .)
b) A reward was offered to the person who found the wallet. (*The person* . . .)
c) A lot of money was left to his wife by an unknown stranger. (*His wife* . . .)
d) The woman who cured him of his sickness has been promised a trip on the Orient Express. (*A trip on the Orient Express* . . .)

5 Work in groups.

a) Look at the notes below about drinks and drink-making. Decide which notes refer to which of the drinks in the box. (One drink is referred to twice.) Expand the notes to make complete sentences, using a passive construction where possible. More than one sentence may be necessary. Example:
Fizzy soft drinks – 5
Carbon dioxide is forced into the liquid under pressure.

fizzy soft drinks	wine	beer
vintage champagne	instant coffee	

1 real coffee – make with hot water – water evaporate – leave powder
2 most expensive bottle – red – sell London, 1985 – $105,000 – 1787 Chateau Lafite – own by third American president, Thomas Jefferson – when open – find undrinkable
3 make from white grapes – northern France – keep in bottles 15 years before drink
4 the process first start 4,000 years ago – Egypt – keep in large pots
5 carbon dioxide – force into liquid under pressure
6 on average in Germany – 150 litres (33 gallons) – drink – per person a year

b) Write the questions which would correspond to your sentences. Example:
1 How is instant coffee manufactured?

EXTENSION 1

Need(s) to be done

1 What celebrations do you have after a wedding in your country? What kind of things need to be organised beforehand?

2 Work in pairs.

STUDENT A
Your son/daughter is getting married shortly. Look at the list of preparations that need to be made for the reception. Find out from Student B what has been done and what needs to be done. Complain about the things that still haven't been done.

PREPARATIONS FOR WEDDING RECEPTION
To be done send out invitations
hire photographer
order drink
buy presents
set up marquee
prepare food
arrange flowers
book chauffeur
borrow glasses

STUDENT B
You are organising the reception. Look at the list of what you have done on page 149. Answer Student A and make excuses and promises where necessary.

Examples:
i) A: *Have the invitations been sent out?*
B: *Yes, they have.*
ii) A: *Has the photographer been hired yet?*
B: *Sorry, that still needs to be done. I'll do it straight away.*

EXTENSION 2

Have (*get*) something done / do it oneself

1 Compare the following examples.
i) *It's OK. We can watch the film I* ***had*** *(****got****) the video* ***mended****. I picked it up from the shop yesterday.*
ii) ***I mended*** *the video* ***myself****. I'm good at these things.*
iii) *Did you* ***enjoy yourself*** *at the cinema last night?*

a) In which example did somebody else (not the speaker) mend the video?
b) Why does the speaker use the word *myself* in example ii)? Is it possible to leave it out?
c) Is it possible to leave out *yourself* in the third example?

2 Complete the sentences below using a word ending in *-self* or *-selves*, or the expression *have (get) it done*. Examples:
i) A: *Did you buy that pullover?*
B: *No, I made it myself.*
ii) A: *Your trousers are filthy.*
B: *Yes, I must take them to the cleaners and have them cleaned.*

a) A: Is she going to look for a childminder for her little boy?
B: No, she ______.
b) A: Where's Jessica?
B: She's gone to the dentist to ______.
c) A: I can't find a jacket big enough.
B: You'll have to go to a tailor's and ______.
d) A: Shall we ask them to book our holiday for us?
B: No, let's ______.
e) A: My eyesight's getting worse.
B: Why don't you ______?
f) A: Your hair is getting very long.
B: Yes, I've made an appointment to ______.
g) A: Did they buy that delicious cake?
B: No, they ______.
h) A: I need a passport photograph.
B: Well, go to the photographer's and ______.
i) A: Ugh! You've got blood on your chin.
B: Yes, I know. I cut ______.

3 Make two lists. One list should consist of the things you like to do for yourself (e.g. *the cooking*). The other list should consist of the things you like to have done for you (e.g. *servicing the car*). Compare your lists with other students in the class.

VOCABULARY

Relationships

1 Complete the following sentences with one of the expressions from the box in the correct form. Use a dictionary to help you if necessary.

go round in circles	on the rocks
heart's in the right place	split up with
love at first sight	fall out about
off the deep end	go out together

a) I'm very sorry to hear that Christine has ________ her boyfriend. What did they ________?
b) When Sebastian and Julia first met it was ________. They have been ________ for years but have never married.
c) Their relationship has been ________ for some time. I don't know why they still live together.
d) We can't keep arguing like this. It's pointless. We're just ________.
e) He's all right. His ________ but unfortunately in a row he always goes ________ and gets very unpleasant.

2 Write down any expressions you want to remember. Write complete sentences to help you to use them correctly.

Sounds: /ɒ/, /ɔ:/, /əʊ/

1 [13.3] Listen to the vowel sounds /ɒ/, /ɔ:/, /əʊ/ in the following words.
g**o**t d**oo**r bl**ow**

2 [13.4] Listen to the words in the box and put them into three groups:
A (/ɒ/), B (/ɔ:/), C (/əʊ/).

str**aw**	thr**oat**	s**o**rry	**o**ff	th**ough**t	
over	**a**ll	g**o**	**o**pen	c**ou**gh	h**o**me
h**or**se					

3 Add some more words to each group. Then dictate your new words in jumbled order to someone else in the class to see if they can put them into the correct group.

SPEAKING

1 Which of the opinions expressed in the articles below and opposite do you agree with? Why?

The mayor has nine wives

Elizabeth, 38, is a smart, bright, modern-looking woman, and the town attorney. She lives here in Big Water with her husband, Alex Joseph, most of his twenty children and all of his eight other wives.

"It's an ideal arrangement for a career woman," Elizabeth, a Mormon, says. "Most American women are trying to juggle their career, lipstick and marriage and not succeeding very well.

"In a plural marriage you can have it all. You never have to worry about who'll look after the kids. You can be fully a mother, fully a professional and fully a woman."

(from *The Independent on Sunday*)

The big question is..

IS MARRIAGE OLD-FASHIONED?

What does marriage mean to you? Just a piece of paper or a deeper and more secure relationship?

CHRIS O'BRIEN

"Yes, it's no different to living together, apart from a bit of paper. I wouldn't bother with getting married, unless my girlfriend wanted to, or we were going to have kids. I think it's important then."

ANNE McLEAN

"No, it's not old-fashioned – I'm married and I highly recommend it! It's rubbish to say that marriage is just a bit of paper, and it's certainly a lot more than just living together."

(from *Catch*)

2 In groups, discuss the following questions and give reasons for your answers.

a) What are the main reasons for getting married and what are the drawbacks?
b) What is the best age to get married? Why?
c) Is there too much social pressure on people to get married? Should other kinds of partnership be more acceptable?
d) Should weddings be religious?
e) Is it acceptable to have more than one partner at the same time?
f) Why do people get divorced? Is it too easy?
g) What problems are there when people decide to get divorced?

Report back to the other groups. What do they agree or disagree with?

3 You have been going out with someone for a while and you have decided to live together. However, before you do so you wish to draw up a personal 'contract'.

In groups, discuss the kinds of things you think it is a good idea to include in such a 'contract'. Things to think about might include:
- when to use the bathroom.
- who cooks the meals and when.
- what happens if you want to go out with other people.

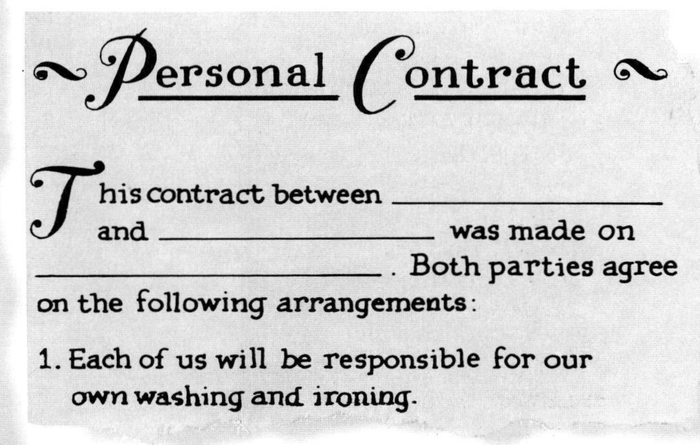

Personal Contract

This contract between ________________ and ________________ was made on ________________. Both parties agree on the following arrangements:

1. Each of us will be responsible for our own washing and ironing.

4 Work with a person from another group. This person is your 'partner'. Discuss what you want to put in your contract and give the reasons. Try to persuade your 'partner'. (Refer to the *Speaking functions* on page 150).

5 Each pair should try to draw up as much of their contract as possible and report back to the class on their disagreements.

WRITING

Writing from notes

1 The text on the right is about a Balinese marriage, but the paragraphs have been mixed up. Read the text and put the paragraphs in the correct order.

2 Discuss the following.

a) What helped you decide on the correct order? (e.g. Which words or phrases refer back to a previous paragraph?)
b) How is the text organised? (e.g. How do you know which paragraphs come at the beginning and end of the text?)

A Discovering what has happened, the girl's family then pretend to be very worried. The angry father is supposed to search the surroundings, asking everyone in the household who took his daughter. Of course, even a close friend who may have helped the daughter pack her clothes, innocently denies any knowledge of the affair.

B First, the couple secretly decides to run away, usually to a friend's house a good distance from the girl's village. On the appointed day, the girl is suddenly carried off by her young man.

C No matter how couples are married, divorce is not difficult. A man merely reports to village authorities that his marriage is finished; or if it is a woman, she simply returns to her home and the children are cared for by the man's family. However, divorce does not often occur. If the situation arises, it is likely that a man takes a second wife, and the first remains as head of the household.

D In Bali, there is one form of marriage, the *negerorod* – marriage by elopement – which is considered exciting for it is preceded by the honeymoon and the man is considered heroic.

E Sometimes even a search party is organised, but the shock reaction is all in fun. Generally the family is well acquainted with the young man and understands that if the daughter took some clothes, she left by her own choice.

3 A British couple, Samantha and Jake, got married in Las Vegas part-way through a touring holiday of the USA. Divide the following notes into four or five sections. Each section should focus on a different stage of their Las Vegas wedding (and form one paragraph).

- Inspected wedding chapels: from Cupid's to Graceland.
- Decided on Little White Chapel.
- Offered choice of 'packages': Economy, Regular and Deluxe.
- Difference: the number of 'give-away' presents: lace hanky, champagne glasses, glossy wedding certificate.
- Chose Economy.
- Got ready: Samantha had brought own dress.
- Jake borrowed western-style tuxedo with flared nylon trousers.
- Collected from hotel in limousine.
- Driven to County Court House to obtain licence: $27.
- Went on to chapel.
- Had civil ceremony: rather flowery.
- Hidden expenses: lady behind counter tried to sell video, recording of vows and white leather-bound photo album.
- Handed envelope: 'Minister's donation: between $40 and $100'.
- Limousine driver said only worked for tips over $25.

4 Rewrite the notes into a coherent description written from either Samantha's or Jake's point of view. Combine the sentences using:
- linking expressions such as *when*.
- adverbs such as *first* and *then*.
- passive constructions where appropriate.

Write the description in draft first and ask other students to suggest ways of improving it. Begin:
On arrival in Las Vegas we spent the afternoon inspecting wedding chapels . . .

Language reference

1 The passive

Passive or active?

In active sentences, the subject of the verb is the person or thing doing the action:

George found the wallet. (Who found it? George did.)

In passive sentences, the action is done to the subject. So the subject is somebody or something to which something happens:

The child was rescued by the police. (Who rescued whom? The police rescued the child. The child didn't rescue the police.)

FORM

The passive is formed by the subject to which something happens (*The child*) + a form of *be* (*was*) + past participle (*rescued*). The word *by* is used when we want to know who performs the action of the passive verb (*by the police*).

In English, a verb can have two objects, an indirect object and a direct object:

He handed ***the invigilator the papers***. (indirect object + direct object)

He handed ***the papers*** *to* ***the invigilator***. (direct object + indirect object)

In these cases two different passive sentences can be formed. (*The papers were handed to the invigilator.* / *The invigilator was handed the papers.* In the first sentence there is more of a focus on *the invigilator.*) This alternative pattern is used with such verbs as: *give, leave, send, promise, show, owe, offer.*

USE

a) The passive is used when the 'doer' is not known, not important or we don't want to say who it is:
   Strips of wood ***are put*** *through a machine.*
   The passive is often used in written texts such as public notices, descriptions of processes and newspaper reports. The passive takes away personal responsibility from the speaker and can be used to make something sound formal and impersonal:
   Income tax ***will be increased***.
b) In English, important new information is often focused on by putting it at the end of a sentence. The passive can be used for this purpose:
   A: *Have you read 'Risk'?*
   B: *Yes, it was written by* ***Dick Francis***.
   Here, it is more natural for B to continue the theme of *Risk* by using *it* and by putting the new information – *Dick Francis* – at the end.
c) Sometimes, when information about the person who does something is expressed in a long phrase, it is more natural to put the phrase after a passive construction rather than in the subject position of an active sentence:
   She ***was left*** *a lot of money by a tall, dark, handsome admirer from Argentina.* (Rather than: *A tall, dark, handsome admirer from Argentina left her a lot of money.*)

2 Need(s) to be done

Need can be followed by a passive infinitive:

The invitations need ***to be sent out***.

The structure need(s) + *-ing* can also be used with a passive meaning:

The invitations need ***sending out***.

3 *Have* (*get*) something done / do it oneself

a) The causative (*have* (*get*) *something done*) is similar to the passive in that it focuses on what happens and not the person who does it. It often conveys the idea that we 'cause' someone (often not mentioning who it is) to perform a service for us:
   Chris ***had*** *his eyes* ***tested*** *last week.* (It doesn't matter who did it.)
   I'm going to ***have*** (***get***) *my appendix* ***taken out***. (The surgeon's name doesn't matter.)
   There is little difference between *have* and *get* in these sentences.
b) When we want to emphasise that something is done by that person and only that person we can use a word ending in *-self*/*-selves* (e.g. *myself*):
   I mended the video ***myself***.
   We made the cake ***ourselves.***
c) In some cases, where the subject of the sentence does something to itself (i.e. when the same person is the subject and object of a transitive verb), it is normal to use a word ending in *-self*/*-selves* (a reflexive pronoun):
   He ***cut himself*** *while shaving.*
   When it is an action we normally (and often) do to ourselves we normally leave it out:
   He ***washed*** *and* ***shaved*** *(himself).*

Note the following expressions:

Enjoy (your)self. (means 'Have a good time.')

By (your)self. (means 'alone')

Unit 14

Mind your manners

SPEAKING 1

1 Look at the pictures and say which actions are acceptable and which are unacceptable in public in your country.

2 Are the following acceptable in public?
- Men and women touching and kissing.
- Spitting.
- Eating food with your elbows on the table.

3 Tick the following sentences which are true for you. Rewrite the others to make them true.

a) I always offer my seat to old people on a crowded bus.
b) I never sit next to the driver in a taxi.
c) I never call somebody by their first name if they are older.
d) It's very rude to arrive late when you are invited to someone's house for dinner.
e) I don't like people to stand close to me when they are talking.

4 Make notes in answer to the following questions.

a) You have invited some strangers to your house for a drink. What kinds of thing offend you? (e.g. someone who brings a dog)
b) What do you regard as good and bad table manners? (e.g. eating noisily)
c) What questions would offend you from someone you have never met before? (e.g. asking how much money you earn)
d) How should children behave in the company of adults?

5 Work in groups. Compare your answers for Exercises 3 and 4, giving reasons where possible.

6 Tell (or show) each other which physical gestures you use:

a) to greet someone of the opposite sex.
b) to greet someone of the same sex.
c) to ask someone to 'come here'.
d) to say goodbye.
e) to say something is OK.

READING

1 This book is about an Englishman who went with his wife to live in Provence, a farming region in the south of France. Guess what differences he found in the way people behaved in public.

2 Read the extract from *A Year in Provence* opposite to check your guesses. Do not use a dictionary at this stage.

"See that? Men *kissing*. Damned unhealthy, if you ask me," our lawyer friend snorted into his beer...

It had taken me some months to get used to the Provençal delight in physical contact. Like anyone brought up in England, I had absorbed certain social mannerisms. I had learned to keep my distance, to offer a nod instead of a handshake, to ration kissing to female relatives and to confine any public demonstrations of affection to dogs. The Provençal welcome, as thorough as being searched by airport security guards, was, at first, a startling experience. Now I enjoyed it, and I was fascinated by the niceties of the social ritual, and the sign language which is an essential part of any Provençal encounter.

When two unencumbered men meet, the least there will be is the conventional handshake. If the hands are full, you will be offered a little finger to shake. If the hands are wet or dirty, you will be offered a forearm or an elbow. Riding a bicycle or driving a car does not excuse you from the obligation to *toucher les cinq sardines*, and so you will see perilous contortions being performed on busy streets as hands grope through car windows and across handlebars to find each other. And this is only at the first and most restrained level of acquaintance. A closer relationship requires more demonstrative acknowledgement.

As our lawyer friend had noticed, men kiss other men. They squeeze shoulders, slap backs, pummel kidneys, pinch cheeks. When a Provençal man is truly pleased to see you, there is a real possibility of coming away from his clutches with superficial bruising.

The risk of bodily damage is less where women are concerned, but an amateur can easily make a social blunder if he miscalculates the required number of kisses. In my early days of discovery, I would plant a single kiss, only to find that the other cheek was being proffered as I was drawing back. Only snobs kiss once, I was told, or those unfortunates who suffer from congenital *froideur*. I then saw what I assumed to be the correct procedure – the triple kiss, left-right-left, so I tried it on a Parisian friend. Wrong again. She told me that triple-kissing was a low Provençal habit, and that two kisses were enough among civilised people. The next time I saw my neighbour's wife, I kissed her twice. *'Non,'* she said, *'trois fois.'*

94

(from *A Year in Provence* by Peter Mayle)

toucher les cinq sardines: shake hands *froideur:* cold personality
'Non,' she said, *'trois fois:* 'No,' she said, 'three times'

3 Read the text again and say whether the following are *True* or *False*. Try to guess the difficult words from the context and check your answers in the dictionary.

a) From the beginning the writer found it easy to adapt to the physical behaviour of Provençal people.
b) In Provence when people meet they always touch each other.
c) You can sometimes get hurt in displays of physical affection.
d) In Paris the customs about how men and women greet each other are the same as in Provence.

4 Answer the following questions about the text.

a) What does this phrase tell you about the English: *confine any public demonstrations of affection to dogs*? (line 7)
b) What does this phrase tell you about Provençal people: *as thorough as being searched by airport security guards*? (line 8)
c) When are you sometimes *offered a forearm*? (line 16)
d) What kinds of *more demonstrative acknowledgement* are there? (line 22)
e) What kinds of *social blunder* can the amateur make? (line 28)

5 [14.1] Before you listen to another extract from the book, guess what the gestures in the pictures mean in Provence. Listen and find out:

a) what the gestures mean.
b) why aerobics never became popular in Provence.

Corrective (contrastive) stress

1 We can stress words to indicate a contrast between two things and to correct what a speaker says. Example:
A: *Has your mother been to France?*
B: *No, but my father has.*
Underline the stressed word in the answers below.

a) A: Did you see Tim on Monday morning?
   B: No, but I saw Jeremy.
b) A: Did you see Tim on Monday morning?
   B: No, I phoned him.
c) A: Did you see Tim on Monday morning?
   B: No, Peter saw him.

2 [14.2] Listen to these answers said in two different ways and write two different questions for each.

a) No, Peter studies in Cambridge.
b) No, I bought a new Volvo.
c) No, the play lasted two hours.
d) No, she's nearly thirty-three years old.

In pairs, practise saying the dialogues, taking turns to ask and answer the questions.

REVISION

-ing or to?

1 Do you agree with the following statement?
Travelling first class is snobbish.
In Britain, the following things are also sometimes thought of as snobbish. Complete the sentences below using verbs from the box in the correct form.

own drink wear tell

a) ________ clothes with a fashionable label.
b) ________ people about your aristocratic friends.
c) ________ fine wine.
d) ________ a holiday home abroad.

What things are considered snobbish in your country?

2 The British still do many things according to their class and background. Is the same true in your country?

a) Which of the statements in the speech bubbles can you imagine being said by someone from the 'upper class' in Britain?
b) From the speech bubbles note down whether an *-ing* form or *to* + base form come after:
   i) a preposition. iii) a verb.
   ii) an adjective. iv) a question word.
   One of these (i–iv) can never be followed by *to* + base form. Which one is it? Refer to Sections 1 and 2 in the *Language reference* if necessary.

My old man enjoys having a game of darts in the pub with the lads.

Before going to the opera, I think it's important to dress up.

I don't know where to exercise my Rottweiler in this place.

PRACTICE

1 Debutantes (or 'debs') are the daughters of rich parents in Britain who make their first appearance in high society at a 'coming-out' party. What can you deduce about the type of people they are and their lifestyle from the article on the right?

These are some of the things people said at the party. Complete the sentences using either an *-ing* form or *to* + base form

a) At a party like this I always find it difficult ______.
b) I never know who ______.
c) What are you thinking ______?
d) Why don't we go outside instead ______?
e) When I got here I was very surprised ______.
f) Are you interested ______?
g) I'm not looking forward ______.
h) No, I don't know what ______.

Debutantes say farewell to their well-spent youth

They are neither the most beautiful, nor the most wealthy, nor the most intelligent young women in town. But for one season, at least, they are judged the most eligible for marriage.

They are this year's debutantes. One hundred and twenty-five of them waved goodbye to their childhoods at the Berkeley Dress Show, at the Savoy, London, on Monday night.

They shed few tears for their well-spent youth. Henceforth, there would be no more Pony Club or ballet classes and precious few piano lessons. This year, their lives begin to get serious. The debs face a busy round of up to four parties a week until the autumn; enough time to make the right sort of connections for life among the upper class.

The guest list included titled names: the Duchess of Argyll, the Countess of Radnor, Lady Maxwell-Scott, Lord Dalmeny ...

(from *The Independent*)

2 [14.3] Listen to Sophie talking about her life as a deb and make sentences about what she says, using the following verbs.

a) enjoy
b) intend
c) arrange
d) carry on
e) hope
f) resent

EXTENSION

-ing or to?

1 After some verbs there is a very different meaning depending on whether the verb is in the *-ing* or *to* form. Match each pair of sentences with the two descriptions below them.

a) *forget*
I'll never forget feeding the parrot.
I'll never forget to feed the parrot.
i) I promise I'll do it.
ii) I remember the occasion very well.

b) *remembered*
He remembered to send the invitations.
He remembered sending the invitations.
i) It's all right. He didn't forget. He sent them.
ii) He had a clear memory of sending them.

c) *regret*
I regret to tell you that I'm leaving.
I regret telling you that I'm leaving.
i) I'm sorry I told you. It was a mistake.
ii) I'm telling you now. Sorry it's bad news!

d) *stop*
We've stopped to have coffee.
We've stopped having coffee.
i) We're not having any more coffee.
ii) We're going to have coffee.

2 Complete the following sentences by changing the verb in brackets to the correct form.

a) Don't forget ______ (*wear*) your bow tie.
b) She remembers ______ (*go*) to the ballet once.
c) I always regret ______ (*not, tell*) my grandmother how much I loved her.
d) When I saw Charlotte dressed in the latest fashion I couldn't stop ______ (*laugh*).
e) Do remember ______ (*bring*) something to read! You'll be awfully bored.
f) I regret ______ (*tell*) you that a seat at this table costs £80. Can you afford it?
g) I shall never forget ______ (*see*) you ride a horse for the first time.
h) Why do you always stop ______ (*look*) in every shop window we pass?

VOCABULARY

Connotation

1 Connotation refers to the feelings or ideas suggested by a word rather than the actual meaning. Example: the word *materialistic* means *interested in possessions and money rather than spiritual matters.* It is usually used to suggest a negative quality. However, words like *practical* and *down-to-earth* suggest something positive.

Which of the adjectives in the box usually have a negative connotation when associated with someone's weight? Use your dictionary to help you.

fat obese portly well-built gross bony plump skinny thin slim slender

2 Which of the adjectives in the box usually have a positive connotation when associated with someone's attitude?

youthful childish mature juvenile child-like grown-up senile adult adolescent

3 The connotation of a word often depends on the context and the attitude of the speaker. Example: The word *shy* usually means *lacking self-confidence and uncomfortable in the presence of others.* However, sometimes, it can suggest a positive quality to mean that a person is *modest* (*The little girl had a lovely shy smile.*)

In the following sentences, what do the words in *italics* suggest? Choose the correct alternative.

a) I think the British are very conservative and *traditional.*
   i) they still do a lot of good things from the past they have always done.
   ii) they are not very modern or up-to-date.
b) You look very *serious*, is anything the matter?
   i) deeply worried.
   ii) sincere and very interested.
c) They're poor but *proud.*
   i) have too high an opinion of themselves.
   ii) have great self-respect.

SPEAKING 2

1 Work in pairs.

a) Identify the nationalities of the people in the pictures.
b) Match the words and phrases in the box to the stereotypical images of those nationalities.

cold friendly hard-working outgoing sense of humour romantic reserved drink a lot of beer loud

c) Do you know anybody from those countries? Is the stereotypical image true of this person?

2 [14.4] You are going to listen to people from Brazil, Japan, Germany, Italy and Sweden talking about a typical person from their country. What do you think they are going to say? Listen and check your answers.

3 In groups, discuss the following questions.

a) Are most stereotypical images positive or negative? Give examples.
b) Why is it often difficult to talk about a typical person from another country? Give examples from the listening texts.
c) In what ways are you typical or not of the country you come from?

Report your discussion to the class.

WRITING

Tourist brochure

1 Which of the following customs and manners are true in your country?

- Punctuality is not important.
- It is normal to bargain in shops.
- You mustn't cross your legs in the presence of a superior.
- Smoking is forbidden in public places.
- It is usual to have a siesta after lunch.
- People say 'Sorry, sorry' when something goes wrong, even though it's not their fault.
- Queueing is not usual.

2 Work with someone else of your nationality if possible and make notes about your country, or one you know well, under the following headings: *Customs*, *Good manners*, *Bad manners*, *Advice to visitors*. Example:

3 You are going to write an entry for the *Local customs* section of a tourist brochure, talking about the customs and manners of people in your country and giving advice to visitors (e.g. *If possible visitors should* . . . ; *Take care to* . . . ; *Make sure you* . . . ; *Visitors should be careful not to* . . . ; *It is unwise to* . . . ; *It is never a good idea to* . . .). Include at least two examples of bad advice but pretend it is good advice (e.g. *Never tip taxi drivers*; *Feel free to smoke downstairs on buses.*) Divide your notes into paragraphs and write a draft.

4 Show your draft to other students (preferably students of the same nationality). Ask them to identify the bad advice and to suggest improvements.

5 Rewrite your entry paying particular attention to the use of *-ing* and *to* + base form.

6 Discuss the customs and manners mentioned. Do you know the reasons for any of them? Are they changing in any way in the modern world?

Language reference

1 The *-ing* form

The *-ing* form of a verb can be used as a noun and can be the subject of a sentence:

__Owning__ a holiday home abroad is a waste of money.

The *-ing* form can also come after the main verb:

I like __owning__ a holiday home abroad.

The *-ing* form is used after prepositions:

__After getting__ the menu you could point to what you want to order.

Many adjectives and verbs are followed by a preposition + *-ing*:

We were very __interested in seeing__ our new house.
Angie's __thinking of leaving__ her job.
I __look forward to seeing__ you. (Here *to* is used as a preposition, not as part of the infinitive *to* + base form.)

2 *To* + base form

Unlike the *-ing* form the infinitive (*to* + base form of the verb) never follows a preposition.

To + base form is used after certain adjectives (e.g. *surprised, difficult, important*):

We were __surprised to see__ how old it was.

Some *to* + base form clauses begin with a question word (e.g. *what, where, when, who, how, whether*):

I want to know __what__ to wear, __where__ to go, __who__ to see, __whether__ to phone up or not.

3 *-ing* or *to*?

When a verb is followed by another verb it is not always easy to tell whether the second verb should be in the *-ing* form or *to* + base form.

Verbs followed by the *-ing* form include *avoid, delay, dislike, finish, practise, risk, suggest:*

I __dislike having__ to get up early.
Have you __finished reading__ the book?
If you go out you __risk getting__ caught in a storm.

Many verbs which are followed by *to* + base form express a concern with the future and are verbs of hopes, offers and plans (e.g. *arrange, expect, hope, intent, mean, offer, plan, promise, want, wish*):

I __arranged to play__ tennis the next day.
She __wants to get__ there early.
He __intended to get__ a job.

Some verbs can be followed by both the *-ing* form or *to* + base form with a small change of meaning (e.g. *begin, can't bear, continue, hate, like, love, prefer, start*). In these cases the *-ing* form normally suggests a general statement and *to* + base form refers to a specific action (often in the future):

I __love going__ to India. I go every year. It's great.
I'd __love to go__ to India next year, but I can't afford it.

I __prefer reading__ to watching TV. (as a general activity)
I __prefer to read__ now so please leave me alone.

She __began playing__ the piano when she was five.
She __began to play__ the piano, but the doorbell rang.

Some verbs can be followed by both the *-ing* form or *to* + base form with a much bigger change of meaning (e.g. *forget, remember, regret, stop*). *-ing* forms are used after these verbs to talk about past events; *to* + base forms are used for present or future events:

Don't __forget to lock__ the door. (in the future)
I'll never __forget seeing__ you fall down the stairs. (It was a terrible sight.)

Please __remember to post__ the letter. (in the future)
I don't __remember posting__ the letter. (in the past)

I __regret to tell__ you you're fired. (So please leave!)
I __regret telling__ you I loved you. (It was a big mistake.)

She __stopped to shake__ hands. (She stopped what she was doing because she wanted to shake hands.)
She __stopped shaking__ hands. (She did something else instead.)

Unit 15

Training diets

LISTENING

Before listening

1 Look at the picture of Jamie Reeves, who won a competition called 'The Strongest Man in the World'. What do you think he had to do to win?

2 Read the article to check your answers.

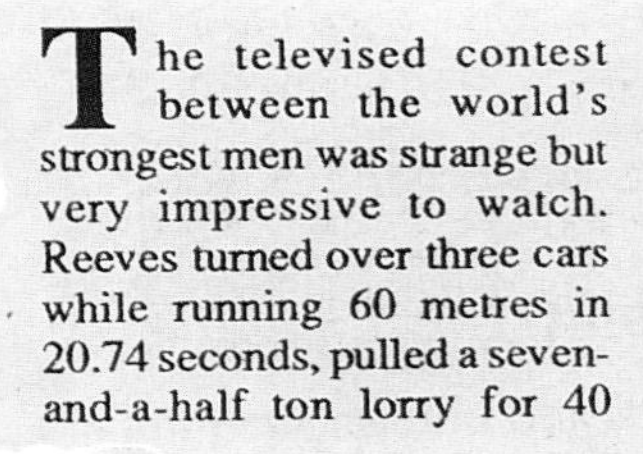

The televised contest between the world's strongest men was strange but very impressive to watch. Reeves turned over three cars while running 60 metres in 20.74 seconds, pulled a seven-and-a-half ton lorry for 40 metres, lifted great logs of wood and walked up and down flights of stairs carrying large containers filled with lead. When it was all over he had dethroned the reigning champion, Jon-Pall Sigmarsson of Iceland.

'It's a decathlon of strength, and the ideal event for me,' said Jamie. 'I'm a strong man who likes all aspects of strength, from power lifting to pulling large lorries. My ambition is to stay healthy and have fun winning things.'

He has to work hard at keeping his large size and fitness. He is 1.95m tall, with 1.54m chest, 55cm biceps, a 55cm neck, a 1.07m waist and 81cm thighs. Daily training and a diet which costs £120 a week maintains his competition weight of 148 kilos.

(from the *Yorkshire Post*)

Listening

1 You are going to listen to an interview with Jamie. In this newspaper report of the interview the journalist has made several mistakes. Can you guess what they are?

'The problem was my parents were small people and I had to eat and train to build myself up. To maintain my weight now I aim at 7,000 calories a day, to gain weight I aim at over 9,000. Most days I eat twice as much as a normal man three times a day. The same food but twice as much. But I am an athlete. I can run 100 metres in just over 13 seconds and 400 metres in just over a minute. I'm big, but I feel fit. When I train I like to do the same routine every day just before my evening meal. I have to be careful to avoid other kinds of sports during the day which may ruin my training. I think when ordinary people train they need to be very careful when they start.'

2 [15.1] Listen to the interview.

a) Were your guesses correct?
b) How is Jamie's diet different before competitions?

3 Devise a menu, based on the interview, to complete gaps 1 and 2 in the extract below.

Jamie's day begins at five o'clock in the morning with a huge breakfast of ____1____. By six he is at the mine welding machinery until lunchtime. The afternoon finds him training at Fitness World, the gymnasium in Duchess Road he runs with his wife Deborah. After an evening meal of ____2____ he is usually in bed by 9.30.

(from the *Yorkshire Post*)

4 Jamie uses nouns of the following words. Can you remember what they were?

a) to compete
b) strong
c) to sprint
d) fit
e) injure

5 [15.2] In the interview, Jamie gave some lists of food, for example: *six eggs, some bacon, some fruit.* When we list things, our voice usually rises on all the items except the last one, when the voice falls. Listen to the recorded example and then practise saying the following sentences.

a) Yes, please. Two eggs, beans, a ham sandwich and a cup of coffee. Thank you.
b) Once upon a time there were three bears: a daddy bear, a mummy bear and a baby bear.
c) I don't like dogs, cats, rabbits or goldfish. Sorry!
d) All the top clubs won yesterday: Liverpool, Arsenal and Manchester United.
e) Nobody likes me: not Tom, Bill, Mary or Sue.

VOCABULARY

Homonyms

1 The words in the box below are homonyms. They have at least two different meanings but the same spelling and pronunciation. In some cases they may be different parts of speech. In the dictionary the different meanings will be shown like this.

type¹ /taɪp/ *n* **1** [C (of)] a particular kind, class or group: *Macaroni is a type of pasta.* **2** (U) printed letters: *italic type*
type² *v* 1 [I;T] to write

Choose five of the words from the box. In pairs, each of you should write a sentence to show one of the meanings. Use your dictionary to help you if necessary. Example: *board.*

A: *There are now two women on the* ***board*** *of the company.*
B: *At four o'clock we* ***boarded*** *the plane.*

board	port	fox	safe	match	can
miss	file	spot	tap	sink	park
light	flat	book	kind	swallow	bat
pick	chest	fine	play		

2 Look at the table below.

HOMONYMS		
WORD	MEANING 1	MEANING 2
board /bɔːd/	*group of directors* (n)	*get on to (a plane)* (v)

a) In your vocabulary records make a table of homonyms from Exercise 1 in the same way.
b) Write down other words you know that have more than one meaning.

Sounds: /l/

[15.3] When we say the word *file* the /l/ sound is different from the /l/ sound in the word *light.* Listen and divide the following into '*file*' words (A) and '*light*' words (B).

a) I'll
b) tell
c) lunch
d) please
e) school
f) careful

Where do (A) sounds usually occur in a word?

A selection of idioms

In list A below the words and phrases in *italics* are examples of informal or colloquial English. Match them with the definitions in list B.

A

a) I'm *fed up with* this cloudy weather.
b) My children are *driving me round the bend.* I'd better take them out.
c) I don't mind what we do. It's *up to you.*
d) Yes, a dishwasher would be very *handy.*
e) If I decide to go, I'll *give you a buzz.*
f) I don't know really. It's *touch-and-go.*
g) I'm sorry I can't tell you *off the top of my head.*
h) He was so funny. I found it hard *to keep a straight face.*

B

1 phone you
2 not to laugh
3 annoying me a lot
4 without thinking about it
5 tired of
6 your decision
7 uncertain
8 useful

REVISION

Quantity

1 In the interview, Jamie Reeves says: *many calories* but *much food*. Divide the following words into countable (***many calories***) and uncountable (***much food***) words.

eggs	damage	people	bread	cornflakes
salt	news	soap	oranges	sugar milk

Add some more nouns to the two lists and compare your lists with a partner.

2 Think of at least one word that can come after each of the following phrases. (Some can be found in the box above.) The first one has been done for you.

a) a pinch of *salt*
b) a slice of
c) an item of
d) a bit of
e) a bar of
f) a teaspoonful of
g) a drop of
h) a piece of

3 Jenny is away and wants to invite some friends home. Diane, her sister, has been looking after the children. Jenny doesn't believe Diane's any good at looking after things in her absence and phones her to check whether there is enough food and drink in the house.

Read the first part of Diane's side of the conversation, choosing the correct alternatives.

'Yes. There are (1) *couple / dozens* of bottles of wine left. White wine? Ah! No, there's (2) *no / none* white wine, (3) *no / none* at all – well, there wasn't (4) *much / many* in the first place. Certainly not (5) *too much / enough* for a party. (6) *More / Most* of the red wine is quite drinkable, though.

Food in the freezer? No, there's not a (7) *great deal / great many* left. The children have eaten nearly everything. There are a (8) *couple / lots* of cakes which they haven't touched. I'd better put them aside or they'll (9) *all / both* be gone before long.

Salad . . . ah! No, (10) *hardly any / all* of that's disappeared too. Lucy gave it to the rabbit.'

4 Work in pairs.

a) Divide the words and phrases in the box below into three groups and complete the chart.
– those only used with countable nouns.
– those only used with uncountable nouns.
– those that can be used with both.
Check with Section 2 in the *Language reference*.

a(n) some any little/a little (bit of)
much many a lot (of)/lots (of) no/
none few / a few hardly any enough
most one / both a great deal (of)
several all / half (of the) (a) whole
more / less a couple (of) dozens (of)

COUNTABLE e.g. *egg(s)*	UNCOUNTABLE e.g. *milk*	BOTH e.g. *egg(s)/milk*
a(n)	*a little*	*some*

b) Complete the rest of Diane's side of the conversation using words from the box above. More than one answer may be possible.

'No doubt if you want __(1)__ sandwich Ben will make you __(2)__. Oh, no, I've just remembered! I don't think there's __(3)__ bread left. Come to think of it, there aren't __(4)__ things we could put in it anyway.

Fruit? There might be __(5)__ a melon left. Not a __(6)__ one, I'm afraid. We had some of it last week. And __(7)__ packets of biscuits perhaps. I know for certain there are __(8)__ packets of crisps. Possibly __(9)__ cheese but __(10)__ of it's any good. What! What do you mean you're going to eat out? I was only joking!'

c) [15.4] Listen and check your answers.

5 Work in pairs to find out if Diane was joking.

STUDENT A
Look at page 149 to find out what food and drink was really in the house. (Do not show the picture to Student B.)

STUDENT B
Ask questions using words from the box in Exercise 4 to find out what the real situation was.

EXTENSION

Compounds of *some*, *any*, *no* and *every*

Compound pronouns and adverbs can be formed from *some*, *any*, *no* and *every*. Example:
***Somebody** saw you steal it!*
They may be followed by *else* (related in meaning to 'other'). Example:
***Somebody else** stole it, not me!* (= some other person)

Rewrite the following sentences using the word in brackets to make a compound. Use *else* where necessary. Example:
I don't know where my wallet is. I can't find it. (where)
*I can't find my wallet **anywhere**.*

a) You're cleverer than all the people I know. (*one*)
b) All the other people were on time. (*body*)
c) All the things in the garden looked lovely. (*thing*)
d) There was no other place to go. (*where*)
e) Another person has parked in my parking space. (*body*)
f) There were no other things she could do. (*thing*)
g) I heard that story in another place. (*where*)

Each, *another*, *both*, *either*, etc.

Work in groups. Look at the extracts from a questionnaire about people's attitudes to health and fitness. Use words from the box below to make as many correct sentences as you can about the attitudes of Simon, Julia and Peter. Start like this:
Each of the people we interviewed thinks that . . .
Simon doesn't think that . . . Julia doesn't either.
Julia thinks that on one day we should . . . and that on another day . . .

all	none	another	neither/nor	both	the other
each	either				

NAME	SIMON	JULIA	PETER
1 Do you think that people work better in the morning or the afternoon?	The morning. Me, I'm exhausted by 2.00...	The morning. In the afternoon people...	Morning, definitely...
2 How much sleep does a healthy adult need?	7 hours or I'm exhausted...	7 hours OK. Better to get 8 hours, particularly...	5hrs. We all sleep far too much...
3 Do you think most people are the right weight for their height?	No, some people are skinny, most are too fat...	No, everyone eats too much nowadays...	Not really...
4 What exercise should a 40-year old get in a week?	...swim or go to the gym twice, every other day.	...go swimming/play tennis, next day go to aerobics.	... exercise is overrated. Why bother?

SPEAKING

1 Read the two extracts below about how some people are obsessed with their health.

a) According to text A why do some people get addicted to exercise?
b) In what ways are the shopping habits described in text B different from your own?
c) Talk about peoples' attitudes to health and fitness in your country.

A

"When we got off the plane, the first thing she did was go for a ten mile run. It used to drive me mad. She would spend a fortune on body supplements and in the end the only thing she cared about was the training. We split up a year ago now."

Dr Cockerill says there are physical reasons why people become hooked on exercise. "The brain has its own chemical 'uppers' called endorphins," he explains. "These are painkillers, released into the bloodstream when the body is under some form of prolonged stress such as childbirth or sustained hard exercise. They produce a sense of wellbeing and some people become addicted to this feeling. Withdrawal from endorphins produces symptoms similar to the 'cold turkey' effect of coming off hard drugs."

B

"These days when I go to the supermarket I won't buy anything with an E-number on the packet. I spend a fortune on health foods every week but it's worth it. Also I drive miles to get my organic vegetables. They're not easy to get round here. I don't trust the experts, though. One minute they're telling you that things like butter are bad for you. The next minute they're good for you."

(from *Bella*)

2 Read the newspaper extract. In what ways are you similar to or different from Steve?

His body building wrecked our love

Sherry Lambert's boyfriend Steve is a gym junkie, hooked on body building. But when he turned to steroids to boost his strength, she watched her gentle man turn into an animal.

Steve even gave up work to fulfil his obsession with building up his muscles.

3 Divide into groups of four: A, B, C and D. Students C and D are going to call on Steve and Sherry and help them sort out their problems. Roleplay the situation.

STUDENT A
You are Steve and you are in love with Sherry. You believe in fitness. However, the obsession is destroying your life.

STUDENT B
You are Sherry. You like Steve and want to help him. However, you can't take any more and are determined to leave him.

STUDENT C
You are a good friend of both Steve and Sherry and want to help them sort out their problems. You live with D and don't believe in exercise and health foods, preferring to eat and drink anything you like.

STUDENT D
You are a good friend of both Steve and Sherry and want to help them sort out their problems. You live with C and are fed up with his/her laziness.

4 Discuss and answer these questions.

a) What were the most interesting parts of the roleplay?
b) What were the most convincing arguments?
c) What language problems were there?

WRITING

Attitude words

1 Complete the following conversation with the most appropriate expression from the lists below. (Most help to convey the personal point of view of the speakers.)

EVE: You sound a bit out of breath. Are you OK?
DEBRA: I'm exhausted!
EVE: Another tough work-out in the gym __(1)__. __(2)__ I think that kind of thing is a waste of time.
DEBRA: The company insists on it – __(3)__. We even have a gym at work.
EVE: __(4)__ they give you time off to go there.
DEBRA: You're kidding! We're expected to go at lunchtime. It's not too bad, though. __(5)__ I get to see Tony. __(6)__ he's in pretty good shape, given how much he eats.
EVE: __(7)__ you're not still seeing him, are you?
DEBRA: __(8)__, we've become very close recently.
EVE: __(9)__ dear Debra, I think you're mad. He's not worth it. He's __(10)__ seeing someone else anyway.

	A	B	C
1	generally	I suppose	really
2	To my mind	Personally	Naturally
3	undoubtedly	seriously	unfortunately
4	Honestly	Broadly speaking	Presumably
5	Frankly	At least	In my opinion
6	Surprisingly	Perhaps	Obviously
7	Certainly	Surely	I imagine
8	Eventually	Consequently	Actually
9	To be honest	Hopefully	Evidently
10	anyhow	strictly speaking	probably

Now answer the following questions.

a) What do you think Eve is trying to persuade Debra to do? Could she have personal reasons of her own?
b) How will Debra respond?

2 Find at least one attitude word or expression in the box below that can be used when you want to:

a) contradict someone.
b) express your opinion forcefully.
c) express surprise.

as a matter of fact	definitely	clearly	apparently	luckily
as far as I know	as far as I'm concerned	between you and me		
amazingly	curiously	funnily enough	strangely	

3 Write a conclusion to the conversation in Exercise 1. Use at least five attitude words or expressions from Exercises 1 and 2.

Language reference

1 Countable or uncountable?

Most common nouns in English are countable, i.e. they have both singular and plural forms: *orange/oranges*.
Uncountable nouns refer to things which you cannot count (like liquids) and normally take a singular verb. Examples:
salt (*a pinch of*); *bread* (*a slice of*); *news* (*an item of*); *sugar* (*a spoonful of*); *milk* (*a drop of*); *furniture* (*a piece of*).
Most abstract nouns are also uncountable (e.g. *advice, excitement*). Some words can be used as both countable and uncountable:
two chickens – the animal; a *piece of chicken* – the meat

2 Quantity words

How we talk about the quantity of a thing depends on whether the thing in question is countable or uncountable. Some quantity words can be used with countable nouns, some with uncountable nouns, some with both.

WITH COUNTABLE	WITH UNCOUNTABLE	WITH BOTH
a(n)	*(very) little / not much*	*no / none*
(very) few / not many	*a little (bit of)*	*hardly any*
a few / fewer	*less*	*some / any*
many	*much*	*half / all of*
one / both (of)	*a great deal (of)*	*a lot / lots of*
several	*(the) / (a) whole*	*(not) enough*
neither (of)		*more / most*
a couple (of)		
dozens (of)		
every		

Note that:
a) The word *some* is used in affirmative sentences as well as requests/offers when we expect the answer *Yes*:
Do you want ***some*** *salt? (I expect you do.)*
The word *any* is used in sentences with negative meaning:
I don't want ***any*** *more to drink.*
Any can also be used in positive statements when there is a choice from every possibility:
You can buy ***any*** *house you like.*
b) *Many* is normally used in negative sentences and questions:
There are not ***many*** *cornflakes left.*
Many is not usually used in affirmative sentences:
There are ***a lot of*** *cornflakes left.*
c) *A little (bit of) / a few* are normally used in affirmative sentences or requests/offers when we expect the answer *Yes*:
Would you like ***a few*** *minutes rest? (I expect you would.)*
d) Most quantifiers (with the exception of *no* and *every*) can be followed by *of* + noun phrase to mean 'part' or 'not all':
Some of this wine *is excellent.*
Compare this with:
Some wine is excellent. (But usually I prefer beer.)

3 Compounds of *some*, *any*, *no* and *every*

Compound pronouns and adverbs can be formed from the words *some, any, no* and *every*:
something/one/body/where; anything/one/body/where nothing/one/body/where; everything/one/body/where
Note that:
a) We use *-one* and *-body* compounds to talk about people. There is no difference in meaning between them (e.g. ***Somebody/Someone*** *saw you steal it!*). We use *-thing* compounds to talk about things (e.g. ***Something*** *is wrong.*) and *-where* compounds to talk about place or position (e.g. *Your wallet must be* ***somewhere***.). In American English *-place* is often used instead of *-where*, i.e. *someplace*.
b) *No-* compounds mean 'not any' but are more emphatic (e.g. ***Nobody's*** *there. There's* ***nothing*** *wrong.*). *No one* is usually written as two words.
c) The rules for using these compounds are similar to those for the first element of the compound, (e.g. *some-* words are usually used in affirmative statements and requests/offers: *I want to give you* ***something***. (NOT ~~*I want to give you anything*~~.) However, *of-* phrases are not usually used (NOT ~~*somebody of*~~).
d) The stress is usually on the first element of the compound: *'anybody*.
e) When *everything* and *everyone* are the subject of a sentence they normally take a singular verb (e.g. *Everyone* ***likes*** *her.*) However, the questions tag is plural (*Everyone likes her, don't they?*).
f) The compounds may be followed by *else* (related in meaning to *other*). Example:
Somebody else stole it, not me! (= some other person)

4 Other determiners/pronouns

Other determiners/pronouns practised in this unit are:
both: ***Both*** *(of) my children go to school.* (I have two children – *both* is used when we take two things together.)
each: ***Each*** *(of them) goes to a different school.* (Every single one of them – *each* is used when we take any number of things separately.)
either: *There's tea or coffee – you can have* ***either***. (One or the other of two.) Remember: *I like maths too. I don't like maths* ***either***. (also)
neither . . . nor: ***Neither*** *(of them) likes maths.* ***Neither*** *Paul* ***nor*** *Judy likes maths.* (Not either of them.)
all: ***All*** *(of) my children speak Japanese.* (I have more than two children – *all* means the complete number/amount.)
the other: ***The other*** *children only speak French.* (The remaining – the ones not already mentioned.)
another: *Would they like to go to* ***another*** *school?* (a different) *Would you like* ***another*** *cup of tea?* (an additional)

A deafening noise

READING

Before reading

1 Think of examples of people in sport who try to influence the results unfairly. What, if anything, can be done about it? Example: *Weightlifters who take illegal drugs should be disqualified.*

2 In pairs, look at the headlines and photographs which appeared on the same day. What story could the newspapers be reporting?

3 Compare your answers with other pairs.

DRUG DEALER PUT HIS MONEY ON ULTRA-SONIC BINOCULAR GUN

(*Daily Mail*)

PLOT THAT COULD HAVE DESTROYED RACING

(*Daily Mirror*)

£15m SONIC FIREWORK BROUGHT DOWN THE FAVOURITE

(*Today*)

Reading

1 Read the article opposite to check your answers.

2 Make notes under the following headings:

- Victim(s)
- Type of crime
- Weapon
- Accused
- Implications

3 In pairs, prepare questions using the cues below and make sure you know the answers to your questions. Then ask and answer your partner.

STUDENT A

a) What happen / racehorse / close to winning post?
b) Why / not discover / the same day?
c) When / first / use?
d) How / harmful / to horses?

STUDENT B

a) How / gun / work?
b) When / jockey / come off?
c) Why James Laming / do it?
d) What kind / bet / criminals make?

4 Are sound guns and light (laser) guns weapons of the future? Give reasons for your answer.

A top racehorse was brought down at Royal Ascot with a shot from a high-tech sound gun, a court was told yesterday.

The gun was built into a pair of binoculars and fired from the crowd as the horse was in sight of certain victory.

The 'technically brilliant' ultra-sonic device – which could not be heard by people – was devised by a back-street inventor. It was to be used with potentially devastating effect in a secret plan 'to destroy the entire system of race-course betting and bookmaking in this country,' defence lawyer Jonathan Goldberg told Southwark Crown Court in London.

He said it had the potential to make a fortune in bets against the favourite because it made sure that the horse would lose.

It was used last year to unseat leading jockey Greville Starkey from Ile de Chypre just before the end of the King George V Handicap, which it undoubtedly would have won, he said.

The astonishing story was told by the defence during a trial in which the inventor of the gun, James Laming, denies drug conspiracy charges.

It came to light because of his alleged connections with a drug baron who wanted to use the gun to help him win large bets.

The inventor is a 49-year-old grandfather and south London car dealer who lives with his mother-in-law in a terraced house in Surrey Road, Peckham.

He told the court that he got all the information on ultra-sonics for the gun from the *Encyclopaedia Britannica* and tested it on horses in fields around Woking, Surrey.

The gun was made from a pair of race binoculars. Showing them to the jury, Mr Goldberg said: 'This device subjected a passing racehorse to a sudden and deafening noise which we human beings cannot hear at all. It is the equivalent in suddenness to letting a loud firework explode in its ears.'

The noise would be 'a horrible ear-piercing shriek' like the feedback from a microphone. Because racehorses were sensitive and temperamental it would have the effect of making the horse swerve and unseat the rider.

'It has the power of a large stereo system' and could be focused like a torch 'right into the horse's ears as it gallops past'.

'It left no evidence of its use and no permanent disability for the animal,' he said.

The plan was to use the gun for horse races and possibly for greyhound races. Mr Goldberg said: 'He would fire it at the favourite or second favourite in a race and would "lay off" a bet – that means you bet against the the favourite or the second favourite winning.

'These criminals, of course, were in a unique position to ensure that the horse lost.'

(from the *Daily Mail*)

5 Match the words in column A with the phrases in column B. Use the context to help you before checking in your dictionaries.

A

a) *devised by* (line 9)
b) *devastating effect* (line 10)
c) *subjected . . . to* (line 42)
d) *the equivalent . . . to* (line 45)
e) *evidence of* (line 56)
f) *were in a unique position to* (line 66)

B

1 had a better chance than anyone else to
2 caused . . . to experience
3 cleverly invented by
4 completely destructive results
5 sign of
6 the same as

6 Find another word for the following in the text.

a) shot (______) (line 5)
b) a good chance (*the* __________) (line 16)
c) lot of money (________) (line 17)
d) piece of equipment (_______) (line 42)
e) likely to change mood quickly (_______________) (line 50)
f) turn suddenly (_______) (line 51)
g) lasting for ever (__________) (line 57)

7 Who or what do the words in *italics* refer to?

a) *It* was to be . . . (line 9)
b) *which* it undoubtedly . . . (line 23)
c) *It* came to light . . . (line 29)
d) tested *it* on . . . (line 38)
e) Showing *them* to . . . (line 41)
f) *It* is the equivalent . . . (line 45)
g) for *the animal,*' he said. (line 57)
h) '*These criminals*, of course . . . (line 66)

8 Replace the word(s) in *italics* with another phrase. Example:
You still see elephants in India. *Elephants* are often used to do heavy work in the fields.
These animals are often . . .

a) Buses cause the most pollution in some cities. *The buses* are often badly maintained.
b) I love Mexico. I've been *to Mexico* many times.
c) We had a pizza in the 'Pizza Express' last night. I've never eaten *in the 'Pizza Express'* before.

VOCABULARY

Sport

1 Work in pairs. Complete the chart with information about sport. There may be more than one possibility.

SPORT	EQUIPMENT	PLACE	VERB
tennis		court	
	trunks/costume		swim
boxing			
	clubs		
football			
		mountain slopes	

2 Make a similar chart for the sports below.

3 Which sport do you think would be suitable or unsuitable for each of the people in the photographs? Give reasons.

Homophones

A homophone is a word which has the same pronunciation as another word, although the spelling and meaning are different.

1 Choose the correct alternative in the following sentences. If necessary, use your dictionary to help you decide and find out how you pronounce the word.

a) There was a long *pause/paws* in the conversation.
b) I bet you can't guess the *wait/weight* of this bag.
c) She resigned on a matter of *principle/principal*.
d) I'll have to *higher/hire* a car for the week.
e) You should *sees/seize* the opportunity immediately.
f) We didn't *steal/steel* it. We found it!
g) When the Queen died the country went into *morning/mourning*.
h) We listened to their *tales/tails* about life on board ship.

2 Which of these following pairs of words are *not* homophones?

a) male/mail
b) where/were
c) late/light
d) pair/pear
e) would/wood
f) shoot/short
g) blew/blue
h) free/fry
i) bare/bear
j) pie/pay

3 Work out how the 'words' in the following list are pronounced. (Look at page 149 to help you.) Then write down two different spellings. If necessary, say the word aloud and try to find words in the dictionary. Example:
/breɪk/ – *break/brake*

a) /weə/
b) /ɑ:nt/
c) /gest/
d) /steəz/
e) /mi:t/
f) /weɪst/
g) /həʊl/
h) /pi:s/

4 Work in pairs. Write the words for the transcriptions in the box as quickly as possible, using the correct spelling. They are all connected to sport. The pair with the highest number of correct answers wins.

/netbɔ:l/ /penlti/ /fɪʃɪŋ/ /faʊl/ /raɪdə/
/tʃes/ /pɪtʃ/ /gəʊl/ /ʃu:t/ /reɪs/
/fi:ld/ /pɑ:s/ /æmətə/ /refəri:/ /skwɒʃ/

EXTENSION

Deduction in the present

1 [16.1] Listen to three dialogues and say which expression means the following.

a) It's impossible that he's out.
b) It's possible that he's out.
c) I feel certain he's out.

2 Answer the following questions.

a) What alternative words are there for the word *may* in the sentence: *He may be out?*
b) If we want to say something is possibly not true do we say: *He might not be out* or *He could not be out?*
c) Correct this sentence: *The light's on. Keith mustn't be out.*

Check with Section 2 in the *Language reference.*

3 [16.2] Listen to three sentences.

a) Which words are most stressed in each sentence?
b) How is *be* pronounced?
c) What happens to the *t* in *must*? What happens to the *n't* in *can't*?
d) Practise saying the sentences.

4 In pairs, take turns to make sentences using the cues in brackets. Example:
A: *There's an ambulance outside number 6.*
B: (old lady ill) *The old lady must be ill.*

a) A: Doesn't that young man look like her?
   B: (Yes – son)
b) A: There's someone at the door.
   B: (not Tom – too early)
c) A: Are they English?
   B: (speaking Spanish)
d) A: When's Helen's birthday?
   B: (don't really know – next week)
e) A: Who's that woman he's with?
   B: (his wife abroad)
f) A: The dog's barking.
   B: (Yes – somebody at door)
g) A: Why are there so many cars next door?
   B: (don't know – a party)
h) A: Whose coat is this?
   B: (not Sue's – hers red one)

5 Work in pairs. Look at the contents of this sports bag. Make deductions about the owner.

6 Write a list of ten things you like in your house. Don't write your name. Divide into two groups. Mix and exchange your lists with the other group. Deduce who the list belongs to.

REVISION

Mixed modals

1 Match the modals in italics in the following extracts with the categories below.

'Why don't you ask me about Buffalo Bill?' His voice was close, at her level. He *must* be sitting on the floor too.
'Do you know something about him?'
'I *might* if I saw the case.'
'I don't have the case,' Starling said.
'You *won't* have this one, either, when they're through with you.'
'I know.'
She then went over to the side

(from *The Silence of the Lambs* by Thomas Harris)

'I do need your friendship though. More than you know. I *can't* go on with it all much longer, even for Vic's sake. *Can* I call on you to help if things get too bad?'
Maurice was afraid of falling down the stairs, so it was with difficulty that he said, 'Yes, of course.'
'It *may* be sooner than you think. It *may* be tonight,' Sylvia answered and kissed him.'

(from *After the Show* by Angus Wilson)

a) possibility b) certainty c) ability d) permission

2 Write down as many modals as you can think of which express:

a) permission (e.g. *may* – ***May** I have a drink?*).
b) request (e.g. *can* – ***Can** you help me?*).
c) obligation or advisability (e.g. *ought to* – *You **ought to** keep that a secret.*).

Check with Section 1 in the *Language reference*.

3 Rewrite the sentences using modals from the box. Example:
I advise you to go the dentist's more often.
*You **should** go the dentist's more often.*

may	must	would	won't	should	might	couldn't
can	ought to	will				

a) *I advise you* to take malaria tablets but *it is essential that* you have a cholera injection. (*You* . . .)
b) *Perhaps* things *will* get better. (*Things* . . .)
c) A lot of the people *didn't know how* to read or write. (*A lot of the people* . . .)
d) *Do you mind if* I take off my coat? (. . . *take off my coat?*)
e) That's a loud knock on the door. It's *almost certainly* Bill. (*It* . . .)
f) *Please* lend me £50. (. . . *lend me £50?*)
g) Steve help? No, never. (*I'm certain Steve* . . .)
h) *Is it possible for me to* use your computer? (. . . *use your computer?*)

SPEAKING

Debating

1 What are the most dangerous sports? Why are they dangerous?

2 Read the openings to two newspaper articles.

3 Work in pairs or groups. Make two separate lists of all the arguments you can think of:

a) in favour of boxing.
b) against boxing.

Use these prompts to help you: *money, injuries, morality, effect on spectators.*

4 What expressions can you think of under these headings?
- Interrupting (e.g. *Excuse me, can I butt in here . . . ?*)
- Disagreeing with someone's opinion (e.g. *I'm afraid I think that's complete rubbish.*)
- Giving your point of view (e.g. *First of all I'd like to explain . . .*)

Refer to the *Speaking functions* on page 150 if necessary..

5 Work in three groups. Debate whether dangerous sports should be banned.

Finish to the Fight

Now that the long-term dangers of boxing have been medically proved, should the sport be banned?

Asked at the end of his career what he liked least about boxing, Sugar Ray Robinson said: "Getting hit."

A fighter's intention is to hurt and disable his opponent. He wears gloves to protect his fists, not his opponent's brain. Most fans of the sport would, if they were honest, admit that they watch in order to see pain inflicted.

(from *The Independent*)

Professional boxing arouses a wide variety of emotions among all levels of society and raises many issues, mainly moral and medical. Moralists would argue as to whether there was place for boxing as a sport.

Read any newspaper and you realise that, unfortunately, society is very violent and boxing, along with other contact sports, seeks to channel that violence in a positive and beneficial way.

(from *The Independent*)

GROUP A
You want to ban any sports that put people's lives in danger. You are also against violence in sport. Why? (e.g. *It encourages violence in spectators.*)

GROUP B
You are against banning any sports. You also believe that some kind of danger and violence are a part of all sports. Why? (e.g. *Banning them would drive them underground.*)

GROUP C
You are in favour of banning some dangerous sports, not others. Decide which. Why? (e.g. *People need to be able to take risks.*) You also believe that taking part in sport is more important than winning.

a) Think of all the arguments which support the point of view of your group and plan what you will say.
b) As a whole class, conduct the debate with one person as chair. As many speakers as possible should put forward arguments based on their group's point of view.
c) Vote on the motion according to what you really believe rather than your group's official point of view.

WRITING

Letter of complaint

1 Give at least one reason why you might write to complain to:
- a shop (e.g. a furniture shop).
- a telephone company or the Post Office.
- government officials or a local authority (e.g. for roads).
- a transport company (e.g. taxi, bus, train).
- a builder, plumber or electrician.
- a language school.

2 Work in pairs.

a) Complete the letter with the words in the box. They all refer back to something previously mentioned. Some are used more than once.

you	the problem		
there	them	this	
ones	it	the	he

b) Divide the sentences into three or four paragraphs.

3 Write a letter of complaint.

a) Choose a situation from Exercise 1 and make notes.

b) Divide your letter into three paragraphs (see the boxes below). Use the expressions in brackets if you wish.

c) Check you have used words like *it*, *the*, *ones* instead of repeating words unnecessarily.

The Manager
Sportscene
Long Street
CARDIFF

66 Chapel Road
CARDIFF

21st May 1992

Dear Sir/Madam,

a) I am writing to complain about a pair of SWIMEASY swimming trunks I bought in your main shop two Saturdays ago and the way your assistant spoke to me when I called in ________ the following Monday to return ________.

b) I bought ________ pair – they were very fashionable ________ – after I saw you were advertising a sportswear sale.

c) However, the first time I wore ________ I realised that there was no elastic in ________, presumably because somebody had taken ________ out.

d) When I explained ________ to ________ assistant ________ told me he couldn't give me my money back because I didn't have a receipt.

e) ________ receipt ________ mentioned was so small ________ must have got lost.

f) I demanded to see the manager but I was told that ________ wasn't possible because ________ were on holiday.

g) I insisted that as ________ weren't there ________ should give me my money back but unfortunately ________ became extremely rude.

h) I enclose ________ pair of trunks and I must ask you to let me have a full refund immediately.

Yours faithfully,

Stuart Blake

Stuart Blake (Dr)

PARAGRAPH 1
Say why you are complaining. (*I'm writing to draw your attention to . . . /to object to . . .*)

PARAGRAPH 2
Give background information, such as precise details of the problem, how you discovered it and how you feel about it. (*I think it's awful that . . . ; I'm very surprised that such a reputable organisation as yours . . .*)

PARAGRAPH 3
Request action. (*I feel something ought to be done to . . . ; It's time you . . . ; I will take further action if . . . ; I demand that you . . . ; Please replace . . . ; I would be grateful if you could . . .*)

Language reference

1 Modals

Modal verbs are used with other verbs to express the speaker's opinion at the time of speaking. They express the speaker's attitude towards an event, a situation or the person they are speaking to. They say such things as whether the speaker thinks something is possible or certain and whether something is desirable or necessary.

FORM

a) The modal verb comes before the main verb. It never changes its form and does not have an *-s* form for the third person singular:
*She **must** think you're crazy.* (NOT ~~*She musts*~~)

b) The negative is formed by *not* or *n't* after the modal verb:
*Stuart **can't** swim.*

c) Questions are formed by putting the modal verb before the subject:
*Where **should we** sit?*

USE

Most modals have more than one meaning. For example, *may* can be used to say that something is possible (e.g. *It **may** rain.*) as well as to ask someone's permission to do something (e.g. ***May** I use the phone?*).

This table shows some of the usual uses of the modals.

	can	*may*	*might*	*could*	*would*	*will*	*must*	*should*	*ought to*
possibility	•	•	•	•					
ability	•			•					
permission	•	•	•	•					
certainty					•	•	•		
obligation/ advisability							•	•	•
request	•			•	•	•			

Note that:

a) *can't / couldn't* can also be used for certainty in sentences like: *It **can't** / **couldn't** be true.*

b) *need* and *dare* also sometimes behave like modals:
*You **needn't** be so rude.*
*I **daren't** tell her. She'll be furious.*

2 Deduction in the present

Possibility

When we want to say that something is possibly true (but we're not sure) we use *may*, *might* or *could*:
*He **may** / **might** / **could** be out. I don't know. I'm not sure.*
(NOT ~~*He can be out*~~.)

When we want to say something is possibly not true we use *may not / might not:*
*He **may not** / **might not** be out. I don't know.*
(NOT ~~*He cannot / could not be out. I don't know.*~~)

Certainty

When we want to say we feel something is true because that is the logical conclusion based on the known facts, we use *must*:
The light's on. Keith ***must** be at home.*

If we know for certain we use *be*:
Keith'***s** home.*

When we feel certain something is impossible because that is the logical conclusion, we use *can't* (or sometimes *couldn't*):
*She **can't** (**couldn't**) have much money. She's always asking me to lend her some.*
*Keith must be at home. He **can't** (**couldn't**) be out. The light's on.* (NOT ~~*He mustn't be out*~~.)

Unit 17

Staying alive

READING

Before reading

Tricia, Andrew and Christopher Clifford are the first British family to sign up to have their bodies frozen after their death, in a new science called 'cryonics'.

"I believe that in a hundred years time there's a real possibility we could be brought back to life." says Tricia, 42.

"I don't want to say 'that's it' in 30 years time. Our ultimate aim is that when the technology is developed we'll be revived and live again as a family, experiencing a second life and a new age. In a hundred years time space travel could be the norm and I'd like to be around to do that."

Alan Sinclair, who set up the first body-freezing laboratory in Britain, says "The moment you give someone an aspirin you have interfered with the natural course of things. We accept a pill to stop conception and birth. What's wrong with a similar scheme at the other end?"

1 Do you like the idea of being able to come back and live your life sometime in the future? What advantages and disadvantages might there be?

2 Do you agree with Alan Sinclair? Do you think governments and religious bodies should support this new science? Give reasons.

Reading

1 Read the text opposite. Which paragraphs talk about:

a) the arguments in favour of cryonics?
b) the technological problems involved?
c) how many people are being frozen?
d) how the head is preserved?
e) why people want to do it?

2 Read the text again and decide whether the following statements are *True* or *False*, according to the text.

a) Dora Kent's body wasn't frozen.
b) 300 people have been frozen in the United States so far.
c) Not everyone regards cryonics as a serious science.
d) There is proof that reanimation can be done successfully.
e) Even if the brain could be thawed, the memory could be lost.
f) Experiments have been done on a human brain.

Shortly after midnight on Friday, 11 December 1987, in California, 83-year-old Dora Kent stopped breathing. Then, with no qualified doctor present, her head was removed from her body and frozen using liquid nitrogen at a temperature of –320°F.

Yet Mrs Kent is just one of an increasing number of Americans who are being 'suspended' when they die, in the hope that one day medical science will be able to bring them back to life and cure what killed them. Like many people Mrs Kent chose to have only her head frozen – after all, a new body could be attached to her head when the time to thaw came round. "You can throw away the computer but if you lose the disc you've lost everything."

This freezing process – known as cryonics – begs many questions, and provides few of the answers. Yet commercial companies such as *Alcor* in California have a membership which is steadily increasing. Over 300 people in America have signed up, although only 20 people and 6 pets have been suspended to date.The story goes that Walt Disney is suspended somewhere in America, and Michael Jackson has booked his place.

Although some people simply regard this trend as just another attempt in the Americans' search for immortality – the next logical step after the jogging, the aerobics, and the healthy eating – others have described cryonics as "the most important science anyone can be engaged in" and say it gives them a broader perspective on the world. They believe that if everyone knew they were going to be around in the next century then they would try far harder to solve the global problems of pollution and nuclear war. A noble thought, perhaps, but what about overpopulation? Cryonicists have an answer to that, too. By the time the technique is commonplace there will be a new world with innovative housing, either underground or in space colonies, they claim.

For those who are convinced by all these arguments, the next question is how feasible the procedure is, and there is yet no firm scientific evidence to prove that thawing of human organs could take place without too much damage being done. This whole area remains hypothetical and difficult to test, although experiments in which a cat's brain was frozen and thawed suggest that the brain does remain viable. But even if a human brain was successfully thawed nobody knows what would happen to the memory. And what would be the point of having an old head on a young body if it has no memory of a previous life and past experiences? After all, our memory is what makes us uniquely human.

One final question remains. Why would anyone want to come back for a second or even third life-cycle? Emilia Marty in the opera *The Makropoulos Affair* knew the secret of eternal life but she also knew it to be a formula for a world-weary and loveless existence. By the time she was 337 she had had enough. For most of us one lifetime is enough.

(from *The Living Dead*)

3 Agree or disagree with the following statements, giving your own opinions and reasons.

a) If you were reanimated it would be enough just to be a physical copy of who you were before – the memory is not so important.
b) If cryonics became more accepted it would give people 'a broader perspective on nature'.
c) Cryonics is human vanity, and is going against nature.
d) Medicine will never be sufficiently advanced to return people to life and cure the illness they died of.

4 Replace the word in *italics* from the text with a word or expression with the same meaning.

a) ... her head was *removed from* her body. (line 3)
b) ... who are being '*suspended*' when they die. (line 7)
c) ... a new body could be *attached* to her head when the time to *thaw* came around. (lines 10 and 11)
d) ... some people simply regard this *trend* ... (line 20)
e) By the time the technique is *commonplace* ... (line 29)
f) ... with *innovative* housing ... (line 30)
g) For those who are *convinced* ... (line 32)
h) ... how *feasible* the procedure is ... (line 33)

VOCABULARY

Suffixes

The suffixes in the box are used to form adjectives from nouns or verbs. (In some cases the noun must be changed.) Examples:
read – *readable*; *innovate* – *innovative*; *science* – *scientific*; *logic* – *logical*; *fun* – *funny*; *child* – *childish*; *hope* – *hopeful*

-able	-(at)ive	-(at)ic	-al	-y	-ish	-ful

1 Change the words in brackets to an appropriate adjective, using one of the suffixes in the box above.

The man who worked here over the summer seemed nice enough. He was always (1 *rely*) as regards timekeeping and so on and, although rather (2 *mood*) and not very (3 *talk*), he had a very (4 *imagine*) and yet (5 *system*) approach to his work. He was quite popular with the rest of the staff as well, because he was very (6 *attract*), with quite a (7 *baby*) face. He was (8 *artist*) and was very (9 *help*) to people who were in trouble, so we were quite shocked when the police told us he was a (10 *profession*) criminal.

2 [17.1] Listen to the recording and check your answers.

Word stress

1 Put the ten adjectives you used in Exercise 1 above into the columns below, according to how many syllables they have. Mark the stressed syllable in each word. The first one has been done for you.

TWO SYLLABLES	THREE SYLLABLES	FOUR SYLLABLES	FIVE SYLLABLES
		re'liable	

2 Listen to the recording again to see if you were correct.

The pronunciation of the letter *a*

1 In the following words, say how the letter *a* is pronounced. Check your answers in a dictionary.

a) attractive
b) talkative
c) artistic
d) babyish

2 [17.2] The following words come from the text on page 121. Put them in the appropriate column according to the pronunciation of the letter *a*.

back	although	America	harder	place
attempt	answer	thaw	happen	space

/ɑː/	/æ/	/ɔː/	/ə/	/eɪ/

3 [17.3] How is the letter *a* pronounced in the following?

a) what
b) many
c) want

Prepositional phrases

1 Put the nouns in the box in lists under the preposition which they usually go with (e.g. *on purpose*). There may be more than one possibility.

purpose	duty	a bad mood	tape	
charge	writing	common	war	chance
mistake	control	fun	rent	a change

AT	*BY*	*FOR*	*IN*	*OFF*	*ON*	*UNDER*

2 Complete the following sentences using one of the prepositional phrases in Exercise 1.

a) It was a mistake. I promise I didn't do it ________.
b) We always go there. Let's go to the Chinese restaurant ________.
c) I haven't got the record, but I might have the song ________.
d) Could you put that information ________, please, and send it to me by Friday?
e) Make sure you keep that dog ________ or I'll report you to the police.
f) It was such a coincidence. I met my brother totally ________ in London. I didn't even know he was there!

REVISION

Reported speech

The Robertson family wanted to go round the world in a yacht. After their boat was sunk by killer whales, they had to survive in a life raft for 38 days before they were rescued.

1 Rewrite the sentences below as direct speech then put them in the correct speech bubbles.

a) Douglas pointed and said it was a ship.
b) Lyn asked if they would be able to see us.
c) Dougal told everyone to get out the flares.
d) Dougal said he was going to use their last rocket flare.

2 Look at the extracts from students' compositions and work out what the person's exact words were. Correct the reporting errors. Refer to the *Language reference* if necessary.

(a) Mrs Young told them not to come.

(b) I remember Alan said me that he can't swim.

(c) Julian asked to me what will I do tomorrow.

(d) Alison said me if I had just bought a new car. I said I didn't.

(e) Simon told that he is living here for two years.

3 Answer the following questions.

a) What usually happens to verb forms when reported?
b) How are *say* and *tell* different grammatically?
c) What happens to the word order of reported questions?

EXTENSION 1

Reporting verbs

1 You want to tell your partner the messages on your answerphone.

a) [17.4] Listen to the recording and make brief notes as you listen.

b) Report the main messages. You don't need to report every word. Use at least one of the words in the box below in each report. (You can also use *say*, *tell* and *ask*.) Example:
Your boss phoned. She ***wanted to know*** *where you'd been all day and* ***warned*** *you that you were in trouble.*

insist	wonder	promise	warn	advise	apologise
want to know	persuade	invite			

2 Write an extract from a newspaper article, telling the story of when the Robertson family saw the ship but were not rescued. (See the *Revision* section on page 123. Do not use *say*, *tell* and *ask*. Use the verbs from the box in Exercise 1 to make your report interesting.

Begin the report:
Douglas, their 18-year old son, was lazily watching the clouds when he sat up with a start. He pointed excitedly and . . .
End the report:
They stared at the speck on the horizon and felt very lonely.

3 Work in two groups.

GROUP A
Read this newspaper report of Martin and Tanis Jordan's travels in the jungles of South America. Underline the reported speech and work out what Martin, Tanis and the barman actually said. Make notes under the following headings.
- What the barman said
- Almost meeting the hunters
- Survival in the jungle
- Provisions
- Peru

GROUP B
[17.5] Listen to Martin and Tanis Jordan talking about their travels and make notes on what they say. Use reported speech and write under the same headings as Group A.

It was miles from civilisation that Martin and Tanis were warned of the dangerous hunters who would often rob and rape. A barman told them to shoot them and throw them in the Orinoco because it acts as a warning to the other hunters. Luckily, as 44-year-old Martin says, they only saw them once while they were running away from a large snake. On that occasion the hunters threatened them but the Jordans managed to escape. But sometimes the Jordans travelled for months on end and only saw a handful of native South American Indians. In spite of all the provisions they had brought with them from England, everything from food to hammocks, to mosquito nets, they never really learned how to survive in the jungle. The only place they say they felt comfortable was in Peru where the air was so clear and fresh. ■

4 Work with a student from the other group and compare what was actually said in the recording with what the journalist wrote in the article. Use your notes as a guide. Group B students must not look at the article.

EXTENSION 2

Reporting tones of voice

1 Replace the words in italics in the following sentences with one of the words from the box.

whisper	scream	grumble
stammer	exclaim	swear
mutter		

a) 'What a lovely day!' Gillian *cried out suddenly.*
b) 'Th-Thank you,' he *said in a hesitating way.*
c) 'Don't touch that wire!' he *shouted loudly in a panic.*
d) 'I want to tell you something,' he *said very quietly* in my ear.
e) 'You're an idiot!' Simon *said in a quiet, unclear way* so no one else could hear.
f) 'Why don't they pay us a decent wage?' she *complained quietly.*
g) 'Damn it!' he *said, using strong words.*

2 The same words can be used when reporting. Make sentences from these cues choosing one of the verbs in Exercise 1 above.
Example:
Janice / when husband dropped shirt on the floor
Janice swore when her husband dropped his shirt on floor.

a) English people / weather / because rains all the time
b) He / in horror / when saw the knife
c) Jane / something my ear / and winked at me
d) I heard her / a threat / under breath
e) Roy / nervously / when gave man's name to police
f) She / at boss / because made her stay late
g) He / in delight / when saw new car

SPEAKING

Discussion

1 Look at the statements below. Tick the ones you agree with.

a) In times of war all healthy people should be made to fight for their country.
b) Teachers should not have to teach sex education in schools. It is the parents' responsibility.
c) Bloodsports such as fox-hunting or bull-fighting should be made illegal.
d) It should be made legal for women to have a baby for a childless couple, and to accept payment for this.
e) Anyone who has been drinking alcohol and is found to be driving a car should be sent to prison.
f) People who want to sell their blood or one of their kidneys should be allowed to do so.
g) If there is a national health service, people should not be allowed to pay for private healthcare.

2 Rewrite the sentences you disagree with so that they reflect your own opinion.

3 In groups, discuss your opinions. Try to persuade people who do not agree with you to change their minds. (Refer to the *Speaking functions* on page 150 to help you.)

WRITING

Presenting an argument

1 A piece of writing which is intended to put forward both sides of an argument is often organised in the following way.

Section 1: Introduction to the essay
Section 2: Presenting the argument
Section 3: Presenting the counter argument
Section 4: Conclusion

2 This is how you might organise an essay with the title: *Experimenting on animals can never be justified. Discuss.*

Introductory paragraph

a) In my opinion we have no choice but to try drugs out on animals if we are going to make progress in discovering ways of curing illnesses like cancer.

b) There is growing criticism about animal experimentation, both in Britain and other countries. Many companies carry labels saying 'Products not tested on animals' in order to sell their products. Yet there is a lobby of people who insist that it's justifiable and necessary to carry out these experiments in the name of science.

Which of the two versions above do you think is a better opening paragraph? Why?

Presenting the argument

a) In the next section of the essay you should:
- i) List all the arguments *for* (or *against*) the statement made in the title.
- ii) Join your ideas together, using linkers of addition.
- iii) Organise them into a paragraph or paragraphs.

b) Look at the text at the top of the next column.
- i) Underline the linkers of addition and enumeration. (The first one has been done for you.)
- ii) Circle the way the writer introduces an example, and put a box round the way a point is emphasised.

There are three main arguments against animal experimentation. Firstly, and perhaps most importantly, it causes a great deal of suffering, which cannot be justified in the name of research and also makes one ask what right humans have to treat animals in this way. Secondly, drugs tried out on animals are not necessarily successful on humans. In fact there have been many cases where humans have been very ill or died as a result of using such drugs, as in the case of the 'thalidomide babies'. In addition to this it is becoming increasingly clear that many serious illnesses are cured not so much by drugs as by social reform such as better food, hygiene, etc. Finally, many drugs are being produced where others already exist, in the name of profit.

Presenting the counter argument

The third section, the points *against* (or *for*) should be connected to the second section with linkers of contrast. Example:
***However**, it is often argued that this kind of experimentation is necessary if there is to be progress.*

c) Write down as many words or expressions as you can which could replace *However* in linking the third section to the second.

d) Make a note of the counter arguments to animal experimentation, and join these ideas together using linkers of addition.

Conclusion

In the concluding paragraph of a 'for and against' essay sum up the main arguments and give your own opinion. Find examples of the expressions the writer uses in the text below to:
a) summarise. b) give opinions.

In conclusion, I think that animal experimentation is only justified in the case of really serious illnesses for which no cure has been found using other means. However, I feel that every attempt should be made to use pain relieving drugs and humane methods, and it should be illegal to use animals in experiments for any cosmetic goods or any drugs which are not essential to save lives.

3 Write an essay with the title: *Cryonics: a step in the right direction or an offence against nature?* or write on any topic discussed in the *Speaking* section. First make notes on the subject. Then organise your essay efficiently. Divide parts into *for* and *against*. Finally, write a draft and check your writing for logical organisation of ideas and clear division of paragraphs.

Language reference

Reported speech

When we report what someone else has said or thought we use reported (or indirect) speech, using such words as *say, tell, ask, answer, advise, announce, beg, believe, convince, emphasise, exclaim, feel, grumble, insist, mutter, persuade, reply, scream, stammer, state, suggest, suppose, swear, think, urge, want to know, warn, whisper, wonder.*

*He **said** / **answered** / **replied** / **insisted** / **emphasised** that he couldn't swim.*

Which verb we choose depends on our attitude or our interpretation of what the person was saying or thinking.

If the reporting verb is in the past then the verbs which are reported are also usually in the past:

'I want to tell you something,' he said.
*He **said** that he **wanted** to tell me something.*

Verb changes in reported speech

Direct speech	Reported speech
*I **want** to . . .* →	*She felt that he **wanted** to . . .*
*Are you **coming?*** →	*He asked us if we **were coming**.*
*Where **have you been**?* →	*He wanted to know where I **had been**.*
*We**'ll help** you.* →	*They said they **would help** us.*
*I **can't swim**.* →	*He explained that he **couldn't swim**.*
*I **must see** you.* →	*She insisted that she **had to see** me. / She said she **must see** me.*
*He **may be** late.*	*They said he **might be** late.*

Other changes

a) Unless the reporters are talking about themselves or addressing the person they are talking to, the first/second person becomes the third person:
I/you → he/she ; me/you → him/her; we/you → they; us/you → them.

b) *This/these* change to *that/those.*

c) Adverbials of time and place often become less specific:
yesterday → the day before; tomorrow → the next day; next week → the week after or *the following week; today → that day; here → there.*

No changes

a) In spoken language, if the statement is still true at the time of speaking or we report something that someone believes will happen, the tense is often not changed:
*Bill **said he lives** in the Sudan. They **said it's going to rain** tomorrow.*

b) The Past Simple only changes to the Past Perfect when we want to emphasise that one thing happened before another:
*Sarah **said she gave** / **had given** it to me.*

c) The modals *would, should, might, could, ought to* often stay as they are.

Note that:

- the reporting verb *tell* is followed by an indirect object:
She told him . . .
but *say* can only be followed by an object with the word *to*:
She said (that) she . . .
She said to him (that) she . . .
- for reporting imperatives the imperative form is replaced by *to* + base form:
'Pick it up.' (direct)
*He told me **to pick** it up.* (reported)
'Don't touch it!' he urged me. (direct)
*He urged me **not to touch** it.* (reported)
- verbs used for reporting imperatives include: *tell, ask, persuade, urge.*
- verbs used for reporting questions are: *ask, want to know, wonder*

Unit 18

Rites of passage

LISTENING 1

Before listening

1 What do you think the photographs have in common?

2 Match the names of the ceremonies in the box to the photographs. Example: *a – bar mitzvah*

cremation	bar mitzvah	baptism	graduation	Aqiqa

3 In groups, discuss what, if anything, you know about any of these ceremonies. Think about:
- the purpose of the ceremony.
- which societies or religions practise it.
- what happens during the ceremony.

Listening

1 [18.1] Listen to a radio programme about the ceremonies in the photographs.

a) Write down the order they are talked about and check that you matched them with the correct words in the box. Example: *1 – d (Aqiqa)*

b) Find out:
i) What 'rites of passage' ceremonies are.
ii) What the purpose of each ceremony is.

2 In pairs, answer the following questions according to the recording.

a) When is an *Aqiqa* held?
b) What happens after the baby's head is shaved?
c) Why does the meat eaten at the *Aqiqa* feast have to be sweet?
d) In baptism, what does washing with water symbolise?
e) At what age does a Jewish boy become a man?
f) Where are the ashes deposited in a Balinese cremation ceremony? What does this mean?
g) In a US graduation ceremony what is the significance of walking across the stage?
h) Why do graduates wear special gowns?

3 Listen again to check your answers.

4 In groups, talk about any interesting 'rites of passage' ceremonies which you have in your own country, or which you know about.

VOCABULARY

Word formation

1 Complete the following sentences using words that are connected with the verbs *to be born* or *to die*.

a) In the middle of our conversation the line went ________ and I had to phone back.
b) Tony is ________ to show you what he's done. He's so proud of it!
c) My grandfather ________ in 1911 and he's still alive.
d) The roses ________ almost at once because the room was too hot.
e) It's her ________ next week. I must buy her a present.
f) You should have phoned to say you'd be late. Your mother was worried to ________.
g) You have to write your place of ________ here – the town and the country.

2 Complete the following sentences, using the correct form of the words in brackets. You may sometimes need to make the word negative.

a) They spent the day ________ on the bed and reading. (*lie*)
b) I thought the manager had been very ________ so I wrote a letter of complaint. (*help*)
c) Did you hear the ________ about the delay? (*announce*)
d) There was a notice apologising for any ________ suffered by customers during the building work. (*convenient*)
e) My wife didn't like it very much but I found the party very ________. (*enjoy*)
f) He ________ on the beach for an hour, but then got bored and went for a walk. (*lie*)
g) The overnight train was cancelled due to engine ________. (*fail*)
h) The most popular ________ paper in Britain is *The Sun*. (*day*)

Euphemisms and idioms

1 Look at the cartoons below.

a) With subjects that people find embarrassing to talk about, such as illness and getting old, other expressions (euphemisms) are often used. What is really meant in each of the situations above?
b) Do you have any expressions like this in your own language?

2 Look at the expressions in *italics* in the items below and decide which is the key word. Then check the meaning of these expressions in your dictionary and complete the sentences in an appropriate way.

a) He's feeling a bit *off colour* so, . . .
b) If you are at a *loose end,* . . .
c) The washing machine has *had it* now, so . . .
d) He found it difficult to keep a *straight face* when . . .
e) He's hardly a *spring chicken*, so I don't know why . . .
f) I don't like living here but *in the long run* . . .
g) I'm *in two minds* . . .

3 Work in groups and take turns to continue the story below, making sure that you use either an idiomatic expression or a phrasal verb. When you have used one of these expressions the next person continues. Anyone who makes a mistake or uses an expression inappropriately should be challenged by the group and will be out of the game.

It was a hot day and Tim was trying to decide what to do. He was feeling a bit off colour so . . .

REVISION AND EXTENSION

Defining relative clauses

1 [18.2] Listen to Imogen describing the photographs in her album.

a) Write down exactly what each of the photographs refers to. Example:
Picture 1 shows the boat which she went round the Galapagos Islands on last year.

b) In pairs, compare your sentences.

2 Note that relative clauses, like adjectives, describe a noun. Example:
*Picture 1 shows the boat **which she went round the Galapagos Islands on** last year.*

a) Look at the sentences you wrote in Exercise 1 and then complete the following notes.
i) The relative pronouns *who* and ______ are used to describe people, and ______ or ______ are used to describe things.
ii) ______ is used to show possession.
iii) ______ is used to talk about a place.
iv) When speaking, prepositions often come ______ of the sentence.

b) Underline the correct alternative in the following note:
The relative pronoun can be left out when it is the *subject/object* of the clause.

c) Check your answers with Section 1 in the *Language reference.* Then complete the sentences below with a relative pronoun. Leave a space if the relative pronoun can be left out.
i) The book ______ was on the shelf has disappeared.
ii) A wombat is an animal ______ lives in Australia.
iii) The meal ______ we had was awful.
iv) The person ______ house we stayed at was away on holiday.
v) The countryside ______ they go walking is really lovely.

3 Look at the following definitions and choose the correct words from the box. (Some of the words in the box will not be used.)

a swallow	a comedy	an obituary	a will
a corkscrew	a widow	a robin	a team
a jury	a thermometer		

a) Something that you take the corks out of bottles with.
b) Something you use for taking people's temperature.
c) A woman whose husband has died.
d) A bird with a red breast.
e) A play which is funny.
f) A document that says who you want your money to go to after your death.
g) A group of people chosen to judge a competition.

4 Work in teams. Think of some more definitions and ask the other teams to tell you what they describe.

Non-defining relative clauses

1 Look at the following sentences. In which sentence (the one with or without the commas) is there extra information which is not essential to the sentence (i.e. which of the two sentences is non-defining)?

a) *The woman who lives next door is really friendly.*
b) *That woman, who lives next door, is really friendly.*

2 Look at Section 1 in the *Language reference* and then underline the correct alternatives in the following sentences about non-defining relative clauses.

a) The relative pronouns *can be / can't be* left out.
b) Non-defining relative clauses are *more common / less common* in writing than in speaking.
c) *Which* is used for *people / things.*
d) *Who* is used for *people / things.*

3 Look at the following sentences and put commas around the non-defining clauses in each sentence.

a) My new boss who I spoke to after work agreed to give me time off.
b) The French students who had failed badly decided not to resit the exams.
c) My uncle who lives in Manchester is retiring next week.
d) That singer whose record is currently top of the charts is doing a concert next month.
e) Our good friend who nobody had expected to settle down got married last year.

Now decide what the meaning of each sentence would be without the commas, and whether it is a likely situation. For example, in the first sentence a defining clause (i.e. no commas) would suggest that there is more than one new boss, and is therefore unlikely.

Intonation of relative clauses

1 [18.3] Listen to the first four sentences in Exercise 3 above.

a) Write down *D* if they contain defining and *ND* if they contain non-defining clauses. The intonation and pausing will indicate where commas would be in written English (i.e. to indicate whether the clauses are defining or non-defining).
b) Practise reading the same four sentences in both ways.

2 Add the extra information in brackets to these sentences, using a non-defining relative pronoun.

a) Joan asked my husband for a lift to work. (*Her car had broken down*)
b) Phil lost the tennis match. (*He had been ill the previous week*)
c) Our postman had a lovely accent. (*He came from Wales*)
d) Pat was in Scotland when it happened. (*Her grandparents live there*)
e) She showed me her pet snake. (*It frightened me very much*)
f) I left my favourite jacket on the bus. (*I had bought it on holiday*)

LISTENING 2

Before listening

Look at the photograph. Guess what is happening.

Listening

1 [18.4] Listen to a talk about funeral customs in China and answer the following questions.

a) What kind of funeral ceremony do the Chinese prefer?
b) What is the government trying to make them do?

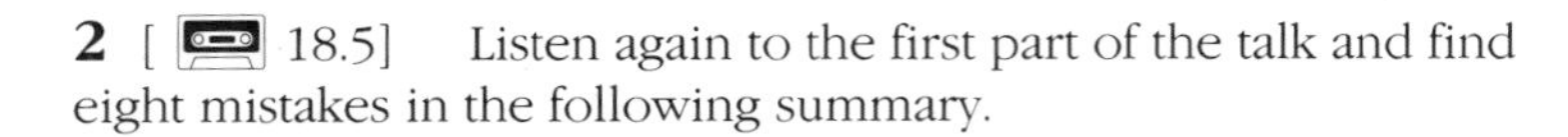

2 [18.5] Listen again to the first part of the talk and find eight mistakes in the following summary.

> The reason for the new policy on burial is that China has 40 per cent of the world's population but only 17 per cent of its arable land so there is no room for graves. National minorities are allowed to bury their dead, but only on agricultural land.
> It is easy to convince the Chinese to accept the new rules as the Chinese are not very superstitious. The cremation rate is now 18 per cent in the cities and 13 per cent in the countryside, where there are no crematoria. Mao Tse Tung, who made the first ruling on cremations 30 year ago, has been cremated himself.

3 [18.6] Try to complete the following summary and then listen to the second part of the talk to check.

> The Chinese believe that the dead can't rest in peace until they ________(1)________. Burial places have to have the right combination of ________(2)________, which can be found ________(3)________ such as ________(4)________. The colour of mourning is ________(5)________ and you will often see exquisite ________(6)________ on the graves.
> Chinese custom means the deceased is also given goods such as ________(7)________ or ________(8)________, which will be needed in the afterlife.

4 In groups, discuss the following points.

a) Why do some cultures bury people's possessions with them?
b) What funeral traditions do you have in your country? (e.g. What clothes do people wear? Is there special food that people eat? Is there a period of mourning?)
c) What is the difference, if any, between modern and traditional ways of mourning?

Word stress

1 [18.7] Listen to the following words from the text being read aloud:
institu*tion* crema*tion*

a) What do you notice about the pronunciation of *io* in the endings?
b) Where is the stressed syllable in these words?
c) Mark the stressed syllable in the words below and write down as many other words as you can ending in *-sion* or *-tion*.
population
regulation
combination
superstition
television

EXTENSION 2

Participle clauses

When the relative pronoun is the subject of the clause we often reduce the relative clause by using the participle form of the verb only, e.g. *the car (which was) parked outside* and *The woman (who was) living* .... The present participle (e.g. *living*) is active and the past participle (e.g. *parked*) is passive.

1 Work in pairs. Student A should look at Picture 1 (on this page) and Student B should look at Picture 2 (on page 149). Describe your picture using participle clauses and find out how many differences there are between your pictures. Example:

A: *In my picture there's a woman wearing a yellow jumper.*
B: *In my picture there's a woman wearing a* **blue** *jumper.*

2 Change the following sentences from relative clauses to participle clauses. Example:
Does he know the girl who lives in the next house?
Does he know the girl living next door?

a) The houses that were designed in Victorian times were quite solid.
b) There's a fast road that leads to the motorway.
c) Trains that leave from platform 5 go to Warsaw only.
d) Is there a man who is called Tim here?
e) I eventually found the letter, which was posted to me yesterday.
f) People who are caught shoplifting will be sent to prison.

Base form of the verb or *-ing*?

1 In the picture on the right which of the verb forms underlined refers to the complete action being observed and which only refers to a part of it?

2 Check with Section 2 in the *Language reference* and then underline the most appropriate form below.

a) When I felt the insect *crawl/crawling* on my arm I flicked it off.
b) I heard the neighbours *quarrel/quarrelling* again last night.
c) I watched the plane *take off/taking off* before I left.
d) I heard them *talk/talking* but didn't interrupt.
e) We watched the workmen *build/building* the house as we were talking. They had just laid the foundations.
f) I saw the cat *catch/catching* the mouse but he was so quick that I couldn't do anything to save it.
g) Did you see the accident *happen/happening*?
h) Can you smell the toast *burning/burn*?

SPEAKING

Designing a monument

Imagine you are asked to design a tomb for a famous person along the lines of the Pyramids or Tutankhamen's tomb in Egypt. In groups, decide who the person will be and then decide on:

a) the kind of monument it should be.
b) the things which should be buried with the person in the tomb to show what their interests were.
c) the kind of things which should be buried to show the times they lived in, so that, in the future, anthropologists would learn something about what made those times special.

Choosing an epitaph

1 Invent an epitaph that would be appropriate for a famous person. Try to make it amusing.

2 Read out your epitaph to the class and try to guess who each epitaph has been written for.

WRITING

Description of a scene

1 Imagine what the ceremony described in the story above was about and what happened when the writer stopped at the scene. On a sheet of paper, write one more sentence to continue the story but do not finish it.

2 Work in small groups. Pass your paper to the next person, who writes another sentence of the story. Go on like this until everyone in the group has written something. The last person should finish the story.

3 Correct 'your' story and then read it out to the rest of the class. Decide on the best story.

Language reference

1 Relative clauses

Relative clauses are like adjectives because they describe a noun. Unlike most adjectives they come after the noun. They can be divided into two types – defining (or 'identifying') clauses and non-defining ('non-identifying') clauses. Defining clauses (without commas) provide essential information about the subject or object without which the sentence makes no sense. Non-defining clauses (with commas) provide extra information not essential to the sentence.

Defining relative clauses

The pronouns *who* or *that* are used for people:
The man ***who/that*** *bought my house is over there.*
That or *which* are used to talk about things:
The car ***that/which*** *won the race is now for sale.*
Whose is used to talk about possession, and replaces *his/her* or *their*:
A widow is a woman ***whose*** *husband has died.*
The relative adverb *where* (or *which* + preposition) is used to talk about places:
It's the place ***where*** *we used to eat /* ***which*** *we used to eat* ***in***.
Relative pronouns can be left out if a relative clause is defining an object:
*The man (****who****) I was talking about is over there.*
*The dress (****that****) she bought was too long.*
*The hotel (****that****) they stayed in was very expensive.*
Prepositions used informally in conversation or writing often come at the end of the sentence:
There is the man (who) I was speaking ***to***.

Non-defining relative clauses

Non-defining relative clauses are less common in spoken English. Intonation and pausing replace the function that commas have in the written form (i.e. separating non-essential information from the main clause).

The pronoun *who* refers to a person in non-defining relative clauses:
My father, ***who*** *lives in Wales, is 83.* (The information between commas is not essential to the sentence.)
Which (not *that*) is used to refer to objects:
The weather, ***which*** *had been very good all year, suddenly turned nasty.*
Whose is used (as in defining clauses) to describe possession:
Jill, ***whose*** *car had broken down, arrived at the dinner party very late.*
Which can also be used to refer to a whole sentence rather than just the subject or the object.
He was very quiet, ***which*** *was unusual for him.*
Non-defining relative pronouns cannot be left out of a sentence.

When, *where* and *why*

When and *where* are used in both defining and non-defining relative clauses and can be left out in defining clauses:
I got there too late, ***when*** *Joan was already asleep.*
*It was the time (****when****) I was working up north.*
That's the restaurant ***where*** *we ate.*
(If *where* is left out the sentence needs a preposition: *That's the restaurant we ate* ***at***.)
Why is only used in defining clauses and can be left out:
*That's the reason (****why****) I left him.*

2 Participle clauses

a) Participle clauses are often used to replace relative clauses when the noun or pronoun (e.g. *the man*) is the subject of its clause (e.g. *the man who is living next door*).
   - Present participle clauses are used to replace defining clauses in the Present Simple or the Present Continuous.
     The man ***who lives*** *next door* becomes *The man* ***living*** *next door.*
   - Past participle clauses are used to replace *which/that* + *be* in passive sentences:
     The car (which is) ***parked*** *outside* becomes ***The car parked*** *outside.*

b) Participle clauses are also used after certain verbs of perception such as *hear, see, watch* to emphasise part of a continuous action:
   I saw him ***running***. */ I saw him* ***opening*** *the door.*
   Compare this with a verb followed by the base form of another verb, which emphasises the whole of the action:
   I saw him ***run***. */ I saw him* ***open*** *the door.*

Unit 19

A mystery!

READING

1 Read the account of a true 'unsolved crime' and answer the following questions.

a) What did D.B. Cooper threaten to do?
b) What do you think he did?
c) Why did he become a folk hero?

THE SKYJACKER who *commandeered* the **Northwest Airlines Boeing 727 flight from Portland, Oregon to Seattle, Washington** was cold, calculating and *ruthless*. He terrified the cabin staff when he opened the canvas bag he was carrying in his lap and showed them a home-made bomb – tightly wrapped sticks of dynamite packed round a *detonator*.

As the jet cruised at 6,000m above the Cascade Mountains, he threatened to blow apart the aircraft, killing himself and the 35 other passengers on board.

But the man who cruelly bargained with the lives of the passengers and the crew *pulled off* something so daring and *lucrative* that he is now fondly remembered as a folk hero, a pirate of the jet age. Songs have been written in his honour, fan clubs have been formed to cherish his memory and thousands of admirers wear T-shirts with his name on. The souvenir industry and the posters in praise of D.B. Cooper would undoubtedly carry his photograph and glowing testimonials about his personal history – if anyone knew what he looked like or who he really was.

But the true identity of the man who *vanished into thin air* with his $200,000 booty still remains a mystery. No one knows who he was, where he came from or where he went.

D.B. Cooper may be a frozen corpse, a broken body lying in a heap of bank notes in an impenetrable forest in the mountains of the northwestern United States. Or he may be sunning himself on a beach in Mexico, and *gloating* over his perfect crime.

2 Read the text again and match the words in *italics* with the definitions below.

a) equipment to make something explode
b) disappeared completely with no trace
c) took control of
d) thinking about something with selfish satisfaction
e) bringing in lots of money
f) cruel
g) achieved

REVISION AND EXTENSION

Deduction in the past

At this stage we don't know exactly what D.B. Cooper did and why he became a folk hero but we can make deductions based on the text.

1 Look at the following sentences and complete the rules below.

D.B. Cooper is remembered as a hero so he ***can't have blown*** *up the plane.*
He had a bomb in his bag, so he ***must have brought*** *it on the plane with him without being seen.*
The cabin crew ***must have been feeling*** *very nervous during the flight because Cooper threatened to blow up the plane.*
Nobody knows if D.B. Cooper is alive or dead. He ***might have escaped*** *to Mexico, he* ***may have died****, or he* ***could have stayed*** *in the mountains.*

a) When we are sure that something in the past is true (because that is the logical conclusion based on the known facts) we use *must* + *have* + ________ or *must* + *have* + ________ + ________.
b) When we are sure something in the past is not true we use ________ + *have* + ________.
c) When we think something in the past is possible we use ________, ________ or ________ *have* + ________.

Check your answers with the *Language reference*.

2 What do you think happened on the plane? In pairs, compare your guesses. Example:
Cooper may have robbed the passengers, because he escaped with $200,000.

Connected speech

1 [19.1] Listen to four dialogues and fill the gaps below by counting the number of words in each sentence. Each contracted word counts as one word (e.g. *can't've* = three words). The first one has been done for you.

a) A: *18* ___ B: ___
b) A: ___ B: ___
c) A: ___ B: ___
d) A: ___ B: ___

What do you notice about the pronunciation of *have* in past modal forms?

2 Listen again and complete the dialogues.

a) A: He ______ car because ______ driven ______ glasses.
B: ______ gone ______.
b) A: ______ run, or ______ popped out ______ shops.
B: It's after five ______ shops.
c) A: Steve ______ window ______ opened.
B: Yes, ______ left ______ night.
d) A: Jane ______ phoned ______ message.
B: ______ decided ______ later.

3 In pairs, practise reading the sentences using the weak and contracted forms in the dialogues.

LISTENING

After the hijack, a journalist wanted to find out information for an article she was writing.

1 [19.2] Listen to the first part of the story and make as many notes as you can under the headings below. Then compare your notes in pairs.

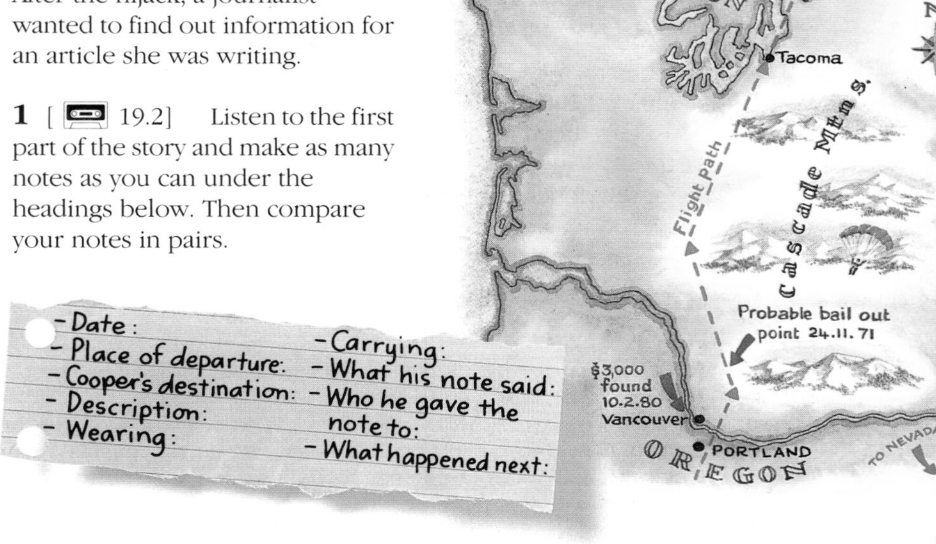

2 [19.3] Listen to the next part of the story. How are the following relevant to the story?

a) FBI agents
b) a trolley of catering equipment
c) a white sack
d) Mexico
e) the black box

3 In groups, discuss the following points, using past modals of deduction.

a) Why do you think Cooper ripped one of the parachutes up?
b) Guess what happened to Cooper in the end.
c) Why do you think he decided to do such a risky thing?

4 There is a lot of vocabulary in the listening text connected with flying and aeroplanes.

a) In groups, write down as much vocabulary as you can remember connected to travelling by plane.
b) Complete the summary below and then, if necessary, listen again to the recording to find the words you couldn't guess. The first letter of a word is given to you (unless the second word is part of a phrasal verb).

After Cooper had c__(1)__ ______ at the airport he waited in the d__(2)__ l______ before b__(3)__ the plane. Shortly after t__(4)__ ______ he summoned one of the c__(5)__ c______ so that he could give his note.
After the plane had t__(6)__ ______ at Seattle and before it t__(7)__ down the r__(8)__, Cooper walked up to the f__(9)__ d______ where the flight c__(10)__ were and gave them orders. Eventually the passengers were allowed to d__(11)__ and go to the t__(12)__ building.

READING AND WRITING

1 Read the last part of the story and decide whether the following statements are *True* or *False* according to the text.

a) Cooper's parachute was found.
b) It is unlikely he could have survived.
c) He must have been going very fast when he landed in the parachute.
d) In the note Cooper said he was hiding somewhere.
e) None of Cooper's money was ever found.
f) It would have been difficult for him to spend the money.
g) It is possible that Cooper could be prosecuted.

The search which followed involved FBI agents, the army, helicopter pilots and frogmen, and yet no trace of Cooper or his parachute was found among the densely wooded, inhospitable mountains in the American West.

His chances of survival seemed pretty slim – he hadn't been wearing protective clothing and in this high altitude the parachute would only have slowed him to a bone-crushing 18 metres per second before he hit the mountain peaks. Only a super-fit expert could have hoped to escape alive and professional experts agreed that Cooper's leap from a speeding jet in a rain storm was suicidal.

Three weeks after the hijack came the first enigmatic clue; a typewritten note, posted in Seattle and signed by D.B. Cooper, was sent to a Los Angeles newspaper.

'I am no modern-day Robin Hood. Unfortunately I have only 14 months to live. The hijacking was the fastest and most profitable way to gain a few last grains of peace of mind.

I don't blame people for hating me for what I've done nor do I blame anybody for wanting me caught or punished – though this can never happen. I knew from the start I would not be caught. I've come and gone on several airline flights since and I'm not holed up in some obscure backwoods town. Neither am I a psychopath. I've never even received a parking ticket.'

This note sparked off a new hunt for Cooper, and as the list of potential suspects dwindled the mountains were combed, looking for clues. There was still no sign of Cooper.

FBI agents were confident that, even if Cooper had survived the jump, he would be nailed as soon as he tried to spend a penny of the ransom money – all US banks and money clearing houses abroad had been alerted to raise the alarm as soon as they began to trickle into circulation.

And as the widely publicised search began to lose steam the first groups of amateur explorers began searching the woods for the ransom treasure.

Not one single dollar of the money turned up, but the mystery hijacker began to gather a cult following from a fascinated public. In 1979 the treasure-hunters started again when an eight-year-old boy playing along the Columbia River near Vancouver found $3,000 of Cooper's cash.

If he is still alive, Cooper can now identify himself. After five years the file is officially closed and he can never be prosecuted for the crime. However, he could face a jail sentence for failing to pay tax on his money!

2 In groups, talk about the following questions.

a) Why do you think Cooper was not wearing protective clothing?
b) Do you think the note was genuine? Give reasons.
c) What do you think he did after sending the note from Seattle?
d) Why do you think the hijack and money gave Cooper 'a last few grains of peace of mind'?
e) Why do you think some of Cooper's money was near the Columbia River?
f) Do you think he is a hero? Give reasons.
g) Do you think it is fair that a file on a crime is officially closed after five years? Give reasons.

3 Imagine that D.B. Cooper was eventually found (alive or dead).

a) In pairs, make up a story about what has happened to Cooper.
b) Write up your story as a short newspaper report. Decide whether it will be a 'serious' or a 'sensational' report. Include information about why he did it and give reasons for what he said in his note (if you think it was genuine).
c) Decide who has the best report.

VOCABULARY

Different sounds

In the recording it says: *The radio **squawked** its message. Squawk* (which is used here metaphorically) means to give a loud sharp cry (like a parrot).

1 Look at the different ways of 'speaking' in the box below and try saying something in the way indicated.

squeak	roar	hiss	murmur	groan	gasp	whisper
scream	grunt					

2 [19.4] Listen to the recording and say which sentence corresponds to each of the verbs in the box.

3 Which of the sounds above can the following make? More than one answer may be possible.

a) a mouse *squeaks*
b) a pig
c) a door
d) traffic
e) a cat
f) a snake
g) a stream
h) the wind
i) a lion

Idiomatic expressions

The words and expressions in *italics* below are used idiomatically in the reading text on page 138. Guess what they mean.

a) His chances of survival seemed pretty *slim* . . . (line 9)
b) I'm not *holed up* . . . (line 39)
c) This note *sparked off* a new hunt . . . (line 43)
d) . . . the mountains were *combed*, . . . (line 46)
e) . . . he would be *nailed* . . . (line 51)
f) . . . the search began to *lose steam* . . . (line 59)

SPEAKING

A press conference

After the hijack, but before the arrival of the ransom note, there was a press conference at which representatives of the world's press were present, as well as the following people:
- the flight attendant, Tina Mucklow.
- the person who checked Cooper in.
- the pilot.
- one of the passengers.
- the head of the FBI operation.

a) Five members of the class should take the roles above. Think about what you are going to say. Say how you felt, and describe the events.

b) The rest of the class will be journalists. Think about what questions you want to ask the five people. Ask about how they felt at the time and what they think happened to Cooper, as well as the details of what actually happened. Decide whether you are writing for a 'quality' or a 'popular' newspaper and ask your questions accordingly. A 'quality' paper will want more factual information whereas the 'popular' press will be interested in information such as personal details about Cooper.

PRACTICE

Before doing the *Practice* activities you might like to refer back to Revision and Extension on page 136.

1 In pairs, take turns to read parts A and B in the exchanges below. Student B should use the cues in brackets to give an appropriate response to Student A. You are required to use present as well as past modals. Example:
A: The milk smells funny. Have you tasted it?
B: (*Yes, must/go off*) *Yes, it must have gone off.*

a) A: Gosh, she looks relaxed and suntanned, doesn't she?
   B: (*must/holiday*)
b) A: Annie used to have straight hair, didn't she?
   B: (*must/perm*)
c) A: Sam's not at work again. I wonder why not.
   B: (*must/ill*)
d) A: Have you any idea where Sue is?
   B: (*might/tennis*)
e) A: Do you know where Ginnie has gone on holiday?
   B: (*can't / abroad / passport here*)
f) A: Their homework is exactly the same, word for word.
   B: (*must/copy*)
g) A: Why on earth has the car stopped?
   B: (*may / run out of / petrol*)
h) A: I wish the dog would stop yapping!
   B: (*must/someone at the door*)

2 Listen to two dialogues and answer the questions.

a) [19.5]
1 Who do you think these people are? Write down the possibilities.
2 What is in the bag?
3 Who do you think Bill is?
4 Who does *her* (in the last reply) refer to?
5 Why does the man say '*Were you followed*'?

b) [19.6]
1 Where did the woman go this morning?
2 What do you think the relationship is between the two people being talked about?
3 What happened last night? (Give reasons for your deductions.)

3 In groups, solve the following puzzles, using *may have*, *can't have* and *must have*. Then share your ideas with the rest of the class.

a) A man lives on the twentieth floor of a block of flats. Every day he gets the lift at the twentieth floor down to the bottom. However, on the way up he always gets out at the fifteenth floor and walks the rest of the way. Why?
b) A woman in a hotel answers the phone in the middle of the night. She says 'Hello' but there is no answer so she puts the phone down and goes back to sleep. The caller is very happy. Who rang?

4 Newspaper headlines are often so short that they are ambiguous. For example: '*Spotted man wanted for questioning*' could mean a man was spotted (i.e. seen) by someone, or it could mean that the man had spots! A lot of British humour derives from this kind of 'play on words'.

a) Work in groups and look at the headlines below. Discuss what some or all of the stories were probably about and also what they *could have been* about. Use your dictionary to check the different meanings of the words underlined.

THREE BATTERED IN FISH SHOP

POLICE FOUND DRUNK IN SHOP WINDOW

BODY IN GARDEN WAS A PLANT, SAYS WIFE

New shock on electricity bills

Meat shortage; Prime Minister attacked

British bird men held by Turkey

b) Share your ideas with the rest of the class.

WRITING

Newspaper article

1 Read the newspaper article based on the '*Spotted man* . . . ' headline in the *Practice* section. Say how the article is organised according to the objectives of each paragraph.

2 Notice the use of participles in the article (*Interviewed*, *Admitting*) at the beginning of two sentences and compare this use with these longer sentences:

i) *When Mr Trimble was interviewed by this paper he told us* . . .
ii) *The 29-year-old bank clerk admitted that* . . .

Using participles helps to make the sentences shorter and often means that more important information can be put first. Rewrite the following sentences to make them shorter and more 'punchy'.

a) When the Prime Minister was asked what he thought about the present economic situation, he said . . .
b) He admitted that unemployment needed to come down and pointed out that . . .
c) Mr Fred Linton, who spent seven years in captivity, spoke to the press today and talked about . . .
d) After the Mayor had welcomed the guests and given his speech . . .

3 Choose one of the newspaper stories from Exercise 4 above and write a short newspaper article based on the model of the '*Spotted man*' article. Organise your information into paragraphs, using participle clauses where possible.

Traffic came to a halt in Oxford Street today and many people came out into the streets to watch as a 'spotted man' was spotted rushing down the street yesterday with two policemen in pursuit.

Interviewed by this paper later Mr James Trimble of West London told us that he was intending to go to a fancy dress party later that day.

Admitting that his strange appearance had probably been responsible for traffic coming to a standstill the 29-year-old bank clerk promised police to go home and change and not to cause a disturbance of the peace again.

Language reference

Modal verbs of deduction

a) *Must have* and *can't/couldn't have* for certainty

We use *must have* + past participle of the verb, or *must have been* + base form + *-ing* (present participle) when we are sure something in the past is true because that is the logical conclusion based on the known facts:

Cooper ***must have brought*** *the bomb without anyone seeing him.* (The speaker feels sure about this.)

Cooper ***must have been planning*** *the hijack for some time.*

We use the negative forms *can't have* or *couldn't have* + past participle or *can't/couldn't have been* + present participle (*-ing*) when we are sure something in the past is *not* true:

Cooper ***can't/couldn't have spent*** *all the money because some of it was found later.*

Cooper ***can't/couldn't have been living*** *normally or someone would have recognised him.*

b) *May have / might have / could have* for possibility

We use *may have / might have* or *could have* + past participle, or *may have / might have been* or *could have been* + present participle when we think something in the past is possible:

Cooper ***might have escaped*** *to Mexico, he* ***may have died*** *or he* ***could have stayed*** *in the mountains.*

Cooper ***may / might / could have been living*** *in Mexico.*

We use the negative forms *may not have / might not have* when we think something possibly did not happen in the past:

Cooper ***may / might not have spent*** *so much money.*

However, the negative *couldn't have* only describes a situation which the speaker is certain didn't happen in the past.

PRONUNCIATION

Have used in all past modal forms (as in the examples above) is usually pronounced with its weak form (/əv/):

He might have (/maɪtəv/) *escaped . . .*

He could have been (/kʊdəvbɪn/) *living . . .*

Revision

READING

Before reading

1 Read the headline and caption. Make guesses about Dorothea's way of life and why she lives alone in the jungle.

2 Write some questions you would like to ask Dorothea. Use *Where?*, *Why?*, *How?*, *Did?*, *Have?*, *Will?* at least once.

JOURNEY INTO THE INTERIOR

For the past 16 years 71-year-old Dorothea Shaw has lived alone in the remote and hostile jungle of Belize with only her animals and a short-wave radio for company.

Dorothea Shaw is 71 years old and nearly blind, and when she chose to isolate herself she went about as far as it is possible to escape 5 humanity.

She lives happily and totally alone – growing her vegetables, tending her trees and looking after her posse of dogs, cats and chickens. Once a month 10 or so an old friend passes by with her provisions and mail. At nights she lies in her hammock in her tiny sleeping hut with the dogs below her, ____(1)____ and one of the hens settled 15 down in a corner of the packed bookshelf and listens for hours to any Spanish, English, German or French broadcasts she can find on her short-wave radio. Sometimes she gets lonely 20 but most of the time the animals and the radio are company enough.

Over the years she has never been embittered in her isolation. She is happy at heart even though her days 25 are filled with the business of survival, from dawn, when she rises and bathes in the river which rushes past her small encampment, to dusk, when she lights her kerosene lamp and settles 30 down with her typewriter or radio. 'You cannot be miserable here if you look and listen,' she says. 'It's impossible. If you use your eyes there are hundreds of different plants and 35 trees and types of birds and insects and creatures. I'm interested in them all. And you can't be miserable or lonely ____(2)____.'

Dorothea was a strange girl, she 40 acknowledges, solitary to the point of reclusion, ____(3)____ and spoke four languages by the time she was a teenager. At 17 she and her parents came home to England. By this time 45 she had come to believe that she was an empath – someone who not only recognised all the less noble and anguished emotions of humanity but also, and sometimes unbearably, felt 50 them as well. When someone was angry, or in pain, she felt that anger, she suffered their actual pain. She was the recipient not only of the more disturbing human emotions, 55 ____(4)____. 'An empath is a receiving telepath who cannot control what he or she receives. I can assure you that to live from childhood to my age now with that particular ability is to live in 60 hell. I know you think I am a completely dotty old woman, ____(5)____ and it is part of the reason why, in the end, I have come to lead my life here.'

65 Recently the very things from which she had fled so far and hidden so well have begun to catch up with her. ____(6)____ by the roar of bulldozers not many miles away. 70 Humanity and the 20th century, once only heard of distantly on the short-wave radio, are now on her doorstep.

A few months ago a jaguar – displaced by the bulldozers to the south 75 of her – came through her place and, in the space of four nights, killed four of her dogs and six cats. 'Fortunately it's the best sort of death they could have. None of them would ever have 80 known a thing about it. I stayed up all night ____(7)____ and banged saucepan lids to try to frighten it away, but of course the silly dogs went and chased after it. It wouldn't attack me – 85 it was frightened and hungry, that was all.'

As the tropical dusk fell, we said goodbye at the edge of her clearing. She came a few paces down the path 90 and took my arm. 'Please don't make me out to be a lonely old embittered lady living a miserable life in the jungle,' she said. 'I'm not really like that.'

(from *The Observer* colour supplement)

Reading

1 Read the magazine article to see if your questions are answered. Then fill in the gaps with the following phrases.

a) who had taught herself to read proficiently by the age of five
b) the cats on the table near the typewriter
c) and went out each time I heard it approaching
d) if you are interested in what is outside you
e) The peace of the jungle has been shattered
f) but I can assure you that what I am telling you is true
g) but those of animals too

2 Work in pairs. Find evidence in the text to confirm or contradict the following statements.

a) Dorothea is unhappy living alone.
b) She has some contact with the outside world.
c) She is insensitive.
d) She has changed a lot since she was a child.
e) Her present life will soon change.
f) She is terrified of wild animals.

3 Look back at the text and guess the meaning in context of the following words in *italics*. Then check your answers in a dictionary.

a) *tending* her trees . . . (line 7)
b) with her *provisions* and mail. (line 11)
c) never been *embittered* in her isolation. (line 23)
d) a completely *dotty* old woman . . . (line 61)
e) the *roar* of bulldozers . . . (line 68)

4 Cross out one of the words or phrases in italics and complete each sentence in any way you like. (Use your imagination where necessary.)

a) I think Dorothea *should have/must have* _______ when she saw the jaguar.
b) She doesn't see *much/many* _______.
c) When Dorothea was young she *must have /can't have* _______.
d) She *insisted/urged* _______.
e) In the jungle you *have to/don't need to* _______.
f) Unfortunately, there are *few/lots of* _______.
g) Do you think she will *stop/regret* _______?
h) In the evenings she *either/neither* _______.

Work with a partner and compare your answers.

VOCABULARY 1

Complete the word puzzle by working out the clues below.

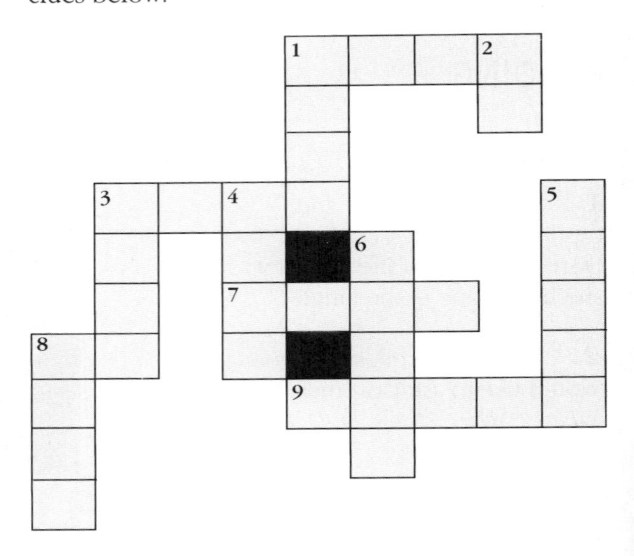

Across

1 Can mean *out of danger* or *a box in which money is locked away.*
3 One way of spelling the word pronounced /mi:t/.
7 Second part of a compound word beginning with *ash.*
8 Suffix to make *nation* an adjective.
9 Suffix to make the noun of *generous.*

Down

1 Can mean *a small mark* or *to notice.*
2 Suffix to make *crowd* an adjective.
3 One way of spelling the word pronounced /meɪl/.
4 Prefix to make *biography* the kind of book which is an account of one's own life.
5 First part of a compound word that describes hair which is not straight. (*-haired*).
6 One way of spelling the word pronounced /weɪst/.
8 Added to *head* or *back* this word makes a compound describing common health problems.

LISTENING

1 You are going to listen to a song called 'I will survive' by Gloria Gaynor.

a) Read the following lines from the opening of the song and complete them in any way you like.

At first I was afraid, I was petrified
Kept thinking I could never _____
But then I spent so many nights
thinking _____
And I grew strong – And I _____

And so you're back, from _____
I just walked in to find _____
I should have changed _____

b) Discuss what you have written with a partner.

c) [📼 20.1] Listen to the first two verses of the song and compare your answers.

2 Talk about the following.

a) Who do you think the person referred to as *'you'* is?
b) Who left who?
c) Why had she (the narrator) been afraid?
d) How has her attitude changed?
e) What caused the change?
f) When she sees *you here* (line 6) what does she regret?

3 Make seven pairs of words from the box according to their rhyme and use them to complete the song. One pair is done for you.

new	alive	goodbye	give	apart	me
door	survive	heart	free	die	you
anymore	live (*verb*)				

Go on now go, walk out the (1) *door*
Just turn around now, cos you're not welcome (2) *anymore*
Weren't you the one who tried to hurt me with ___(3)___
Did you think I'd crumble. Did you think I'd lay down and ___(4)___

Oh no not I
I will ___(5)___
Oh as long as I know how to love
I know I'll stay___(6)___
I've got all my life to___(7)___
I've got all my love to___(8)___
And I'll survive,
I will survive

It took all the strength I had not to fall___(9)___
Kept trying hard to mend the pieces of my broken ___(10)___
And I spent oh so many nights just feeling sorry for myself
I used to cry, but now I hold my head up high

And you see me, somebody ___(11)___
I'm not that chained up little person still in love with ___(12)___
And so you felt like dropping in and just expect me to be ___(13)___
But now I'm saving all my loving for someone who's loving ___(14)___

4 [📼 20.2] Listen to the whole song and correct your answers.

5 Give your opinions on the following statements, referring to the text where possible.

a) The narrator has always been an independent person.
b) She has found a new partner.
c) Her old partner (*'you'*) doesn't respect her.
d) She is still in love with her old partner.

6 Write a letter from the narrator to her old partner or from the old partner to the narrator at the time of the broken heart.

VOCABULARY 2

1 Organise the words in the box into five groups. The words in each group should have a link in meaning.

reception	globetrotter	appoint	clutch
ceremony	overtake	burglary	trip
employer	honeymoon	bail	gears
applicant	arrest	licence	stopover
slow down	explorer	prosecution	recruit

2 Complete the following sentences with a word from the box below. Some words are used more than once.

round	at	up	of	in	on	out	with

a) Listen to this! It's just _______ your street.
b) I'm _______ two minds whether to go or not.
c) I hear that Gillie has split _______ _______ her boyfriend.
d) In our arguments we keep going _______ _______ circles.
e) Graham's not very keen _______ football.
f) I'm sorry. I've run _______ _______ petrol.
g) Can I come over? I'm _______ a loose end.
h) Are you interested _______ movies?
i) I promise you the job will get better _______ the long run.
j) You must be fed _______ _______ waiting. Let's go home.
k) Honestly, I didn't spill the coffee _______ purpose. It was an accident.
l) Have you got rid _______ that cold yet?

3 Brainstorming.

a) Work on your own. In five minutes make a list of as many idiomatic expressions and phrasal verbs as you can which have been practised in this book but which do not appear in the vocabulary exercises in this unit. Make sure you know what they mean. You may look through the book to help you.
b) Work in groups. Check each other's lists. If the words have not been practised in this book or the person who wrote them doesn't know what they mean cross them out.
c) As a group, agree on the ten most useful expressions and phrasal verbs.

GRAMMAR

Verb forms

1 Look at the pictures which show some of the things that have happened to Pauline and guess:

a) what Pauline's problem is.
b) what her life must be like.

2 Choose the most appropriate verbs in the text below.

Pauline Shaw hardly looks the most shocking woman in Britain and yet, at 46, this grandmother-of-one frequently (1 *gives / is giving*) off at least ten times the normal amount of static. In the past six years she (2 *blows / has blown / blew*) twelve television sets, six tumble driers, four food processors, two videos, plus irons, toasters and countless light bulbs. On one occasion the television refused to (3 *switching off / be switched off*) while she was near it; on another the washing machine continued (4 *to work / work*) even after the door (5 *opened / was opened*).

All these things she has to (6 *get mended / mend*) and she reckons her problem has cost her at least £8,000 – "that's the most shocking thing" – and most manufacturers won't let her (7 *have / to have*) a guarantee when she buys things.

The problems began when Pauline (8 *would work / was working*) in a dry cleaners and she made all the machines (9 *go / to go*) wrong. After that, two inch long sparks (10 *were flying / would fly*) from her fingers and her hair would stand on end. Even (11 *to embrace / embracing*) her husband was a problem. One terrible day she boiled the tropical fish: her mere presence (12 *used to cause / had caused*) the tank thermostat (13 *overheat / to overheat / overheating*) the water. On top of that her house (14 *is struck / has struck / has been struck*) by lightning three times.

Pauline decided (15 *to give up / giving up*) her job. "If anything (16 *would go / went / would have gone*) wrong, I knew I (17 *would blame / would be blamed*)." To avoid trouble she even stopped (18 *shaking / to shake*) hands with people. "Nowadays, if I (19 *won't shower / wouldn't shower / don't shower*) and wash my hair for twenty minutes at least three times a day, the static builds up. One of these days if I'm not careful I (20 *start / 'll start*) a fire!"

3 Use a future form to complete the sentences. If you think of more than one answer, explain the difference in context and the attitude of the speaker.

a) Don't worry. I ________ (*help*) you. I'm an expert in 'electrical sensitivity'.
b) I understand from your letter that you ________ (*set up*) a company in Tokyo.
c) Before the end of the week we ________ (*run*) out of money.
d) The sea voyage across the Atlantic ________ (*last*) six days.
e) This time tomorrow, we ________ (*play*) golf.

4 Work in pairs. Student A is a journalist and Student B is Pauline Shaw's husband. Roleplay the interview.

STUDENT A
You are a journalist. You want to interview Pauline Shaw's husband to find out about what it's like living with an 'electrical sensitive' person. Write down some of the questions you will ask him. Example:
Does she get bad headaches? Can she see ghosts?

STUDENT B
You are Pauline Shaw's husband. Make notes on some of the problems for both you and Pauline, for example:
– what life is like during a thunderstorm.
– the people who want to interview her.

WRITING

Correcting errors

Correct the errors in the following sentences.

a) Katherine wrote to her a lovely letter.
b) My motorbike I bought last year is fantastic.
c) Do you know anyone having seen her?
d) However he's not very good at his job, he earns a lot of the money.
e) What an awful weather!
f) Elizabeth dropped suddenly the cup.
g) We're looking for place you told us about.
h) Planes leave from Heathrow are always late.
i) Let's meet next week in case we get the time.
j) My wife who works in New York is having a baby.

INTEGRATED SKILLS

1 Look at the picture below. It illustrates a poem called *Happiness* by the American, Raymond Carver. Try to guess the reason for the title.

2 Try to complete the poem, using the picture to help you.

3 [20.3] Listen to the poem and check your guesses.

HAPPINESS

So early it's still almost .... (1) .... out.
I'm near the window with .... (2) ....,
and the usual early morning stuff
that passes for thought.
5 When I see the .... (3) .... and his friend
walking up the road
to deliver the .... (4) ....
They wear caps and .... (5) ....,
and one boy has a .... (6) .... over his shoulder.
10 They are so .... (7) ....
they aren't saying anything, these boys.
I think if they could, they would take
each other's arm.
It's early in the morning,
15 and they are doing this thing together.
They come on, slowly.
The ...... (8) ...... is taking on light,
though the ...... (9) ...... still hangs pale over the ...... (10) ......
Such beauty that for a minute
20 death and ambition, even love,
doesn't enter into this.
Happiness. It comes on
unexpectedly. And goes beyond, really,
any early morning talk about it.

4 Listen to the poem again and answer the following questions.

a) *the usual early morning stuff that passes for thought.* (lines 3–4). What kind of 'early morning stuff' do you think about? Practical things, like what you're going to wear or general things like whether you're happy or sad?
b) *I think if they could, they would take each other's arm.* (lines 12–13) Why do you think they can't take each other's arm?
c) i) Which phrase refers to delivering papers in line 15?
ii) The poet says *Such beauty* (line 19). What is beautiful in the scene before him?
iii) Which word refers to happiness in lines 22 and 24?
d) Which is more important to the poet: his normal morning thoughts or the scene before him? Give reasons for your answers.

5 Work in groups. Read the newspaper extract and discuss the questions below.

> A stable extrovert has the best of all possible worlds - a lot of positive happiness and very little misery. As obvious extroverts, Mel Brooks and Peter Ustinov would be capable of great happiness. Extroverts would be seen as sociable, impulsive, lively and excitable. Stable Chris Evert would be unlikely to feel extremes of unhappiness, whereas apparently neurotic John McEnroe could be expected to suffer high levels of misery. People like Richard Nixon are seen as introverts: reserved, thoughtful, controlled and serious.
>
> (from *The Sunday Correspondent*)

a) Do you agree that people who are mainly extroverts are more likely to be happy than people who are mainly introverts? Give reasons.
b) Is the poet in Exercise 3 an introvert? Do you think he is generally 'happy'? Give evidence from the text.
c) In your experience how important to happiness are 'external' factors (e.g. relationships, money) or is personality more important?

6 Choose either of the following writing tasks.

a) Write a short poem about a happy experience you have had.
b) Write the poet's diary entry for the day he wrote the poem *'Happiness'*. Include what happened before and after he saw the boys.

Additional material

Unit 8 (page 54)

Space quiz

1. 1969.
2. Every 365.25 days.
3. True.
4. Because he was the first person to be rocketed into space and to circle the Earth.
5. 385,000 km; 240,000 miles.
6. Russian (Valentina Vladimirovna Tereskova).
7. No, it is no colder than the Antarctic in winter.
8. Jupiter (143,000 km / 89,400 miles in diameter).
9. Carbon dioxide.
10. It is moving through space. (Every point on the Equator is moving at about 1,600 km/h or 1,000 mph as the Earth spins on its own axis.)

Unit 18 (page 133)

STUDENT B

Unit 13 (page 93)

STUDENT B

PREPARATIONS FOR WEDDING RECEPTION

To be done | *send out invitations ✓*
hire photographer
order drink
buy presents
set up marquee ✓
prepare food
arrange flowers
book chauffeur
borrow glasses ✓

Unit 15 (page 107)

STUDENT A

Pronunciation

CONSONANTS

symbol	key word
/ p /	**p**en
/ b /	**b**ack
/ t /	**t**ea
/ d /	**d**ay
/ k /	**k**ey
/ g /	**g**et
/ tʃ /	**ch**eer
/ dʒ /	**j**ump
/ f /	**f**at
/ v /	**v**iew
/ θ /	**th**ing
/ ð /	**th**en
/ s /	**s**oon
/ z /	**z**ero
/ ʃ /	fi**sh**
/ ʒ /	plea**s**ure
/ h /	**h**ot
/ m /	co**m**e
/ n /	su**n**
/ ŋ /	su**ng**
/ l /	**l**ed
/ r /	**r**ed
/ j /	**y**et
/ w /	**w**et

VOWELS

symbol	key word
/ iː /	sh**ee**p
/ ɪ /	sh**i**p
/ e /	b**e**d
/ æ /	b**a**d
/ ɑː /	c**a**lm
/ ɒ /	p**o**t
/ ɔː /	s**aw**
/ ʊ /	p**u**t
/ uː /	b**oo**t
/ ʌ /	c**u**t
/ ɜː /	b**ir**d
/ ə /	Chin**a**

DIPHTHONGS

symbol	key word
/ eɪ /	m**a**k**e**
/ əʊ /	n**o**t**e**
/ aɪ /	b**i**t**e**
/ aʊ /	n**ow**
/ ɔɪ /	b**oy**
/ ɪə /	h**ere**
/ eə /	th**ere**
/ ʊə /	t**our**

Linking expressions

Function	Linking parts of a sentence together (conjunctions)	Linking ideas across sentences (adverbs)
TIME	after, before, when, while, as, as soon as, until, since, once	*finally, then, later, eventually*, afterwards, in the end, meanwhile, beforehand, firstly, secondly, lastly
ADDITION	and*, as well as, in addition to, besides	*also*, as well*, too*, in addition, furthermore, moreover, besides, what's more
CONTRAST	but*, although, while, whereas, even though/if, in spite of/despite	nevertheless, nonetheless, however, yet, even so, still, on the other hand
REASON AND RESULT	because, as, since, so*	*therefore, consequently,* because of this, as a result, that's why
PURPOSE	(in order) to, so that	
CONDITION	if, unless, in case, so/as long as, provided that	

Position of conjunctions in a sentence
Conjunctions marked with an asterisk (*) usually only go in the middle of a sentence. All the other conjunctions can go either in the middle or at the beginning of a sentence.

Position of adverbs in a sentence
Adverbs marked with an asterisk (*) go at the end of a sentence. All the other adverbs usually go at the beginning of a sentence. However, those in *italics* can also be placed after the subject (e.g. *Tom **finally** understood).*

Speaking functions

1 Agreeing
I couldn't agree more.
(I agree) absolutely.
Exactly!
So do I. / Neither do I.
I take your point.
That sounds a good idea.
Yes, to a certain extent . . .

2 Disagreeing with someone's opinion
Do you (really) think so?
Well, actually I'm not sure I agree with that.
I disagree entirely.
Rubbish!
You must be joking.
I can't accept that.
You've missed the point completely.
I'm afraid I think that's complete rubbish.
On the contrary, I . . .
I agree up to a point but . . .

3 Giving your point of view
First of all I'd like to explain . . .
It's quite clear to me that . . .
As far as I'm concerned . . .
I think it's absolutely awful that . . .
I think . . . is right because . . .
That's why I feel that . . .

4 Interrupting
Just a minute!
Excuse me, can I butt in here?
Sorry to interrupt but . . .
Before you go on, let me . . .

5 Asking for and giving clarification
Could you explain what you mean by . . . ?
I'm afraid I don't quite understand.
What I mean is . . .
All I'm trying to say is . . .
The point I want to make is . . .

6 Transition
Mind you . . .
Now . . .
To turn to . . .
To move on to . . .
As far as . . . is concerned . . .
Having said that . . .

7 Adding things
As well as that . . .
Not only that but also . . .
Besides . . .
What's more . . .

8 Suggestions
What/Where would you like to . . . ?
What do you suggest we . . . ?
Is there anything in particular . . . ?
What/How about . . . ?
Why don't you/we . . . ?
Would(n't) you like to / be interested in . . . ?
If I could make a suggestion, we could . . .
Might I suggest that we . . . ?
Let's . . .
We could . . .
Why don't we . . . instead?
Wouldn't you rather . . . ?
Wouldn't it be better . . . ?

9 Personal interests
Do you take much interest in . . . ?
Are you into . . . ?
Well, I'm not particularly keen on . . .
I'm rather more interested in . . .

10 Plans
I was wondering if you had anything in mind for . . .
Have you got anything fixed up for . . . ?
Well, as a matter of fact, I've arranged to . . .

Tapescripts

Unit 1

RECORDING 1

Extract 1

INTERVIEWER: So where would you say your motivation comes from?

GLORIA ESTEFAN: Well, I'm just a survivor, Number 1 and I'm a very positive person. I always try to look at the good side of things and try to, no matter what experience it is, only concentrate on how it could be better or what I can do about it. If there's a problem I'll try to look for a solution and if there's no solutions then I just won't worry.

I: Would you say you were a sort of determined stubborn character?

GE: Very – very determined and I think if you ask my family they'd say stubborn in some ways, when it's something that I really want – when I have a goal that I really want to achieve – I just focus on that one thing and whatever I have to do to get there I'll do it.

Extract 2

I: Do you think that's something you've inherited from your father, because he sounds like quite a tenacious character?

GE: And my mother also. My mother's also very determined. When she came to the States she had a PhD in Education from Cuba and they ripped up all the papers so she had to start over, and she went to the university again and got all her credits again and eventually became a teacher and then got her Master's so, I come – and my grandmother also, she learned to drive when she was seventy-three in the States because my grandfather had passed on and she didn't want to be a burden on anyone, so she also was a very, very strong-willed woman and I guess it comes in my genes.

I: You've mentioned Emilio quite a lot. Would you say he's the biggest influence in your life?

GE: Definitely. My grandmother and Emilio are my two biggest influences. She was a feisty old woman that really did everything that she always ever set her mind to do and she gave me a wonderful example of a strong woman, and in her lifetime – I mean she was, she wanted to be a lawyer when she was nine years old and she never achieved her goal because she had to work for a living in Cuba, but at that time for a woman to want to do that was unbelievable, and her whole life was an example to me. And Emilio who's really helped me blossom as a person. There's never been any jealousy between us. On the contrary he's always tried to do and bring out the most in me and encourage me and motivate me to do more and more things. I'm a couch potato, I really never would have – I'm a very contented human being so I never would have thought well let me go this step further and he really has brought me into the person that I am today.

Extract 3

I: Let's talk about your music. How does it work for you?

GE: I'm not the kind of person that like Diane Warren who worked with me on this album, who gets up every morning at 8 o'clock and all she does is write, cos that's her life. I need some kind of inspiration or an idea or some emotional cue to spur me into writing. My song writing has always been – music to me has always been a very emotional thing. I've been singing since I was three and to me it was my catharsis. I was very introverted and shy so when I wanted to cry or laugh I would just go in my room and sing, and to me that was my way of pouring out my emotions, rather than you know the standard way, and my song writing has turned also into that – into sometimes ideas that I have, cos I love to observe things in life and just sometimes very deep feelings and sometimes the more difficult the feelings the easier it is to write.

Unit 2

RECORDING 1

Extract 1: Lucy

My mum's always playing opera music in the car with the windows right down and it's really embarrassing. And I just hope I never see anyone I know when we're driving through town. And she plays it really loud. My father will never cook anything but sausages and spaghetti – which gets a bit boring as Mum's never around because she goes to work.

Extract 2: Ben

Thomas is the worst, I reckon. He plays his music too loud and he always gets his own way when he's watching the television. If I want to watch something he always wants to watch another and then – cos he's bigger than me – he always seems to get his own way.

Thomas keeps coming into my bedroom and taking things or borrowing things – so if I've been out somewhere I'll come home and sort of find the lid off something or something's out of place and I know that somebody's been, like Thomas, has been fiddling with things or trying to work out how to use it or switching on the television and lying on the bed and all sorts. He's got his own television in his room but he often watches mine for some funny reason. And now he alway keeps coming in there without asking and that really annoys me.

RECORDING 3

1 A: Well personally, I'm strongly against mixed education.
B: Are you? Why?
A: If you ask me, kids learn much better in single sex schools. They can concentrate better.
B: Do you think so? I'm not sure I agree with that, actually.

2 A: I think that old people's homes should be closed down! People should look after their old relatives themselves.
B: So do I! I couldn't agree more.

3 A: As far as I'm concerned the police should be allowed to carry guns. It's too dangerous, otherwise.
B: Absolute rubbish! I disagree entirely.

Unit 3

RECORDING 2

GILLIE: Oh, come on! It kills the imagination. I mean, you've heard that term 'couch potato' – I mean, people sit there like vegetables.

MARK: I disagree. No, I disagree. What – and anyway, what would they be doing if they weren't doing that?

G: Well, probably sport, activities, I don't know, but it's . . . so addictive. I mean, they just sit there day after day, night after night and I'm sure it causes bad behaviour in kids.

M: I disag. . . how can – there's no – there are no statistics to prove that, absolutely none. On the contrary, it's a – it's a way of bringing people together. I mean, it's the only time families get together – they sit round – round the TV. It's a friendly, relaxing presence.

G: How can you say families get together?

M: But they do. It brings people together, it keeps kids off the street, keeps them entertained.

G: They don't communicate.

M: Course they do. Family life goes on around it. It's just there – it's just on. This is a very middle-class view, you know, I mean it's like saying that – it's like saying that people would be reading if, if they weren't watching television. Well there's no evidence to show that.

G: I'm sure they would. And instead of reading, instead of playing musical instruments what are they doing? They're sitting in front of this television with no intellectual quality at all – a load of rubbish.

M: That's – that's nonsense – that's absolute nonsense. I mean, there are lots of good programmes on. All you've got to do is be selective. All you've got to do is act with a little bit of judgment. I mean there's a lot of educational stuff broadcast – there's a lot of stuff that you can learn from and if you watch sensibly you can learn a great deal.

G: Yes I know, but I mean, I've got kids – kids like adverts, kids like soap operas, that's what kids want. I mean, you sit them in front of an 'educational programme', they're not interested.

M: Yes, but if you will use the television as a babysitter then that's what's gonna happen, isn't it? I mean, you're just using it to occupy your kids. And all right, while we're on the subject – soap operas. Now soap operas, a lot of people say they're rubbish – no doubt you would – but they can be very educational. They – they bring up all kinds of social issues – they teach people about AIDS, they're engaged in the world.

G: That's complete rubbish, Mark. Come on! People spending three to five hours every evening watching television – watching things like soap operas, you cannot tell me that they're going to intellectually advance themselves.

M: Now that's not fair. We're not saying that they're watching three to five hours of soap operas.

G: And one thing that really upsets me is the amount of violence on television and I'm sure that has an effect on children. I'm sure it makes kids aggressive.

M: How? How?
G: Well, I'm sure they watch – you know, they watch things like Kung Fu or whatever, and I'm sure they just try and imitate it – even cartoons. Tom and Jerry – very violent. The whole cartoon's based on violence.
M: Are you saying that kids are in some way manipulated by this violence? They have the capacity to distinguish between fact and fiction. They know that Ninja turtles are fictional – they know that Tom and Jerry cartoons are fictional.
G: Well, they're out there playing it!
M: Well, what's the matter with playing it? That's fine.
G: But they're actually copying this, they're actually imitating this aggression, as if aggression equals good.
M: Oh come on, come on! Kids are far too sophisticated to assume that – to be affected by the violence in some way. They know it's storybook stuff.
G: Well I'm not convinced. I mean I don't think they do distinguish that much between fact and fiction – see, what they see on television to them is real, you know. I mean fairies are real to children, Father Christmas is real, you know . . .
M: So you're saying that when they watch – they think Ninja turtles are real? Come on, come on, what sort of kids have you got? I mean . . .
G: No, I really believe they do!

Ninja turtles and *Tom and Jerry:* TV cartoon characters

RECORDING 5

Police have not yet found the nineteen-year old university student who vanished while she was on her way to a lecture last week.

Police all over the country have been looking for her for three days but haven't had any useful information yet which would help them with their inquiries. They have already interviewed the girl's boyfriend and her flatmate. If anyone has any information, please phone 081-223765.

Unit 5

RECORDING 1

WOMAN 1: Well the body's rough. I'd quite like to hear it running really to give a proper opinion on it.
INTERVIEWER: Confirmation about what I suspected: my car was on its last legs, but 'Gwenda's', named after a famous 1920s woman racing driver, is flourishing after humble beginnings last May. But why did three women join up for this venture?
WOMAN 1: Well, we needed a job for a start. We just all got together and opened it up after a lot of planning.
WOMAN 2: There aren't any opportunities for women in the motor trade, very, very few if, if at all and so if we wanted to get work, the only way we were going to get work was to create our own jobs. And the second thing is that we wanted to offer women a service they felt they could trust.
I: Unusual in the first place I suppose to train as a motor mechanic if you're a woman?
W1: Yes, but I think that a lot of women would like to do things that are outside of the traditional things that women normally do and if you've got a car or a motorbike I think it's obvious, that women as well as men would want to maintain them, and that's how we've got started really, from having our own vehicles and wanting to maintain them, which was the most sensible thing to do really.
W2: And that's what we actually hope: to encourage women as well, like if women come here and we talk to them about their cars then maybe they can look at that part another time. We run a class for women as well on maintaining their cars and things.
I: Looking at you now in the middle of your garage and looking at all the grease and oil on your hands, that's often the reason given for women not wanting to . . .
W1: I know but this, this amazing sort of invention: it's called soap and water, and that's what we do at the end of the day, we wash just like everybody else . . .
W2: Heavy lifting – that's the usual one: they don't think we can lift.
W3: The toilet facilities.
W1: Yes, toilet facilities, lack of toilet facilities: we haven't got any facilities for women to go to the toilet.
W2: I think that women actually do a lot of lifting, carrying shopping bags from town, on and off buses, they do a lot of lifting around the house and they do a lot of dirty work, cleaning, and cleaning ovens and washing floors and things like that. I don't think that it's only mechanics that get their hands dirty. I think women often in the housework get their hands dirty as well.
I: And this partnership feels that women can have an uncomfortable time in garages run by men.
W3: When a woman, a woman car owner driver takes a car to the garage, then she can be told anything basically. I mean I'm not saying that she's necessarily going to be ripped off, but you know she's going to be given a load of explanation that she doesn't understand, doesn't feel able to ask questions as to why and, you know what, what exactly is happening, and I think like that something that's important is that we want to, customers to feel they can ask us so that, you know, we'll offer them an explanation that they can understand.
I: Well, what do the women customers think? Do they feel happy with motor mechanics of their own gender? Linda Emery was waiting for work to be completed on her car.
LINDA: It's a woman's garage and I think the advantage of that is that instead of bringing your car in and not knowing what's happening to it, they actually show you what they're doing, why they're doing it and how it connects up with other things in the car, so it takes away the fright when you lift up the bonnet and don't know what the hell's happening. I think that's, that's the advantage of bringing it here.
I: So you've had more explained to you at this garage than other garages?
L: Oh, absolutely. A hundred per cent more. I mean unless you ask specific questions at another garage which you wouldn't know how to ask anyway because you don't know anything about your car, they won't explain anything to you. All you usually get is the bill and recommendations about further work that needs to be done, and you can't make a judgment on whether it's, it's an emergency thing that needs to be done or whether it can be left for a bit. You have to trust them, and basically I don't trust garages, I think, except for Gwenda's, and I know there that I am getting good advice about my car.

RECORDING 7

A: Where are you from?
B: I'm from Turkey.
A: Have you been to Edinburgh before?
B: No, this is my first visit to Scotland.
A: How long did it take?
B: Only six hours from London.
A: And where are you staying?
B: In a hotel near the centre.
A: How far away is it?
B: Not far.
A: What's it like?
B: It's quiet, but my room's a little small.
A: How did you come?
B: I got a taxi.
A: Whose drink is that?
B: I don't know. It's not mine. I haven't had anything to drink yet.
A: Would you like me to get you something?
B: Yes, please. A lemonade.
A: How do you like it?
B: With a little ice, please.
A: How many languages do you speak?
B: Turkish of course, as well as Arabic and a little English.

RECORDING 8

GILLIAN: Yes, before he went to the interview he was in quite a state really. Wondering what questions they'd ask him. Luckily he's very confident and he's got excellent shorthand. Anyway, when he got there they couldn't believe a man would want to do a job like that. But they didn't ask him anything that people normally ask at interviews. Things like his experience or his reasons for applying. Just kept on about why a man should apply for a job like that. Anyway, to everyone's surprise, he got the job. Of course when he started work the other secretaries wanted to know how he'd learned to type. But none of them offered to help him. It was sink or swim all the way.

Unit 6

RECORDING 3

Every Sunday they made me go to church which I didn't mind too much, I enjoyed it. I had my friends at church. We sang in the choir but I was made to go. Weekends they allowed me to go into town on my own. Sometimes they let me go to a football match when I was twelve or thirteen. They allowed me to go to the youth club. They didn't let me go to the Roman Catholic youth club; I had to go to the right youth club which was our church youth club. They let me go to anything that was sporty that I wanted to do. I was allowed to join the tennis club, I could go swimming on my own. All those things they let me do without anybody with me. I was allowed to go on my own as long as they knew who I was with and when I was coming back.

Unit 7

RECORDING 1

A: Well, I was coming up, coming up a slight hill on the London Road, the slight hill where it approaches the bend and I was doing about, doing about forty, close to the limit and – what time was it? – it must have been, yes, it must have been four, four-twenty I should say. I'd just done a drop and I don't like to get there too early cos they're usually having their tea, so yeah, about four, four-twentyish, and anyway as I say I was coming up this hill and suddenly in my mirror I saw a BMW, and it was flying along and I had to slow down at that point because of the bend. I pushed it down a gear, slowed down for the bend, then suddenly this BMW was overtaking me, flying past. She can't possibly have seen where she was going because I was right on the bend by that point. On top of that it was just beginning to get dark, visibility was pretty poor – I think it was about to start raining as well. Anyway, so I'm coming round the bend, and then suddenly she flies past me, and after that there were just cars everywhere. I think there were a few people around as well but I can't really tell you much more than that.

B: Look, officer, it's what I've already told you. There I was about half-past four, driving perfectly safely. You know I've got a BMW. I had plenty time. I checked my mirrors, I checked the road, everything was fine. What happened? I started to overtake. No problems. Loads of time to get back in when that stupid lorry driver accelerated. It's typical! That is exactly what happens. He looked in his mirrors and what did he see? A woman driver in a BMW. This is a bit of fun, he thought, and went faster. If it hadn't been for him, everything would have been all right. I would really like to talk to him. Honestly, you have got to disqualify him. He's not safe to be on the roads. I drive thousands of miles every year and I have never had an accident.

C: It was just after four o'clock and I had just picked the kids up from school. I was in a bit of a hurry because I had to get home to make dinner and I was driving along behind this taxi, driven by a lady driver and she had slowed down to turn left and indicated that she was going to turn left, so I had a look at the road ahead and it was perfectly clear and I indicated to overtake her and I was speeding up to pass her, going just over forty miles an hour, when suddenly the other car driven by the woman came screaming round the corner. I tried to avoid hitting her but couldn't, and we touched each other and span into the nearside lane forcing the taxi off the road. There was a chap standing at the side of the road hitchhiking and I'm sure he must have seen everything that happened.

D: Well, what happened was this basically. I was travelling along at about forty miles an hour, the speed limit as far as I know on that road is, is forty. I was travelling along up to collect my fare, further along the Birmingham road, and it was a fairly clear day, I think the time as far as I remember was about ten-past four, in fact I'm sure it was because I had a fare, my fare was due to be picked up at four fifteen and no problems, you know, going along enjoying the drive, when, when suddenly out of the blue this, this bloke behind, I think, I think in a Volvo Estate, I dunno, some sort of estate car, overtakes me. We were almost at the bend. He clearly wasn't concentrating on what he was doing. He was, I think he was turning round at, looking at or talking to his kids. He overtakes and at the same time round the bend this woman comes like a bat out of hell, I think in a BMW or something like that, and the next thing I know I'm in the ditch. It was absolutely incredible. It all happened so fast. Now, you know, there was a turning off to the left. I wasn't, I wasn't indicating left, you, there was no reason why I should be and really it was, you know, it was not my fault. These two maniacs were clearly at fault and you know I'm pretty fed up about the whole thing to be quite honest. I drive a taxi for a living and you know it my car is now going to be off the road for, for weeks if not months and, you know, as I say, I'm fed up and you know you don't expect this sort of thing on, you know, a nice September afternoon, so there you are. That's my story.

Unit 8

RECORDING 2

DES: Looking fifty years into the future is very difficult indeed, of course. It'll all be very different from the way it is now. I suspect because of overpopulation of the planet we'll be living in places which we're not living now. I think we'll be living under the sea, I think we'll be living on satellites circling the Earth, maybe on other planets even.

In terms of transport I reckon, well I hope anyway, that we'll have found a form of transport that won't pollute the environment quite as much as our present system. And I think, because of pollution and over-population, we'll be eating very different kinds of food from what we're eating today, probably highly-processed food and artificial food.

In terms of work, well I think people will be doing very different kinds of jobs from what they're doing today. I think it's not really possible to predict very much about what work will be like fifty years from now. I'd like to think, though, that people will be working *with* each other rather than *against* each other, in some kind of spirit of cooperation, I suppose.

RECORDING 3

Extract A: Whitley Strieber and the aliens

And then there was the story of the home-loving dad who claims he was experimented on by space alien scientists. Human guinea pig Whitley Strieber suffered a terrifying brain examination as he lay naked inside the hi-tech surgery of the cruel creatures' spacecraft. The writer of the best-selling book *Communion* wants the world to know extraterrestrials are out there – and they're not friendly. Whitley trembled as he recalled his operation millions of light years from Earth.

'I had been captured like a wild animal and it was like they were trying to tame me,' said the 41-year-old.

'They performed bizarre medical procedures on me and inserted a thin metal instrument into my brain.'

Whitley claims his outer space tormentors were like giant-sized insects.

They were bald, with massive liquid-like narrow eyes, yellowish-brown skin that felt like leather, two holes for nostrils and big, floppy lips.

And to prove his chilling time with the beings actually took place, he agreed to take a lie detector test – and passed!

The New Yorker says his nightmare began when an army of aliens invaded his home while he slept.

He was unable to move as they ripped off his pyjamas, poked him with their wrinkled hands, then took him off to their waiting craft.

'They told me they were going to do an operation . . .'

Extract B: Mrs Coe and the aliens

Yes, the aliens have landed. Only yesterday they stepped out of their spaceship and went for a walk in the park. Three giant creatures twelve feet tall with tiny heads and wearing bluish metallic clothing chose Russia for a very close encounter with the human race.

Their arrival was heralded by a shining ball seen hovering over the local park by residents of Voronezh, 300 miles east of Moscow.

The UFO landed and out came the giants, similar to humans and accompanied by a small robot.

'They went for a walk near their spaceship,' said the official news agency Tass. 'Then they disappeared back inside. Onlookers were overwhelmed with fear that lasted several days.'

The landing was authenticated by staff from the Voronezh Geophysical Laboratory, whose head, Genrikh Silanov, is a respected scientist.

Tass said: 'Scientists confirmed that a UFO landed in the park. They also identified the landing site and found traces of aliens.'

Silanov's men discovered a twenty-yard depression in the park with four deep dents and two pieces of rock.

'They looked like deep red sandstone. But analysis showed that the substance cannot be found on Earth.'

There was speculation among UFO experts in Britain that the aliens could have been those that Mrs Coe said landed in her garden last month in a spacecraft which was surrounded by bubbles of light. According to her amazing story the aliens grabbed her by the arms and lifted her up a beam of light into a kind of room. Mrs Coe was reported as saying she felt they meant her no harm and that when she came round she was in her garden and not hurt in any way.

Unit 9

RECORDING 2

MICHAEL PALIN: There was a passenger ferry to Alexandria, there was a ferry down from Suez to Jeddah, after that it was just going on cargo vessels and the most primitive one we went on was the one across the Persian Gulf which had you know no radar, no radio and we were just . . . we slept on top of the cargo – (this was the dhow) – under clear skies, this was the dhow.

INTERVIEWER: You say when you were on that that the crew became like your family, in a way, because you were with them for what six, seven days?

MP: Yes, I mean there were eighteen of them and just lived all together on the deck, and I mean you washed together and went to the loo – well, you didn't go to the loo together – but I mean (it's public) everything was open and *al fresco* and so you just you know . . . we needed them desperately, we didn't know – it was unfamiliar territory for us, we had to make friends . . . and they repaid our friendship so well and they were so kind and they looked after us and bring us little mugs of that very sweet tea the Indians like.

I: Did you, did you ever sort of feel a point where you thought, oh just for a bit of privacy, that would be so nice?

MP: Yeah, I did, especially on the dhow when I felt ill. You just, when you're ill you don't want, you feel horrible, you feel grotty, you just don't want anyone to see you really, you just want to go away and hide and you couldn't there because it was so hot and there was, you know, you were in amongst all these people, and just you know you weren't fit, you feel you just wanted to be home and in bed. It was as simple as that really.

MP: There was a parrot I met in Hong Kong, in the place called the bird market which is a long, long street full of all manner of birds because in China and Hong Kong it's just this incredible bustle and everything is used, every sort of bit of wildlife is used, and they either use them for song birds or fighting birds – it's very popular – they get birds over from nationalist China who are really stroppy . . . (*noise*) birds like that, and they fight and gamble – people gamble on bird fights (*Oh!*), and there's also, you know the decorative birds, birds, there's birds you can eat and there were these wonderful parrots and one of them bore a distinct resemblance to the parrot which John Cleese used to smack on the counter in the pet shop sketch, and I was talking to it – and this other big bird – I think it was a cockatoo with a great big beak was sort of nibbling gently at my trouser leg, so I called the camera over and said 'Oh, look at this' – it's rather nice – you know, St Francis of Assisi scene – Michael surrounded by admiring birds, and it wasn't admiring at all – it wanted to tear my leg off and it actually had to be prised off my trousers with half the trousers in its beak.

I: You've not always travelled in style. I mean you were quite happy to go and sort of use the local rooms and you balanced it with some of the style, five star hotels and stuff. On reflection would you prefer local rooms or the big hotels?

MP: I much prefer local rooms. On reflection, that's the important thing. Looking back, they are terrific. You learn much more from those places and you make friends, but you also take risks, you can have really unpleasant, at the time they can be very unpleasant and very uncomfortable, whereas the five star hotels that we stayed in or four star, three star, were always havens of, so delighted to get to them because they were usually after a hard period of travelling and you could get your things washed and laundered, you could have a hot bath, you know you could have a drink of wine or something like that – I missed my wine, going round the world – and so you know I would say at the time those big hotels served their purpose and kept me going, but the experiences all lie in the sort of the smaller places because they are typical of the country.

RECORDING 6

HELEN: The train gets in about six in the morning from Tokyo. I'll try and meet you at the station but I'm teaching that morning.

MRS BAKER: I'm sure it'll be all right, dear.

H: The trouble is it's very difficult for me to get the time off. They're very short-staffed at the moment.

MRS B: It's all right. It's not as though we're not used to travelling.

H: Anyway, you just get a taxi to the golf course which is where the main road ends. Unfortunately, the taxis don't like going any further because the roads get pretty rough after that.

MRS B: It's all right, we'll walk if it's not too far.

H: Yes. Just leave your suitcases at the clubhouse – the man at reception speaks English – and we'll pick them up later. Anyway, don't worry. I'll send you a map showing you the way from there.

MRS B: No problem. It'll be an adventure.

H: Now when you get there, the lady next door will bring you in a real Japanese breakfast: rice, miso soup . . .

MRS B: Miso soup? What's that?

H: It's made from soya beans. It's nice when you get used to it. What else? Mm, grilled fish, pickles, raw eggs beaten with soya sauce and seaweed . . .

MRS B: Raw eggs and seaweed!

H: Yeah, it's great. I really like it now. I know you like exotic foods. Anyway, listen. I'll finish work at about twelve, so have a rest, maybe take a little walk and get a good look at that incredible view we have of the mountain. It's fantastic at this time of the year. It'll be quite safe to walk around. I'll be back about half past.

MRS B: It sounds wonderful. We're really looking forward to it. Unfortunately Dad's legs aren't what they used to be but he can still get about. How long are you going to let us stay?

H: Don't ask such questions. As long as you like of course. I'll drop you a line to explain all this . . .

Unit 10

RECORDING 1

'I've been dying for a smoke for the last half-hour,' she said, lighting a cigarette.

'Then why didn't you smoke?'

She made a furtive gesture back towards the house, then grinned mischievously.

'Oh I see,' I said.

'Guess what? I've got a boyfriend now.'

'Oh yes?'

'Except I'm wondering what to do. I haven't made up my mind yet.'

'Quite understandable.'

'You see, he's making plans to go to America. He wants me to go with him as soon as I finish studying.'

'I see. And you want to go to America?'

'If we go, we're going to hitch-hike.' Kikuko waved a thumb in front of my face. 'People say it's dangerous but I've done it in Osaka and it's fine.'

'I see. So what is it you're unsure about?'

We were following a narrow path that wound through the shrubs and finished by the old well. As we walked, Kikuko persisted in taking unnecessarily theatrical puffs on her cigarette.

'Well, I've got lots of friends now in Osaka. I like it there. I'm not sure I want to leave them all behind just yet. And Suichi – I like him, but I'm not sure I want to spend so much time with him. Do you understand?'

'Oh perfectly.'

She grinned again, then skipped on ahead of me until she had reached the well. 'Do you remember,' she said, as I came walking up to her, 'how you used to say this well was haunted?'

'Yes, I remember.'

We both peered over the side.

'Mother always told me it was the old woman from the vegetable store you'd seen that night,' she said. 'But I never believed her and never came out here alone.'

'Mother used to tell me that, too. She even told me once the old woman had confessed to being the ghost. Apparently she'd been taking a short cut through our garden. I imagine she had some trouble clambering over those walls.'

Kikuko gave a giggle. She then turned her back to the well, casting her gaze about the garden.

'Mother never really blamed you, you know,' she said in a new voice. I remained silent. 'She always used to say to me how it was their fault, hers and Father's, for not bringing you up correctly. She used to tell me how much more careful they'd been with me, and that's why I was so good.' She looked up and the mischievous grin had returned to her face. 'Poor Mother,' she said.

'Yes. Poor Mother.'

'Are you going back to California?'

'I don't know. I'll have to see.'

'What's happened to – to her? To Vicki?'

'That's all finished with,' I said. 'There's nothing much left for me now in California.'

'Do you think I ought to go there?'

'Why not? I don't know. You'll probably like it.' I glanced towards the house. 'Perhaps we'd better go in soon. Father might need a hand with the supper.'

But my sister was once again peering down into the well. 'I can't see any ghosts,' she said. Her voice echoed a little.

'Is Father very upset about his firm collapsing?'

'Don't know. You never can tell with Father.' Then suddenly she straightened up and turned to me. 'Did he tell you about old Watanabe? What he did?'

'I heard he committed suicide.'

'Well, that wasn't all. He took his whole family with him. His wife and his two little girls.'

'Oh yes?'

'Those two beautiful little girls. He turned on the gas while they were all asleep. Then he cut his stomach with a meat knife.'

'Yes, Father was just telling me how Watanabe was a man of principle.'

'Sick.' My sister turned back to the well.

'Careful. You'll fall right in.'

'I can't see any ghost,' she said. 'You were lying to me all that time.'

'But I never said it lived down the well.'

'Where is it, then?'

We both looked around at the trees and the shrubs. The light in the garden had grown very dim. Eventually I pointed to a small clearing some ten yards away.

'Just there I saw it. Just there.'

We stared at the spot.

'What did it look like?'

'I couldn't see very well. It was dark.'
'But you must have seen something.'
'It was an old woman. She was just standing there, watching me.'
We kept staring at the spot as if mesmerized.
'She was wearing a white kimono.' I said. 'Some of her hair had come undone. It was blowing about a little.'
Kikuko pushed her elbow against my arm. 'Oh be quiet. You're trying to frighten me all over again.' She trod on the remains of her cigarette, then for a brief moment stood regarding it with a perplexed expression. She kicked some pine needles over it, then once more displayed her grin. 'Lets's see if supper's ready,' she said.

RECORDING 2

Supper was waiting in a dimly lit room next to the kitchen. The only source of light was a big lantern that hung over the table, casting the rest of the room into shadow. We bowed to each other before starting the meal.
There was little conversation. When I made some polite comment about the food, Kikuko giggled a little. Her earlier nervousness seemed to have returned to her. My father did not speak for several minutes. Finally he said:
'It must feel strange for you, being back in Japan.'
'Yes, it is a little strange.'
'Already, perhaps, you regret leaving America.'
'A little. Not so much. I didn't leave behind much. Just some empty rooms.'
'I see.'
I glanced across the table. My father's face looked stony and forbidding in the half-light. We ate on in silence.
Then my eye caught something at the back of the room. At first I continued eating, then my hands became still. The others noticed and looked at me. I went on gazing into the darkness past my father's shoulder.
'Who is that? In that photograph there?'
'Which photograph?' My father turned slightly, trying to follow my gaze.
'The lowest one. The old woman in the white kimono.'
My father put down his chopsticks. He looked first at the photograph, then at me.
'Your mother.' His voice had become very hard. 'Can't you recognize your own mother?'
'My mother. You see, it's dark. I can't see it very well.'
No one spoke for a few seconds then Kikuko rose to her feet. She took the photograph down from the wall, came back to the table and gave it to me.
'She looks a lot older,' I said.
'It was taken shortly before her death,' said my father.
'It was the dark. I couldn't see very well.'
I looked up and noticed my father holding out a hand. I gave him the photograph. He looked at it intently, then held it towards Kikuko. Obediently, my sister rose to her feet once more and returned the picture to the wall.
There was a large pot left unopened at the centre of the table. When Kikuko had seated herself again, my father reached forward and lifted the lid. A cloud of steam rose up and curled towards the lantern. He pushed the pot a little towards me.
'You must be hungry,' he said. One side of his face had fallen into shadow.
'Thank you.' I reached forward with my chopsticks. The steam was almost scalding. 'What is it?'
'Fish.'
'It smells very good.'
In amidst soup were strips of fish that had curled almost into balls. I picked one out and brought it to my bowl.
'Help yourself. There's plenty.'
'Thank you.' I took a little more, then pushed the pot towards my father. I watched him take several pieces to his bowl. Then we both watched as Kikuko served herself.
My father bowed slightly. 'You must be hungry,' he said again. He took some fish to his mouth and started to eat. Then I too chose a piece and put it in my mouth. It felt soft, quite fleshy against my tongue.
'Very good,' I said. 'What is it?'
'Just fish.'
'It's very good.'
The three of us ate on in silence. Several minutes went by.
'Some more?'
'Is there enough?'
'There's plenty for all of us.' My father lifted the lid and once more steam rose up. We all reached forward and helped ourselves.
'Here,' I said to my father, 'you have this last piece.'
'Thank you.'

Unit 11

RECORDING 1

Extract 1

I honestly think that a journalist's job is solely to be a professional recorder of the news, to convey to his audience, or to his readership or her audience, her readership, as clear and accurate and unambiguous a factual account of what's happening as possible. I think it's up to the people themselves when getting as accurate a picture of what's going on as possible, to decide their own point of view and then effect the changes, or effect the help – humanitarian help in the case of a famine, because they have been stirred by an accurate picture of what's going on. I don't think it's a journalist's job to do it. I think it's a propagandist's job to attempt to present things to gain a particular effect one way or another and I don't think journalists should be propagandists.

Extract 2

It's a very difficult question for a reporter. Clearly in a famine situation, and particularly in the 84–85 famine, I felt that it was my job not just to tell the facts of how many people were dead and dying and how many were likely to die and why, but also convey a feeling of what it was like to be there and in a sense, going even further in that particular instance, almost what I felt – what it felt like for me to be there. Now I think in a famine that that was a fair thing to do and a fair journalistic thing to do. It is not the sort of thing that I would do for instance covering a domestic political story where there are, you know, conflicting political views about something. But I think the famine was such a gut human disaster that I felt it needed that extra dimension to try and provide as many extra dimensions to enable people to feel what it was like to be there.

Extract 3

It is terribly difficult because it's very difficult to be an impartial observer – it's very difficult because in those circumstances, because we were European, because you know, we had transport and all that sort of thing people thought we were doctors. And we had people sort of bringing their dying children and saying you know, 'save my child' and under those sort of circumstances one feels as a journalist totally useless – as a recorder of events, what is more useless than that? You know how I wish I'd been better at physics and chemistry and biology and become a doctor or a nurse or an Oxfam worker or something or even somebody who could dig a hole, you know as part of a water project. You do feel, as a journalist, totally useless and it's it has a great impact on you, it's a very depressing feeling merely to be a recorder of events under those circumstances.

Extract 4

Yes. I mean that's bound to be the case, isn't it? I mean, to put it at its crudest if you've got a million people dying of starvation it is a quote great news story, isn't it? On the other hand it has been my experience as a newspaper reporter, radio reporter, television reporter, that while we may feel very sensitive to the crass actions of journalists in disasters it's quite often the victims of disasters and the relatives of the victims of disasters don't have the sort of sensitivity that we impute to them, particularly people who starving whose interest is merely to focus attention on their particular plight so that help may come. They don't, I think, commonly feel exploited – in that particular way – in a way that we as outside observers might think that this misery was merely being exploited for titillation purposes.

Extract 5

Oh, I think they're absolutely vital, aren't they? I mean there are some extraordinarily talented writers who are able to conjure with their words both the facts and the emotions of occasions like that but nothing can substitute for pictures, and nothing particularly can substitute for moving pictures of what is happening when it is an event. When it comes to famine and war and things of that nature, visual events, I mean the pictures just are so so essential, pictures complemented by words and information and that extra – I mean nothing, nothing can compare with that, not even the most talented writer could possibly have had the same impact with a newspaper story in 1984–85 – or even a radio story – as the television pictures which took you there.

RECORDING 4

CLARE SHORT: I say that anything I do in my public life is a matter for scrutiny by the media. If I'm a hypocrite in any way between my private and public life that is to be exposed, if I'm corrupt in any way that is to be exposed. But I am a human being and it isn't right – I mean I have a normal human life. I have a bath. I mean if the *News of the World* put a picture of me in the bath on the front page it would be true that I do have baths but it wouldn't be right. And it's both for me as me the human being but also for all of us. I think this behaviour drags our press and our culture into the gutter. It's nothing to do with investigative reporting, it's just to do with linking everyone up with something to do with sexuality that's supposed to be ideally a little bit hidden and deviant. And I think if we had a privacy law we'd actually help our press out of the gutter and we'd get very much better investigative journalism.

Unit 12

RECORDING 5

SAM: It was all my fault. I mean I wish now I hadn't been so thoughtless. I used to come back late from work, after stopping off at the pub on the way home, and didn't lift a finger to help when I did get home. I should've helped more with the baby and things like that.

FRIEND: Well yes, the main thing if you ask me is that you shouldn't have taken on that new job in London when she'd just had a baby.

RECORDING 7

SAM: I know, I mean I'd just collapse in front of the TV and show no interest in what her day had been like or anything, I was so tired. And then there were a lot of other things like we never went out on our own anywhere because I couldn't be bothered to get a babysitter – we never did anything together. I used to shout at the dog, which she loved, all the time. I never really said anything nice to her – I don't blame her for leaving me, actually.

Unit 13

RECORDING 1

INTERVIEWER: Satish, you've married your wife twice. Can you explain why?

SATISH: Yes, well my wife, Barbrȯ, she's Swedish and my parents, they are Gujarati Indian, and so we had two ceremonies, one to satisfy my parents' wishes and one to satisfy Barbrȯ and her parents' wishes.

INTERVIEWER: How did the Swedish ceremony compare with the Hindu wedding?

SATISH: Different . . . very different, in for example length. The Hindu wedding took seven hours, the Swedish wedding in church took maybe thirty-five, forty minutes at the most. The number of people, the Hindu wedding had up towards 800 people, the ritual was very different. In the Swedish wedding I knew what the priest was saying. I knew . . . I could understand every single word. Everybody was listening to what was being said by the priest. In the Hindu wedding . . . I was being asked to do things by the priest. The priest would give me the instructions in a language, Swedish or English, that I could understand but the Hindu priest said everything in Sanskrit, which is a very old language, which . . . of which I have no knowledge whatsoever, so that was also very different. We weren't the centre of attention in the Hindu wedding: families were meeting; we were seeing people that we hadn't seen for a long time; perhaps future marriages were being arranged because everybody was dressed very smart, we were all of the same caste there, so there were all these aspects. And one other thing is actually timing; the Swedish wedding I had to get there to the church at five o'clock. I had to get out by a certain time, the car was going to pick us up at a certain time, etcetera. It was very time-oriented. The Hindu wedding, it started when it got round to starting and it carried on and it finished when it finished. There was no time element to it.

INTERVIEWER: Of the two weddings, which was the real one for you?

SATISH: I have to say that they were both because I belong to two cultures, both a Gujarati one and a Western one for want of a word and they were equally important; the first one when I married, when I got married in Sweden was something very important for my wife and her family and my Western friends; and the wedding that I had in Britain with my family there was very, very important to them.

INTERVIEWER: Do your parents share that view?

SATISH: Well, for my parents, the real wedding came when we were in Britain, when we had the Hindu ceremony. Because, for example, when people have a registered marriage according to different . . . according to their Government, their country, this is just seen as a bureaucratic OK, whereas the Hindu wedding is the one that counts for them.

RECORDING 2

INTERVIEWER: Your marriage wasn't an arranged marriage. Is that because you don't believe in arranged marriages?

SATISH: My marriage wasn't an arranged marriage because it wasn't something for me. My, my older brother for example, three years older than myself, his marriage was arranged. He and his wife are very happy, all of . . . , nearly all of my friends who have got married have had arranged marriages and they're also happy in theirs. I'm also happy in mine. It just means that it wasn't for me.

INTERVIEWER: How can you defend arranged marriages to somebody who doesn't believe in them?

SATISH: Arranged marriages have a faith for tomorrow. What I mean by that is, it's not only your feelings, what you feel that day. In a relationship you meet somebody and it's very exciting and you learn to know each other and you do many things together and it's great fun, it's a wonderful feeling. But when those original, when these fresh feelings begin to die off and you still have each other you know a lot of each other. Is that a time then to throw away the relationship and start all over again or can you build upon it? An arranged marriage is where, although you don't have this love for each other you know that your love will develop, you will learn to love, but in fact in an arranged marriage people, the people who meet they know each other before their marriage, or at least their parents know each other's background, your family backgrounds are known, you've been checked out, they know that you are not a bad person or a drunk or somebody who's aggressive or etcetera, and therefore in some ways you know each other before you've met. I'd like to make an important point here I think: an arranged marriage is exactly that: it's arranged, it's not necessarily forced. Some people, of course, I think a minority have had a forced marriage where this person has been told that you're going to marry this other person but in the case of my friends, and my brother who had an arranged marriage, they had met one or two or three people. My brother had met one or two or three girls before he found somebody who he thought 'I am compatible with this person' and therefore it was arranged. My brother didn't have the choice of getting married or not but he did have the choice of marrying the person that he wanted to marry.

INTERVIEWER: How do the courtship rituals differ?

SATISH: Well, an arranged marriage courtship is under supervision. People, the couple that were engaged would, could go out together but it would be for a few hours and they'd get back before a certain time, no overnight stays or anything of that kind. It's done so that the, both the bride and groom keep their respect of each other up until the wedding ceremony, the idea being that both will be pure up until the wedding ceremony.

Unit 14

RECORDING 1

The instrument of warning and argument is the index finger, in one of its three operational positions. Thrust up, rigid and unmoving, beneath your conversational partner's nose, it signals caution – watch out *attention*, all is not what it seems. Held just below face level and shaken rapidly from side to side like an agitated metronome, it indicates that the other person is woefully ill-informed and totally wrong in what he has just said.

Describing a sudden departure needs two hands: the left, fingers held straight, moves upwards from waist level to smack into the palm of the right hand moving downwards.

At the end of the conversation, there is the promise to stay in touch. The middle three fingers are folded into the palm and the hand is held up to an ear, with the extended thumb and little finger imitating the shape of a telephone. Finally, there is a parting handshake. Packages, dogs and bicycles are gathered up until the whole process starts all over again fifty yards down the street. It's hardly surprising that aerobics never became popular in Provence. People get quite enough physical exercise in the course of a ten-minute chat.

RECORDING 3

SOPHIE: What's it like being a deb? Well, it's actually quite fun in a lot of ways simply because the kinds of things we do are the sort of things I like doing anyway. I love going to parties and meeting people and having fun and not really having to have a serious conversation about anything, but there are certain drawbacks as well. It is actually quite boring when you're not in the mood having to go out and be polite and friendly, particularly when there's the older generation around. A lot of these parties you get the parents and all of their friends there and sometimes I'm just not in the mood for being a sweet, friendly person, but I think it's probably quite good in, in a way to have to train yourself to be sociable even if you don't feel like it.

The plans I've got for when I actually come out are mainly just carry on having fun actually. I hope that I'll be able to keep up with a lot of the people who I've become friendly with. In fact, I think I might be going on holiday with a couple of people I've met.

My engagements for the coming week, I've actually got quite a full agenda. I'm going to a cocktail party tomorrow night and I'm going along with a friend of mine who's also doing the deb season so it's quite nice, I can go along with her. And then after that I'm going for dinner with some people I've met who've invited me round for dinner. I suppose some people would say we are privileged, because we spend a lot of money and that, that is true. It is entirely a frivolous activity but I I tend not to worry about that really because it's always been like that. Some people have money and some people don't and those that do might as well spend it.

RECORDING 4

CASSITA: Usually, the Brazilians are lively, outgoing and friendly, easy to get along with, and they, although they have many problems, as you see in documentaries on TV coming from abroad, the poor people in the *favellas*, they seem happy. It's also important to focus the mixed races we have in Brazil especially São Paulo, there are many Japanese already Brazilians and many Italians who are Brazilians, the mixed races makes the race very beautiful.

RIEKO: Well, a typical Japanese person is rather shy and they are not so accustomed to mixing to other people but they are very interested in the news of other countries and so many people like reading newspapers, and magazines and seeing movies of other countries.

WOLFMANN: For the foreigner a German seems to be very serious at first glance but I think a German isn't only serious, a German can be very, very funny. He's normally a bit silent. He's not as loud as many people think and he doesn't want to play an important role in the world as many people think as well but he keeps on old traditions.

MARIA CRISTINA: Really, if you are asking me what an Italian is I wouldn't know how to answer because we are coming from such a different kind of countries all together and Italy was made just only last century. And we are completely different for culture, background, even physically different and so I will answer what I feel is an Italian. . . . We are very friendly, . . . every foreigner is welcome but we are very, very jealous about what is going to happen or what is our house, our home. Home is completely apart from the public and this is another point that goes together with the fact that we likes clothes because we like how we appear and I would say that for an Italian would be much more important how you look likes than how you are and for this reason I thinks that even if you are wearing cheap clothes, clothes or dress you are very careful about matching the colour or things like that because for an Italian it is very important to be smart, to appear.

YNGVE: What we all have in common in Sweden is that we love the countryside very much and we are used to having a lot of space around us and therefore many Swedes they go to the north of Sweden fishing and climbing the mountains, doing things like that where they can be completely alone for weeks and they just enjoy the silence around them.

Unit 15

RECORDING 1

INTERVIEWER: Have you always been a large and a strong man? Where did you get the idea for instance to go in for competitions of this kind?

JAMIE REEVES: I've always been very big, my parents were very big, so to do this much in the sport I've chosen, obviously like any other sport you've got to be genetically gifted so with big bones, etc. I were very gifted at this and also at 6'4 I'm a very big man anyway. 'The Strongest Man in the World' is a competition which is devised to test all aspects of strength, so to actually become the strongest man in the world you need all-round body strength. It's a kind of a question as who's the decathlete of strength, so I try and train all of my body not just certain parts.

I: Give me an idea then of your training regime day to day. What kind of training you have to do.

JR: What I try and do is split me training up into three days: on day one I would do legs and abdominals, on day two I would do chest, shoulders and triceps, and day three I would do back, biceps and front deltoid.

I: What about sports, apart from just training? Do you play any sports to make it more interesting?

JR: I like all kinds of sport but obviously I'm restricted with me training. I like to add a little swimming into me training, maybe do some running, some sprinting, maybe a little football, any kinds of sport. I don't mind. I like all kinds of sport.

I: Let's have a look at diet . . . what you eat in a normal day . . . it would be very different from a person's normal meal, so take me through your normal diet.

JR: My normal diet really consists of just more or less the same food as an average person but I try and eat every three hours and consume about three times as many calories per day, so most of my food is just good all-round balanced food but maybe three times as much.

I: So give me an idea of your breakfast, your lunch and your dinner, what you actually eat.

JR: It differs from day to day what I actually eat but what I try and do is consume thirty grammes of protein every three hours, good balanced carbohydrates, greens for irons and minerals and water for body clearance but in general just more or less the same as a normal person but three times as much.

I: So, an average breakfast for instance would contain what?

JR: Maybe six eggs, some bacon, some fruit, some fresh fruit, maybe a little toast or a little bran.

I: What about your main meal of the day? What quantities? What would that contain about?

JR: The main meal of the day for me would be taken around 8 o'clock at night after training. I maybe train around 7 then eat around 8 which would be maybe fish, potatoes, rice, chicken, greens and some milk.

I: Any special foods though you need particularly, say, when you go in for a competition? Any foods for strength?

JR: Not really. Strength's built throughout the year. The food I would maybe eat before competitions or lifting would be such as spaghetti or pasta, rice for carbohydrates for a lot of energy on that day, so I know that physically I was performing to the best of me ability. Use a lot of nutritional products, from a lot of protein drinks and high supplements . . . a lot of high protein drinks, things like that.

I: Any foods you have to avoid?

JR: Not really. Before a competition I always cut out a lot of fats for maybe two months, I avoid fats with eating so much to keep me cholesterol level down and keep pretty healthy. So, yeah, fats I avoid more or less.

I: You're a pretty good athlete as well though

JR: I've run the 100 metres, I've been timed in under 12 seconds, at around 11.97, and I've also been timed on the 400 at 56.

I: What about tips for ordinary people and the training they can do to be fit?

JR: I think whether it's fitness or power-lifting or strength or just general aerobics or whatever, it's very important to start off properly, to start off very light and then work your way up nice and steady, nothing too strenuous to avoid injury and then progress from there.

I: I don't suppose there are many people come up to you in a pub and pick a fight, are there?

JR: No, only very silly ones.

genetically gifted: born with big bones
biceps: the large muscles in the upper arm
deltoid: large muscle that covers the shoulder joint (used for raising the arm to the side)

RECORDING 4

DIANE: Yes. There are dozens of bottles of wine left. White wine? Ah! No, there's no white wine, none at all – well, there wasn't much in the first place. Certainly not enough for a party. Most of the red wine is quite drinkable, though.

Food in the freezer? No, there's not a great deal left. The children have eaten nearly everything. There are a couple of cakes which they haven't touched. I'd better put them aside or they'll both be gone before long.

Salad . . . ah! No, all of that's disappeared too. Lucy gave it to the rabbit. No doubt if you want a sandwich Ben will make you one. Oh, no, I've just remembered! I don't think there's any bread left. Come to think of it, there aren't many things we could put in it anyway.

Fruit? There might be half a melon left. Not a whole one, I'm afraid. We had some of it last week. And several packets of biscuits perhaps. I know for certain there are lots of packets of crisps. Possibly some cheese but none of it's any good. What! What do you mean you're going to eat out? I was only joking!

Unit 17

RECORDING 1

The man who worked here over the summer seemed nice enough. He was always reliable as regards timekeeping and so on and, although rather moody and not very talkative, he had a very imaginative and yet systematic approach to his work. He was quite popular with the rest of the staff as well, because he was very attractive, with quite a babyish face. He was artistic and was very helpful to people who were in trouble, so we were quite shocked when the police told us he was a professional criminal.

RECORDING 4

1 Hi, this is Bob. I'm phoning from the States to tell you that Pat and I will finally be getting married in Britain on August 10th, so keep that date free. We'd like you to come to the wedding if you can. Cheers!

2 Fred here. Just to warn you that the motorway is still choc-a-bloc with cars – bumper to bumper. It took us nearly four hours to get home. So if you're still thinking of doing this journey tomorrow it would be better to take the A120 road. Good luck!

3 This is the Mr Andrews from the library. Just to jog your memory about the book you ordered from us. It's been here for a week and I'm afraid if you don't collect it soon we'll have to let someone else have it. There's quite a long waiting list because it's just come out.

4 Hello, this is Janice Weston. I never seem to be able to get you these days but I simply must have that translation by Monday at the very latest. I'm sorry to put you under so much pressure but it's really important.

5 Hello, Tim darling. It's Mummy here. Please try to get down for lunch on Sunday. I know you and Pam are so busy but I'll make you a special meal if you come. I'll phone again when you're in – I hate this machine!

RECORDING 5

MARTIN: Yes, the barman said. 'Damned hunters! Shoot 'em. There's plenty of places to bury them.' We could hardly believe our ears! 'Make sure you don't bury them right by the Orinoco river. When the rains come, the river'll wash the bodies down here and the tourists don't like that.'

TANIS: Luckily we never actually came face-to-face with these awful hunters, though I'm pretty sure we were followed on occasions.

M: Yes, do you remember walking along that beach and seeing that beautiful lizard? I tried to catch it and as I was chasing it into some long grass, I saw a man hurry away. We became really nervous after that.

T: We survived in the jungle – by trial and error, I guess. We hadn't brought much from home, just a tent and a medical kit. Everything else we got on arrival.

M: The one thing we never seemed to have enough of, though, was mosquito cream. Do you remember Peru? That was the worst place for mosquitoes. When we went to bed there were so many on our net that we couldn't see out.

Unit 18

RECORDING 1

Nearly all societies hold 'rites of passage' ceremonies, which observe a person's entry into a new stage of life. The most common rites of passage are occasions such as birth, marriage and death. Most rites help people to understand and accept their new roles in society and help others to learn to treat them in new ways. And now we're going to hear about five different ceremonies.

Muslims hold a ceremony a week after a baby is born, which is known as an Aqiqa. The ceremony is intended to protect the baby from dangers in its life, and it has several parts. The child's head is first shaved so that it's completely clean, and then the weight of the cut hair is given in gold or silver to the poor. This is the baby's first act of charity towards others. After this, the baby is named, and the ceremony is followed by a feast. Goats and sheep are cooked and sweetened, as it's believed, that sweet food will make the child good-natured. Two thirds of the meat is given to the poor.

Another religious ceremony which babies often go through is called baptism. This practice involves a symbolic washing with water to indicate the washing away of sins and the start of a renewed life. Most churches consider baptism to be the main ceremony which signifies a person's entry into the Christian community. Children are often given their first name at this ceremony, and there is usually some kind of party afterwards.

A Jewish *bar mitzvah* celebrates the reaching of spiritual adulthood, which is, for a Jewish boy, at the age of thirteen. A crucial aspect of the bar mitzvah experience is when the father lets his son go, accepting that he is now his own person, responsible for his own actions. The father is thanking God for his son's manhood when he says: 'Blessed is he who has released me from responsibility for this child.' From the following day the boy is expected to observe all the relevant commandments and to be responsible for his own behaviour.

Nearly all religions include the belief that human beings survive death in some form. For many people, such as the Balinese, a funeral symbolises the passage from one life to another, rather than an end of a person's existence. In Bali, a cremation is therefore a time of joy and celebration. On the morning of the cremation, friends and relatives gather to pay their last respects and to eat and drink with the family. There is then a procession to the cremation ground, some men carrying the corpse in a tower built of bamboo and paper, and other men carrying a special container called a sarcophagus, which may be in the shape of a cow or a bull. At the cremation ground the body is transferred to the sarcophagus and when it has been reduced to ashes and the soul released there is a happy noisy procession to the sea, where the ashes are scattered. This last ceremony represents cleansing and purification.

Not all 'rites of passage' are religious, and other kinds of 'rites' in modern times would include the 'key of the door' which young people get at the age of eighteen or twenty-one, the right to vote, or a driving licence. People often pass through rites as a group. In graduation ceremonies in the United States, for example, students first stand together in a special area, away from their friends and relatives. Then they walk across a stage to symbolise the transition, and change the tassels from one side of the cap to the other to indicate entry into society as graduates. The graduation gowns symbolise their temporary separation from society.

RECORDING 2

TIM: That's nice. Why have you got a photo of a boat in your album?

IMOGEN: Ah yes, that's the boat which we went round the Galapagos Islands on last year. It was wonderful – really comfortable.

T: What a lovely cat!

I: That's Basil. I'd forgotten about him! He was our first cat, the one that won a prize at the local cat show.

T: Who's the woman in this photo?

I: Ah, that's Suzanne. She's a girl – one of many! – who used to be engaged to my brother.

T: I see. And is that the flat where you used to live?

I: That's right – in Rome. And the last picture is of a really great Portuguese family whose house we rented one summer.

RECORDING 4

The Shanghai crematorium might almost be called a model institution in the Chinese leadership's new drive to spread the practice of cremation from China's cities to its rural areas. The altogether plausible argument is that, with a quarter of the world's population but only seven per cent of its arable land, China just hasn't got room for graves. The new regulations specifically ban burials on agricultural land or scenic spots and, although burials are still to be allowed in certain circumstances – for instance, for national minorities – there must, the government says, be no use of what it calls superstitious burial objects. The problem is that it's not an easy matter to persuade the intensely superstitious Chinese to accept cremation as an alternative to burial. Since Mao Tse Tung's first pronouncement on cremation thirty years ago the cremation rate – as the Chinese call it – has risen to 80 per cent in the cities. However, in the countryside, even where there are crematoria, it's still only thirty per cent. Mao, in his own death, scarcely helped – his embalmed uncremated body lies on display in a mausoleum in Peking.

The way the Chinese have traditionally seen it, a dead man can never rest in peace until he's properly buried under ground. The right spot has to be found with what's termed in Chinese the right *feng-shui*, or combination of water and wind, and that can be literally anywhere.

Whatever the government's stand on such things it's many a time travelling around China that I've already come across what one might call fresh 'wild cat graves' by the road or field-side, complete with exquisite wreaths of white paper flowers. In China, white, not black, is the colour of mourning.

But it's not enough just to find the right spot for burial – the deceased has, in Chinese custom, to be given the goods he'll supposedly need in the afterlife – specially printed paper money for petty bribes in the nether world and sometimes, in this electronic age, paper television sets, cassette recorders, even paper cars, bikes and sewing machines.

It's feudal superstitions like these that appear, much to the disquiet of the powers-that-be, to be making something of a comeback in China.